Remembering China from Taiwan

Woe unto you, ye souls depraved!
Hope nevermore to look upon the heavens;
I come to lead you to the other shore,
To the eternal shades in heat and frost.
And thou, that yonder standest, living soul,
Withdraw thee from these people, who are dead!

Dante, *The Inferno*, Canto III (Cary Translation)

Remembering China from Taiwan

Divided Families and Bittersweet Reunions after the
Chinese Civil War

Mahlon Meyer

Hong Kong University Press
14/F Hing Wai Centre
7 Tin Wan Praya Road
Aberdeen
Hong Kong
www.hkupress.org

© Hong Kong University Press 2012

ISBN 978-988-8083-86-2

All rights reserved. No portion of this publication may be reproduced or transmitted in any form or by any means, electronic or mechanical, including photocopy, recording, or any information storage or retrieval system, without permission in writing from the publisher.

British Library Cataloguing-in-Publication Data
A catalogue record for this book is available from the British Library.

Digitally printed

Contents

Acknowledgements		vii
Introduction		1
1	Degrees of Escape	15
2	Mixing Memory and Desire	57
3	Low Lie the Shattered Towers	119
	The second generation	120
	Low lie the shattered towers	121
	Death outside	128
	Social change: Taiwanese versus the rest	159
	The grandchildren: Two sketches in memory	164
4	Overseas Connections	179
	Bugged: The story of Tan Zhefu	179
	The factory worker	186
	Liu Rong: Stranger in a strange Land	199
	Missing	210
Conclusion: The Other Shore		219
Notes		223
Index		231

Acknowledgements

As this book goes to press, there are over one million people from Taiwan working in mainland China. For the first time in sixty years, there is direct travel between Taiwan and the mainland. President Ma Ying-jeou has opened up air travel so that, when I was conducting my last research, I was able to fly directly from Taipei to Qingdao! As I conducted that last research, I came to believe that the events described in this book help explain why Taiwan and China are becoming increasingly integrated. They may even be a prelude to some form of unification by explaining what caused it.

Despite these developments, there are still sensitivities on both sides. So in the interest of protecting the people who gave oral histories, I changed names if there was any question of political or other sensitive issues. The use of oral histories is sometimes questioned by some academics but at the same time some of their colleagues argue that oral history will become increasingly important, particularly in Chinese studies, since a whole generation of Chinese people who lived through the major events of the twentieth century is passing away.

Some of the people I wrote about—it will become clear who—I have known for twenty-five years, and have lived through many of their (and my) major life events with them. I have been part of one family in particular and their extended relatives on the mainland, as I explain in the introduction. This has meant that people would open up much more than to other historians or journalists. Of some of the events I wrote about in detail, I was literally there when they happened. I traveled with the person involved and/or was told exactly what that person was thinking and feeling at the time. In many cases, because I was a foreigner, who speaks fluent Chinese, family members would share secrets with me that they either did not want other family members to know about, or they would tell me intentionally so that I would then relate the piece of information to another member of the finally. Obviously, this utterly desolates the principle of objectivity, unless you count my own judgment and perspicuity in helping to maintain somewhat of a bubble of awareness. In other cases, I was introduced to the people I interviewed through friends or close business acquaintances which created a sense of trust between us that allowed them to open up more. In each case, I spent many more hours and days with the individual I interviewed than I actually needed. The most was twenty-five years. The least was a day. The rest were somewhere in between.

As you may know, there are many different ways of writing Chinese using an alphabet. There is the Chinese pinyin. There are older forms, which are sometimes jumbled together and are still in use in Taiwan. Then there are those forms that are based on the individual choice of the person. I have respected the choice of each individual, how he or she wants his or her name to be romanized, and where I have tried to protect the individual with an altered name, I have also tried to follow the same romanization as the original name. Generally speaking, though, individuals from mainland China use pinyin while those from Taiwan have different forms.

This book is dedicated to Page.

Most of all I want to thank R. Kent Guy, whose support has sustained me for years, who is a model as a scholar, teacher, and writer. His irony and humor about and fascination with Chinese history are infectious for anyone who comes into contact with him, who reads Faulkner before writing about southern China and who is able to see both the tragic and the comic sides of things. Thank you.

Others I want to thank include Tom Reilly, who helped me find a focus and fundamental theme for this book, actually turning it from a jumbled piece of writing into the semblance of a book. And for the care and compassion he took with the manuscript. Thank you.

Thank you to Doreen Weisenhaus who, in reviewing the book, alerted me to specific gender issues that helped me make important improvements and for other insightful comments.

Thank you to Pat Ebrey for spending so much time and energy on the manuscript and also for tremendous support, in one way or another, throughout many years.

Those who read part or all of it and offered comments include Stevan Harrell, who brought his tremendous intellectual resources, scholarship, and undying commitment to his students and critiques; Bill Kirby, whose dry sense of humor in teaching Chinese history is nonpareil; Carol Thomas, who helped me in innumerable other ways, including teaching me how to line edit; Richard Johnson; Jonathan Spence, who read one section; and Ron Perey, for his careful reading.

I did not take all of the suggestions or comments offered to me and, more often than not, followed my own predilections. So whatever is wrong with the book is owing to me alone.

I could not have researched and written this book without a grant from the Fulbright Foundation and the generous and loving support of Wu Jing-jyi, a gifted playwright, an inspiration and a godsend, who helped me far, far beyond his role as Fulbright coordinator in Taiwan.

I want to thank Chuang Yin for giving me a glimpse of how powerful oral histories from mainlanders can be.

Michael Kwan of National Chengchi University has helped me in so many ways, I cannot even count them. He helped me find a place to live, offered emotional support, and provided a base of emotional and intellectual support with him and his staff. He is someone special in my life.

President Ma Ying-jeou has always been one of the most forgiving and generous men in Taiwan. Early on, he opened up to me about his ancestors and himself. When I wrote articles critical of him for *Newsweek*, he continued to see me (unlike other prominent leaders). When I returned to Taipei to start working on this book and went to visit him, he saw how nervous I was and hugged me. As mayor, he also enabled me to gain access to the Taipei municipal archives. As president, he has not changed, except for being a little tired, perhaps.

It has been a fortunate and pleasurable opportunity to work with Michael Duckworth, the publisher at Hong Kong University Press, whose sensitivity and humor are matched by his charisma. His receptivity to others' ideas combines with his own compelling vision. Thank you.

Clara Ho, the assistant managing editor, has helped me remain calm through the final stages of the book with her patience, expertise, and kindness.

I also want to thank Winnie Chau, the marketing manager, and Jenifer Lim, the marketing executive, at Hong Kong University Press for their help.

Thank you, deeply, to the gifted copy editor who worked with the manuscript, whose knowledge of Taiwan and China was helpful and whose sensitive eye picked up on nuances of construction and writing that improved the book a great deal.

I want to thank Dorinda Elliott who shared with me her love of China and Taiwan, guided me for years in ways that transcended writing and reporting and mentored me in a new sense of sensibilities.

Thank you to my mother for proofreading the manuscript.

Thank you to my family and friends in Taiwan for supplying photos and to Ying Sheng Quo, a world-renowned photographer, for preserving and providing the cover photo of his mother, Shen Hsueh-yung, on the mainland years before she was forced to leave for Taiwan.

Through writing this book, I have also come to realize the importance of my own family. It was my parents who first got me the opportunity to make this a book. My father, a noted China scholar, whose books and recovered Chinese silent films have made an unparalleled contribution to education about early modern China, helped me on this process in unparalleled ways. As I faced the challenges of putting this book together, I have also realized how important it is to have a family behind you.

Introduction

I hope this book will not have the same effect on you as it did on one of my friends. The friend in question is a well-known Taiwanese journalist who helped me on countless occasions, bringing perspective or knowledge to my newspaper and magazine articles. Whenever I wanted to tackle a new topic, I would simply call her up and she would help me outline the main points of my piece, feeding me background information about all the people I was interviewing and generally throwing in her opinion and perspective. She was a mentor and a good friend. But after hearing me simply mention the topic and characters involved in this book, she rose up rudely, in anger, and stormed out of the coffee shop where she had been taking refreshments with me, knocking chairs out of the way and promising never to contact me again. She had not read a single word of the manuscript.

The above story is true, and just goes to show how inflammatory this topic is in current-day Taiwan. The journalist friend in question is the daughter of mainland refugees, whose stories are the focus of this writing. She said she was overwhelmingly perplexed at my tendency to use a soft touch in dealing with her parents' generation. She told me that she was outraged that I presumed to describe them as innocent survivors of invasion, civil war, and finally exile rather than condemn them as predators who had come to Taiwan from China to murder and harass the local Taiwanese. When I protested that the piece was focused upon the *memories* of these men and women which they clung to even harder now given their recent loss of position and status, she left without looking back.

My friend had gone over to the "camp" of the native Taiwanese, whose representative was, at the time, in the presidential palace. She was working, during that highly emotional period, as a television commentator aligned with the Taiwanese party, the Democratic Progressive Party. As a mainlander, in fact the second generation of a group that terrorized or held sway over the locals for almost half a century, she was appearing on nightly talk shows supporting the locals, the group that she believed her parents and their generation had wronged. After her outburst and sudden departure, I walked the streets of Taipei for hours, trying to sort out how I felt about her, this book, and myself. Besides my sadness over the encounter, I began thinking that I had, perhaps, failed in what I had wanted to do. I had wanted to show that the oral histories given me by aging exiles from China showed the beginning of a new sense of being Chinese that would ultimately result in the closer integration of Taiwan and China. I interviewed these exiles after their political party had lost power for the first time in Taiwan. They were facing a second defeat, the first one being the loss of their homes on China at the end of the Civil War when they were separated from their families, crossed the Strait to Taiwan, and were born into a new life.

No one was disputing that the Kuomintang, of whom all the subjects interviewed in the book were members, was one of the most disappointing regimes in history. Conceived as a revolutionary party to save China from warlords and foreign exploitation at the start of the twentieth century, the party soon allied itself with gangsters and triads and eventually warlords. When Chiang Kai-shek took over the leadership, he copied organization and ideology from the Nazis.[1] Mass conscriptions of peasants, staggering corruption and economic failure alienated southern and coastal China and eventually contributed to the loss of the entire country to the Chinese Communist Party, led by Mao Zedong. Eventually, the Kuomintang fled to Taiwan. Fifty years of rule on the small island—roughly the size of a small US state—started in 1945, when the Japanese colonizers handed the island back to China, and the government of Chiang Kai-shek began transferring over from China. But starting only two years after taking over the island, Kuomintang troops began massacring tens of thousands of people. Many natives simply disappeared into the labyrinths of the security forces. Execution cells and firing squads became a way the government dealt with dissenters, and the souls that once screamed and perished there are said by local historians to still exist, as ghosts, beneath the central institutions of government.

One of the most haunting events for the Kuomintang, as it began to set its sights on Taiwan as a possible base for a retreat, was the 2–28 Massacre, named for the day and month in 1947 when it started. It was through this slaughter, which started when a local woman was harassed for selling contraband cigarettes, that the party launched its regime in Taiwan by hunting down and killing up to 30,000 locals in the massacre that lasted over a year. Many of the victims were students and leading citizens. The reign of terror is now understood to have mimicked Stalin's in Poland, aimed at wiping out the intelligentsia before taking possession of the new land.[2]

But it was not only Taiwanese that suffered. Poet Ya Hsien writes of "heads nailed to a cross" and saw cities "mutilated by iron."[3] Writer Bo Yang was penned up in Green Island for years for loosely translating the captions of a Popeye comic strip that made Chiang Kai-shek think he was being mocked. When he emerged, emaciated and with his skin sagging, he wrote another book entitled *The Ugly Chinaman*, writing that the Chinese people had brought a curse down upon themselves. But by the time he was released, he was safe; he was an international celebrity and the days of White Terror were already over. Both men were immigrants from mainland China and had held literary appointments with the central government.

Most of the mainland immigrants, however, just went along with the regime's way of handling things, it is true. The Kuomintang's soldiers, civil servants, and other functionaries of the central government were heavily subsidized and remained so for the rest of their lives. Wang Shu-chih, one of those who provided an oral history for this book, lived in a number of government-subsidized compounds. The first one, however, was a cramped warehouse divided into small units with blankets, each one packed with a single refugee family. Although these mainland refugees (or invaders, as the locals at the time called them) often attribute their success, and the success of Taiwan, to their own enlightened efforts, such as Chiang Kai-shek's land reform, some of it came down to the luck of having two American wars in the region that stimulated the island's economy.

This group of "mainland refugees" or "mainland immigrants," that could also be called "mainland settlers,"[4] who lost their homes in China only to build others in Taiwan, represents a remnant of a cultural ideology that died out elsewhere. Whatever atrocities their soldiers and government may have committed, they brought with them a now-unique way of patterning their world. This would change as they lived and developed in Taiwan, but would still emphasize essentially moral elements. These elements show up in their memories transformed into guilt, anger, and shame. Even so, many of those interviewed here were on the periphery of the Kuomintang regime and were not directly responsible for the violence perpetrated by its government and military. Their struggles have more to do with repetition of loss, both as children on the mainland, when they lost their homes, and later, as adults in Taiwan, when they lost their ruling-class status. My interpretation, as I believe this book shows, is that these aging exiles continually re-imagined their identities, to adapt to the times, and ultimately came to identify themselves with their former enemy, seeing themselves once again as Chinese, but now as part of a rising economically-superior China. For close to forty years, they had been staring across the Taiwan Strait, gazing at the other shore, the mainland, where they had left families behind. Meanwhile, their relatives in China had been looking to their shore with longing, regret, and hostility. It has taken another twenty years, a democratic election in Taiwan, and growing affluence in China, for both sides to see beyond the other shore to something bigger, which is what this book is about.

I still think my friend misunderstood my enterprise. I do not mean, in the first two chapters, to portray these aged "Chinese refugees," or "mainland immigrants," as I call them, as victims. On the contrary, I intend to use their own feelings of impotence and shame, and self-victimization to gain a richer understanding of their experience. Later, I talk about what happened to their children and the relatives they left behind in the mainland.

The Kuomintang held power in Taiwan from 1945 until 2000 when a popular democratic election thrust them from ruling status. Their reaction on election night, when their representatives used violence to try to overturn the election, was one indication of the shock. Never before had the mainland immigrants realized the full extent of their minority status. They and their descendants occupied only about fifteen percent of the island's population. And suddenly they were living through the greatest social and political upheaval since they had come to Taiwan. The society they had dominated for half a century was now going through the kind of turbulence that they had experienced in the mainland a half century earlier. Would it be a prelude to the same violence and disaster they faced then, which sent them fleeing to Taiwan in the first place? The familiar sense of terror, grief, and shame came welling up like a genie out of a box. It was their trauma surfacing again, even as the local Taiwanese were trying to escape from theirs. The result for the mainlanders: emotional and social chaos and the

Introduction 5

resurrection of feelings of shame and helplessness at the inevitability of displacement. To explain this kind of dislocation, loss of status and power, a leading psychiatrist at Taipei Veterans' General, Chou Chih-sui, who treats old soldiers and displaced mainland immigrants, said: "The biggest event in the second part of these peoples' lives was their loss of political power in Taiwan. This election and the democratic reforms that brought it about was a huge blow to them. They have reacted with rage and disorientation. It has caused them to start to question their entire lives." An entire website is devoted to the expressions of rage and sadness of mainland immigrants.[5] One letter is excerpted, as follows. Here, "Nei Di Ren" refers to refugees from China.

> **The Last Generation of Nei Di Ren**
> **Written by Xin Huai-nan; translated by K C Lu**
>
> We are a minority among minorities. Fifty years from now, when Chinese historians study this period, they will find that we, the Nei Di Ren, are a unique group of people.
> We were born into a chaotic time marked by continuous warfare. If we had not escaped to Taiwan, I believe at least one third of us would have perished under Mao Tze-Tung's communist regime.
> We spent our childhood in Taiwan; some in the northern cities, and others in the southern fields . . . Although we were short on material possessions, we never went hungry. Many of us grew up in "Juan Cun" (literally spouse village), a compound of state-provided housing for the dependents of government and military personnel. Many criticized us for never learning to speak Taiwanese and not being "Taiwanese" enough after spending our formative years on the island. However, this was not our fault. The government at that time was trying to establish Mandarin as the official language on the island. We had no opportunity to speak Taiwanese at school and could not learn it from our parents at home since they themselves did not speak it. It is unreasonable to place the blame on us.
> Too often we are made to feel like some forlorn traveler listening to the blowing of the political winds in a lone boat picked out by the moonlight. In Taiwan, first we were called Nei Di Ren; later, we were addressed as Wai Sheng Ren (people from other provinces) to differentiate us from the provincial Taiwanese. Yet when we go to China, we are treated as Taiwanese.
> In terms of political beliefs, we rejected the "White Terror" perpetrated by Chiang Kai-Shek's government. Nor could we identify with the "red terror" that

> is the communist one party dictatorship practiced in China. We love Taiwan more than we love China, but we are not the "New Taiwanese" who deny their Chinese heritage.
>
> To some degree, we try to be true to Confucius's belief that a man must expand his resoluteness because he accepts the challenges and realizes his burden will be heavy and his path long. We are not the greatest generation of Chinese; we are simply the last generation of Nei Di Ren.

Another clear expression of their shame and rage, came through in the 2006–07 demonstrations in front of the presidential palace. Mainland immigrants came roaring out of their apartments and condominiums to demonstrate against the (native Taiwanese) president. They rioted in front of the presidential palace. They frequently appeared on television, making wild threats, and pounding on drums, as if they were going to lead a battalion into battle. Notable figures from this disenfranchised generation, such as Chen Lu-an, a former defense minister and son of a major Kuomintang General, and Hu Chih-chiang (Jason Hu), constantly rallied crowds against the president. Fist fights broke out, instigated by ethnic tensions between the local Taiwanese, who usually supported the president during those days, and the mainland immigrants who wanted him out of the presidential mansion and a return to their days of power.

Anger spread through the society. Television news on channels owned or influenced by the Kuomintang, which still controls vast resources in Taiwan, carried nothing but news items attacking President Chen Shui-bian. Influenced by these programs, citizens of Taipei flocked to the protests, with little more reason than that they had heard news broadcasters announcing that he was corrupt. Through October, November, and December of 2006, the hysteria spread. Crowds attacked the president's car. Meanwhile, in the south, where locals predominate, support for Chen Shui-bian remained high. The island was poised, for the first time in more than fifty years, to split apart along ethnic lines: the local, native Taiwanese on the side of the president, the mainland settlers represented by the Kuomintang, along with those locals who had joined their cause and transformed it, on the other. Then what seemed like a sacrifice was offered. The courts found the nephew of Chen Shui-bian guilty of corruption. He was sentenced to eight years. The hydra of the Kuomintang had proved its strength after all. But Chen Shui-bian remained in the presidential mansion. After the whole thing was over, and the Kuomintang retook the presidency, he too was sentenced to twenty years.

It was in this atmosphere, when society seemed turned upside down to the older mainlanders—the "years of chaos" as one Kuomintang historian put it—that the oral histories for this book were taken at the moment of greatest despair for the mainlanders. This book is a snapshot of those moments, of those eight years, when their deepest fears were realized. It is a snapshot of a time, of a moment. But the feelings of loss and shame are still driving them. Just for a moment, they believed they had not only lost China but Taiwan as well. Old wounds, filmed over with fifty years of scabs, were ripped open and started to bleed. To stop the flow, they began thinking in new ways, about themselves and about their former enemies, the Communists in China.

Their position was a little bit like other elites from earlier times in Chinese history, toppled from power, but encouraged to write their own histories. Throughout Chinese history, scholars from a previous dynasty, crushed by the current one, were asked to write the history of their defunct dynasty. They were asked, by new rulers, to tell the stories of their past adventures and their defeated masters. This happened during the Qing dynasty, when scholars were wooed back after experiencing profound alienation with the new dynasty that had waded into power through rivers of blood. The promise of an exam which, if passed, would qualify them to write the history of the Ming dynasty they had once been loyal to, eventually pulled many of them back to the official halls. These scholars, then, actually wrote the history of the Ming dynasty under the supervision of the Qing, who were their new masters.[6] How they dealt with their guilt and the realities of working under the enemy, how they transferred their sentiments over to their new masters, how aware they were of the oppression they must have felt themselves subject to, and how all these complexities appeared in their writing, are all questions that would have to be looked at bit by bit in the Ming history they wrote. The position of these Ming scholars is similar to that of the mainland refugees in Taiwan—both tell a history of their own past, not as victors, but as the defeated—no longer even masters of their exile government but, rather, subject to a hostile regime. After being in power for fifty years in Taiwan, these mainland settlers began to lose power two decades ago after their party gradually opened its doors to local Taiwanese. Eventually, democratic reforms catapulted them from their privileged seat. Like their Ming counterparts, the mainlander refugees in Taiwan told their stories as if their lives were flashing before their eyes, never knowing when their lives as they knew them would end.

By linking the stories of the family members who escaped to Taiwan with their relatives left behind, I am suggesting that what are usually taken as two separate stories are actually one. The devastation of the Maoist movements in the mainland is actually part of the same narrative that describes the crushing weight of Kuomintang repression in Taiwan. I am suggesting that this book offers a new way of unifying the experiences of all Chinese over the past four generations, generations that were ravaged and left desolate by war as one community marked by dislocation and changing identities. The mainlander exiles, for their part, are still coping, still trying to re-imagine their past and present. Many have tried to return to China, to visit lost relatives or marry wives, and found that a half century of nostalgia has clouded their memories—or made them more corrosive. When Ko Jen-tao left home at the age of ten, his mother was thirty, plump, and had dark, sleek hair and a seamless round face. When he finally found her again, over fifty years later, she was in her eighties, with white sparse hair, toothless gums, and a face like a crumpled sack, heavily wrinkled and sagging after a lifetime of waiting.

His memory of her, which had helped keep him alive, was part of a grander memory of a past glory—and of how that glory was stripped away. It was almost as if the entire group of mainlanders ached for memories that they might have forgotten. What they found was shame for being cast out from their privileged position, shame at having to live with the knowledge that not only they themselves knew this but their enemies knew this as well, and shame that they needed to reinvent themselves so late in life. Perhaps even shame for what they believed had happened to their civilization. For if one event delineates the People's Republic from past Chinese history, it was the systematic elimination of the elite, landlord class, which for most of Chinese history played the major role in transmitting culture. It is safe to say that many of those who survived the pogroms were among the roughly two million who fled to Taiwan around 1949. In a sense, capturing oral histories from the first generation of survivors is capturing some ethos of that extinct class, that lost civilization which was once imperial China. They had endured the loss of their homeland. They had endured fifty years of exile in Taiwan. They had endured a second exile—from power and status. And they had reinvented themselves again.

Table 1
Subjects interviewed, occupations, provinces of origin and ages[a]

Mainland Immigrant	Biographical Data[b]
Chang Ching-tan	civil servant; Fujian, 82
Lin Ching-wu	soldier-educator; Fujian, 85
Hu Yao-hen	professor; Hubei, 77
Weiwei Furen (Yin Tsai-chun)	newspaper columnist; Nanjing, 74
Ko Jen-tao	police chief; Nanjing, 83
Ku Chi	banker; Shanghai, 77
Shen Hsueh-yung	opera singer; Sichuan, 78
Wang Shu-chih	civil servant; Henan, 77
Tan Hua-shen	soldier; Shandong, 78

a. The limited number of interviewees was compelled by the emphasis on a qualitative, rather than quantitative, approach to the subject. The attempt to explore the mindset, as deeply as possible, of the subjects, necessitated a close, detailed approach, much as in recent works in American History such as the award-winning *A Midwife's Tale: The Life of Martha Ballard, Based on Her Diary, 1785–1812* (New York: Vintage Books, 1991) by Laurel Thatcher Ulrich. A more "Chinese" approach of selecting interviewees involved seeking out friends and acquaintances of the principal family of Ko Jen-tao. Anthropologists call this approach "snowballing." But, in this case, my approach assumes that friends and acquaintances, like a family, share certain characteristics of temperament and experience that create a cohesive whole not unlike a village or family.

b. Taiwanese-style romanization is used for names, unless the person came from mainland China within the last few decades in which case I use pinyin.

The mainlander

Ko Jen-tao is talking about his problems.[7] His wife works thirteen hours a day. She works as a nurse's aide in the hospital. In the morning, she prepares her food, her breakfast, and her lunch. Her dinner she buys at the hospital. The problem is that Ko is lonely. At eighty-three, his face sags more than ever, his pot belly comes and goes depending on his state of sadness, and when he complains it sounds like a great foghorn. "My wife is never around to take care of me," he says.

He married her ten years ago when she was a lithe beauty from Qingdao with white skin and a figure that seemed to suck the velvet dresses she slipped into tight against her hips and breasts. His sons insist she married him for his money. (The mainland in most places is still poorer than Taiwan.) When he met her, through a fellow police officer, she was living alone with her two sisters and father in a tiny shack in that port city where fog grips the horizon like a milky white hand half the time. His first wife had died, a horrendous death as cancer ate away her bones until they cracked. Soon after, he married Liu Rong. Their wedding picture, taken several years after the event, shows a happy, if perhaps slightly cynical, couple arrayed in colored costumes. She appears haughty and wise. He, on the other hand, looks like some gamester, some kingpin of Macau or other small-time city in greater China. They seem suited for each other.

Yet now, their unhappiness seems boundless. Liu Rong has a son from a former marriage. The son just never seems satisfied with what he has. He walked away from a school in the heart of an agricultural district because the water was laced with salt and fertilizers. Now he stays at home playing computer games and talking with his grandfather. This is the reason why Liu Rong, his mother, works seven days a week, thirteen hours a day, folding hospital quilts and removing catheters. She wants to get him out, out of China; she dreams of sending her son to New Zealand. Once there, and having earned a visa, he will buy a house, with her money, and eventually be able to bring herself out to New Zealand also. "I won't go," says Ko, wretched. He hates the son. And he is furious at being left alone. "She should take care of me," he says. "This is her real job."

Today is a rest day for Liu Rong. She is having hot flashes from menopause and flits around the house, boiling water, sitting and fanning herself, and listening to the oral history delivered by her husband. Her cotton dress is short and rides up her hard, white thighs when she sits down. At fifty, she is still very beautiful, with wide, intelligent eyes and long limbs. "She really takes care of herself," says Ko, as if she is a commodity, as if she keeps herself in splendor so that, if she fails in this marriage, she can find another. In their moments of despair, they seem united in a single false belief, belied at other times, but hovering now in their terror that her body is all that she has.

Ko deteriorates every moment he sits on the couch watching her, speaking about his life. The black dye he uses on his hair has faded at the periphery so that his hair appears to molt around his collar. Deep sacks with surfaces fading from black to grey pucker under his eyes. His clothing is that of the old man in Taiwan—an undershirt with no sleeves and loose shorts. Even his toenails are sick. They are stunted, curving like elephant tusks, yellowing with decay. Liu Rong, flitting around in hormonal frustration, her dress flying up as she sits down in a chair, now on the couch, now as she paces by, might be his daughter, trapped in an obscure old apartment with a single couch, a tiny, hot kitchen filled with steam, tied to her aging father in a dance of hate and recrimination.

"I used to be able to run all the way around the Sun Yat-sen Memorial. Do you know how far that is? If we block out the streets like this, and this, you see, it is a perfect square. I used to be in really good shape. My colleagues all envied me."

His wife brushes by again, apparently without having heard the comments: she's heard them before. Ko repeats every anecdote, every sentence many times. In the old days, such repetition used to be a sign of hospitality, such as the hospitality I was offered when I came to his house for dinner. In those days, the dinner table overflowed with food. Chicken, fish, tofu, vegetables, duck, plus the inevitable bottle of brandy. He presided at his dinner table once a week, when his work permitted him to come home.

I would give up; a little more food would be eaten. Or I would have more brandy forced on me. Against my better judgment, I would take a sip or two, and the issue would be settled. Although, for the rest of the evening, Ko would rumble, "Ah, you didn't eat anything."

For many of these refugees, like Ko, trauma—or despair—did not show its face until old age. Something happened. A fall. An accident. The death of a parent. The loss of prestige. Then old age came sifting down like leaves, or ashes, and suddenly the past became all too real. I wanted to capture that past before the mainland settlers gave up wanting to talk about it. Each oral history ranged from about one hour to over four hours, depending on the respondent's willingness to draw forth memories. Each of the refugees was eager to talk, eager to imagine and re-imagine his or her identity in the context of the present. For Ko, it was the advent of bone spurs, that prevented him from taking his daily run, that began to transform him. A police officer for over thirty years, the loss of the use of his physical frame hit him particularly hard. He put on weight, he slowed down, he grew tremendously frustrated.

The decline of his body mirrored the decline of his ability to control his life. When first married to Liu Rong, he bought her a two-story, white and brown brick house looking out into the harbor of Qingdao. The house, now rented to a Japanese businessman to pay for her son's schooling, is painted to resemble an Alpine chateau. But it's not enough to cover his wife's plans, he says, frustrated. The income goes to her son and Liu Rong continues to work; studying in New Zealand takes enormous sums. Ko has a lot to think about. He'd like to talk to her about it but he has to let her sleep, so she can do well in her job. He wakes up naturally at five or six in the morning—the only hour he can get an erection—and looks at his wife sleeping soundly next to him. "I don't dare to wake her, that's when she's having her soundest sleep." In the morning, after she has gone, he writhes in agony. "I feel if she had to choose between me and her son, she'd choose her son."

Each of the eight individuals featured in the early chapters and their relatives who remained in the mainland were touched by the same explosion of invasion, flight, trauma, rebuilding and ultimate displacement. Each mainland refugee lost a whole other life in China through war, then rebuilt his or her fortunes in Taiwan as a new ruling class, finally to have his or her position in society knocked away like a child's building blocks.

Even later, after their party returned to power, they continued to face other disillusionments, other challenges. Foremost among them was how to understand the rise of a powerful China, the homeland they lost, and how to convince themselves that they are still a part of it.

Ko, who was born in Shanghai, and came to Taiwan as a child with the retreating Kuomintang armies in 1949, is a member of a group of Chinese refugees who share a unique fate in modern Chinese history. Defeated by the Communists, yet masters of Taiwan for almost half a century, they faced a period of profound alienation. Having lost the mainland, they found they had lost political and social control of Taiwan as well. The final disaster has been the attempt over the past two decades to return to mainland China in various ways—through business ventures, marriages, even actual immigration. But some of these have been nearly as unsuccessful as their battle against the Communists and subsequent retreat. Now these mostly seventy-, eighty-, and ninety-year-olds face the disillusioning task of taking stock of their engagement with China, their birthplace and land they have been banished from for most of their lives. Their final reckoning is important in another sense, for it may also impact the way Taiwan and China come together in the future. These refugees, old soldiers and dispossessed landlords, though deracinated, yet cling fast to traditional moral elements that they see lacking in mainland China, subject as it was to decades of communist purges and emaciating poverty. Leading intellectuals and the media in the mainland are unceasingly fascinated with the experiences and value systems of their former enemies. Television shows in China now focus on the lives of the mainland settlers. Some Chinese scholars even feel nostalgic about Chiang Kai-shek.

It has taken both sides over half a century to get there. When the mainland settlers first arrived in Taiwan, there were no familiar landscapes, buildings, or routines. So they rebuilt a life there that eventually surpassed the original in prosperity and abundance. They didn't want to forget what they had been. Chinese art, transported out of the war zone and ensconced in hills in the center of the island before being resurrected in an artificial palace built in the capital, served both to spur and legitimate memory. Their leaders sought to mimic the China they had lost by turning Taipei into a map of mainland China, taking possession of the land with a series of ornate rituals centered on naming things and reflecting Chinese philosophical cosmology. As they developed their mimetic land, and held onto, for a while at least, their dream of retaking mainland China, they were less successful in dealing with the trauma of their wartime experiences.

Now, sixty years later, the mainlanders have been remembering their pain so long that they are trying to forget. They had lived so long in memories that when they started to come out of them, when they were awakened by their loss of power, they found that they no longer had anything to hold on to, except those memories and the success of their families they had once left behind. They now want to feel that they are part of that success, of the pride of a China they once remembered only with shame.

1
Degrees of Escape

Hatred of Japanese invaders is almost too big for the mainlanders to get their minds around. Yet one also gets the sense that these feelings, while arising from historical fact, are also some kind of ritual, something they learned from their leaders. For decades within the Kuomintang, hatred of Japanese was played up along with love of China. Lin Ching-wu, a short, balding, eighty-five-year-old man from Fujian, is talking about the Japanese. He glares furiously and jumps up and beats his chest.

> I was just a kid and I saw the most horrible things. The Japanese would fly their airplanes over our school. We'd all dive down under our desks. And when the pilot didn't see any movement, he'd head out to the countryside and shoot dogs. They would drop bombs on stray dogs just to watch them explode. As I got older, I saw them dropping bombs on farmers out in the fields the same way. They just wanted a pretty picture of heads and bodies spread all over the ground.

Other instances of Japanese depredation appear throughout the stories told by this group of refugees. As Ko Jen-tao describes a scene from the Japanese invasion, his words take on a virtually repetitive tone. As he recounts the scene, his speech quickens, propelled by trauma, horror, or some combination.

> There was this girl that used to boss me around at school when I was a kid. She made my life hell. One time, when she was going outside the city with some of her friends, I decided to follow them. I think I thought they were doing something wrong and I would catch them at it and could get her in trouble. I was just a kid. I was just following them like kids do. I was pretty far behind them when I saw a whole group of Japanese soldiers approaching. I instinctively ducked down in some weeds. At that age, I couldn't

understand what was going on. The Japanese soldiers were pulling off their clothes and pushing them down to the ground and lying on top of them. I went back home and told my older brother what I had seen. He said that the soldiers had been raping them. Now I know they weren't just raping them, they were gang raping them. I remember them, one after another, on top of each of the girls.

Formerly an assistant police chief, whose awards indicate he rose to his position through sheer bravery and doggedness in tracking down and apprehending criminals, he has in the last two decades seen a staggering falling-off in his own preeminence in society. Once a member of the ruling class, governed by members of his own core of two million refugees who crossed the Taiwan Strait, after losing the Chinese civil war, he has just seen the government change hands. He has seen the people whom his people once conquered rise up and unite and form their own party and take power. Along with the rest of the elite mainland settlers, he has witnessed the kind of change he never could have imagined. A party of the locals, the Democratic Progressive Party took over. It was through an election, the second presidential election held on the island. But it was a loss of power they felt they just couldn't handle and still remain whole. It was a loss of power to the local 20 million descendants of poor farmers who arrived hundreds of years before the conquering mainlanders arrived. Since these locals have memories of massacre, displacement and oppression at the hands of his group, they were waging a desperate battle to disenfranchise people like Ko Jen-tao.

In personal ways, as well, the loss of power experienced by his group of refugees has seemed to resonate through his life. His four children, no longer bound to him by the ties of obedience taught in an authoritarian society where people like him were at the top, now rarely visit him. His mainland-born wife, exploiting conditions of her marriage to a citizen of the island, also seems to ignore him. He seems, to himself, a feather for each wind that blows, so much is he at the mercy of others who once were his dependents. As he recounts the repetitive rapes of the Japanese, his frustration almost seems to find expression in his heated, heavy language, not to mention the choice of the image itself to respond to a broad question about the War of Resistance, meaning the fight against the Japanese invasion of China in the 1930s.

It was mostly resentment, and shame, that they felt about the Japanese aggression. They were forced to flee. Their enemies were too strong. The rapes were the worst kind of memories of all, memories of shame and helplessness that one frustrated old man has been carrying with him like a walking stick for most of his life. Drunkenness and death are two other images that stick with him as he sorts through his memories of the Japanese. It is almost as if, with the loss of power in his own society, Ko Jen-tao and his cohorts are reliving their loss more than half a century earlier. The old memories mingle with the new pain, the new confusion and suffering. At this moment in their lives, their memories seek out new images that will express the pain, sorrow, and shame they felt then and are feeling now.

Ku Chi, a seventy-seven-year-old native Shanghainese, whose shriveled face resembles the side of a dim sum dumpling, sums up his father's death by attributing it to heartbreak, which led to alcoholism, brought on by Japanese bombing of his clinic.

> It was all the Japanese. My father had only been a moderate drinker before the war. He would drink two glasses of liquor before bed as his medicine, as he called it. But after the Japanese bombed his clinic, he lost all his clients. They all went to other parts of the city. Then he really began to drink. He would start in the morning and by the end of the day he could barely see. He fell down some stairs and killed himself.

Ku, who retired from a bank twenty years ago, explaining that he only wants to "eat, drink, and be happy," has an extremely complex history that will emerge later. But, like others, in the early parts of his story, he attributes the disruption of dreams, lives, and prosperity to large, blunt historical forces: invasion and war. But his willingness to speak of it, of a loss so personal, comes at a time when he is facing a new crisis: his displacement in Taiwanese society. In other words, Ku's own lack of livelihood, his failing status, and his loss of eminence in a rapidly-changing society, in which he is no longer a member of the ruling class, are the context for his candor.

> The bombing didn't just kill my father. It killed thousands of others. I remember walking the streets and seeing corpses lying out of windows and doors like fish. The Japanese bombs were quite effective. Houses all along our street were flattened. One day, I showed up at school and the school was missing. There was only a pile of rubble and bricks on the side of the street. One moment my school had existed, the next it was gone.

The loss was of a kind that would haunt a man for the rest of his life. And the description of it is just as haunting. These kinds of images of loss and destruction are buried just under the surface of the minds of mainland refugees like Ku. The images come to the surface at times, especially recently, when they knew they were losing ground again. Anyone who saw the virulence of the protests against President Chen Shui-bian during those years, can hardly doubt the existence of deep tensions lingering in Taiwanese society—particularly among the mainland refugees. The anger and humiliation felt by the whole class of mainland émigrés as they reckoned up their loss of power and status over the past two decades was like a fire rekindled after sixty years. For many of the mainlanders, it is as if time blurs and one loss follows another until the past and the present are united in one moment of shame, humiliation, rage, and helplessness.

Their memories are like wild dreams, in which they search for safety, knowing that safety was lost long ago, but still willing to make any sacrifice for a return to normalcy. As they tell their stories, at a time when they feel unsafe again, these two parts of their past come out strongly. In the tale of a childhood inundated with the Japanese invasion, Chang Ching-tan gives us clear instances of both, of a need to portray himself as having made a sacrifice and of the need to seek safety and shelter after doing so. Chang has a freckled head under his thinning hair. He stands squarely, gesturing with his sweater-clad arms as he narrates his past. He was born and raised in the southern, hilly province of Fujian. His pride in his region of birth comes out in many ways, such as in describing the special task force of civil servants from his province who were trained to take over Taiwan after it was relinquished by Japan. They spoke the same dialect as the natives on the island, for one thing.

But that was much later. When the Japanese invaded the area in 1937, Chang was only twelve. His brother and his family had gone into retreat. Chang had agreed to look after his brother's second-hand clothing store. Someone had to do it. It was the only income for the family. And Chang was the only one without dependents to care for. So he volunteered to stay behind. Everything would have gone smoothly except that the day before, someone had sold a Nationalist (Kuomintang) uniform to the store. His brother, unthinking, had bought it. It was good quality material. Perhaps it could be cut up for sale. But word had spread. And soon the Japanese found out. They came. They arrested Chang. And they led him off with other prisoners. He ended up in a small cell along with a handful of other prisoners. There was only one small pitcher of water for everyone in the cell.

After a day, all the men in the cell were brought out. They were made to line up in front of the Japanese soldiers. This is when Chang was traumatized, perhaps for life. At twelve years old, when a boy's sexuality is just emerging, any such shock can scar it irreparably.

> When they brought us out of the cell, they led us into a square where they had a fire going and were eating dinner. I was about twelve or thirteen but small for my age. We were standing in a line. One of the Japanese officers came over and unzipped my fly. I was too scared to do anything. He pulled out my penis and let it hang there in the open. The other officers were laughing. Another one of them was fighting with a stray dog. He got a hold of it and brought it over close to me. He was trying to get it to bite off my penis. But fortunately for me the dog was just as scared as I was. So finally the Japanese officer let it go. He made some comment in Japanese. I imagine he said something like, he's too small. But I was just thinking how lucky I was; it wasn't a Japanese military dog.

After recounting the traumatic experience of having a stray dog pushed to bite at his exposed genitals, Chang immediately downplayed the severity of the trauma. "The Japanese officer was just having fun," he said. He particularly stressed that he was fortunate to have saved his brother and his family from a similar fate.

> It's not that I am brave. Not at all. It's just that I knew that if my older brother had been caught, he might have been killed, and then his entire family wouldn't have had anyone to support them. No, I felt I was lucky to be young without a wife or kids. I was ready to die.

It is probable that the twelve-year-old boy did in fact feel such stirrings of honor and concern. It is likely. But what we do know for certain is that, over the past two decades, mainland immigrants, such as Chang, have continually harped on a similar theme: they have always been responsible. They were responsible for Taiwan's stunning economic growth. They, as a people who had sacrificed all—their homes, their past, their prosperity—for the good of the island ought to be acknowledged. Obviously, the truth of the matter is much more complicated. But the belief that they have made sacrifices and endured trauma for others might be part of a more traditional value system. Or it might just be the way a man fights his way out of memory. The image of the little twelve-year-old boy bravely defending his home against the Japanese, sacrificing even his private parts, is the first sacrifice. Later, as they continued their journey of flight and rebuilding, a whole class of people justified their lives as sacrifices to the building up of Taiwan. As he tells the story of the brave little boy that he once was, the husky arms of the old man are now swaying in his sweater, his feet gripping the floor. He is still talking about a value that he believes he embodies, the value of sacrifice. Now he believes he is facing a crisis again. He and the other refugees have lost their place as leaders of their society. And this time, Chang doesn't know what to sacrifice. The people he believes he has sacrificed his life for are now rising up against him. It is a great betrayal.[1]

Eventually, the Japanese grew tired of taunting the boy. And Chang was let go. For the moment, at least, he could forget the idea of sacrificing himself, an idea which had probably helped him endure the ordeal. He comforted himself with food. And then, as a final release, he allowed himself to cry.

> Eventually, the Japanese got tired of us and let us go. I wandered around in the dark in the countryside unable to cry. I kept thinking to myself, if I can just see some light I'll be okay. I eventually did make it back to Fuzhou. I still had some money and the first thing I did was find one of those stalls selling fish balls. These are a kind of traditional food they sell there. I drank the broth too quickly and then real tears came to my eyes and I was no longer ashamed to cry.

Presently he found a way to escape to the interior where his brother and sister were hiding. There he again indulged himself in food. Soon he had unremitting diarrhea. He had returned to normalcy, or so the narrative would suggest. If trauma is timeless, as some believe, then the desire for an escape out of trauma, for a return to a state before trauma, must also partake of that timelessness. Chang is talking about what all the mainland refugees talk about: the desire to return. It does not matter whether this is a return to Taiwan under martial law, before democratic reforms spoiled the absolute power of the mainland refugees, or it is a return to a childhood before the Japanese invasion, when a father still lived and offered a far different future than the one later meted out by fate. Or whether it is a return to the arms of a soldier husband whose life was squelched out on a battlefield in 1949. All the memories generated during an exploration into the history of the mainland immigrants show some desire to return to some other state, no matter how far back in the past.

The Japanese invasion marked a point of no return for China. It was not just the tens of millions who died, nor the swathes of land laid waste. Documentary accounts from former Japanese soldiers testify to the rage and indiscriminate attacks of the Japanese army on Chinese civilians. Reports showing just how barbaric the Japanese soldiers were have filtered out of Japan in recent years.[2] Retired Japanese soldiers, in their eighties and nineties, told a Japanese documentary maker how they had tied women to bales of straw, inserting straw in their vaginas, then set the entire fixture alight. Others confessed similar acts of brutality.

Yet immediate history overshadows even this. It offers an antidote, an alternative, a panacea. It impacts the way Chinese refugees tell their stories. The refugees have moved on. They have found a new way to talk about themselves. The rise of mainland China, economically and militarily, relative to Taiwan, over the past two decades has proved a concrete fixture in the minds of mainland Chinese refugees recounting their pasts. Many of the refugees interviewed have gone back to China in recent years, now that the blockade is over. They have sunk thousands of dollars into alleviating the plight of relatives. Some have failed when they tried their hand at business ventures. One sign of this newfound familiarity with China is the slather of Chinese jargon that finds its way into the mouths of its refugees, fifty years after they fled for the first time. Ko Jen-tao speaks repeatedly of *danwei*, or work units, as if he had grown up with the specifically Chinese term. Ku Chi, the retired banker, lards his entire account with words of Chinese origin which he picked up during his annual pilgrimages.

More profoundly, the refugees now look back into their memories for signs of the Communists' power. They have come to paint the Chinese Communists as awesome, fearsome, better informed and more effective logistically than the Kuomintang soldiers ever were. Even ten years earlier, when the shadow of the KMT still held sway after half a century of rule, such a representation would have been impossible. The mainland settlers have a new way of seeing things. They have seen the demise of their party. Locals infested it and it finally fell from power. They have seen the rise of the Democratic Progressive Party, representing those locals. But they have also seen the rise of China as a super power. Thus, we have Tan Hua-shen, a farmer turned soldier, in awe of the Communist educational tactics: upon arriving at camp, the Kuomintang soldiers could sleep. But the Communists had to endure a long ordeal of study sessions. Only with such discipline, he argues, were the Communists able to lure in the entire population of every district they encountered. Again, twenty years earlier, Tan would have been shot for such a description. Perhaps, then, the two decades since have merely loosened tongues. But they have also changed perspectives.

Through their memories, we see a change in attitude towards China, and the kind of identity that can be wrought from identifying oneself as Chinese. In the initial rush, twenty years previously, when restrictions on cross-strait travel were first lifted, mainland refugees such as Ko Jen-tao rushed to their hometowns to dispense gold watches, jewelry, and hard currency. By identifying themselves as Chinese, by binding themselves to their families, they could escape the growing intolerance of them by the natives in Taiwan. They had become, overnight, denizens of China, a great country. They could reap the respect from the rising superpower that they had lost at home. But eventually, their hopes were shattered. Most of their investments in China failed. They found themselves alienated from their relatives. And they married younger Chinese women only to find their whole families opposed. The common culture formed out of these experiences was one of profound sadness and confusion. Nevertheless, elements of it still remained strong in the memories of the refugees.

Tan Hua-shen used to be a farmer in a small corner of Shandong Province. His accent is strong. So strong that it sounds like his tongue is simply clacking in his mouth. He has black splotches covering his face. When he turns his head, his face appears as thin as a reed. But when he talks, it becomes solemn and long. Across his forehead stretch a myriad of tiny wrinkles, like ridges on sand. He was a colonel in the Kuomintang army, fought with Communist soldiers hand to hand, and still retains enough unfazed swagger to crush out lighted cigarette butts between his bare fingers. Through the haze of his deep accent, which now sounds like insects scratching, now like sticks breaking, he first describes a battle scene in a manner reminiscent of other battle accounts.

> I was running on the battlefield when I saw my first Communist. It was really misty and I couldn't see well. He came up out of the fog and I stabbed him in the shoulder. It didn't go in far. Just about half-an-inch. He pulled it out and threw my gun to the ground. Then I saw he was actually much bigger than I was. We had a rule on the battlefield. If the enemy is bigger than you, run. If he's smaller, fight. I started to run and he yelled at me. He yelled, "Don't move." Then another one came in. I held up my hands and said, "I surrender." The big one still stabbed me. I held up my hand to stop

it and I still have a scar across my palm where the blade went in. After that, I ran again.

Such a forthright account would not have been tolerated during Taiwan's forty-year period of martial law, when the slightest word against the government or the party (roughly the same thing) would have led to disastrous consequences. Nor would any admiration shown for the enemy have been tolerated. The Chinese Communists were continually referred to as the "Land Bandits," who won China through thievery, skullduggery, brainwashing its people, and massacring millions. The narrator's standpoint becomes more vehement when, a little further on, he describes his foe's methods. In what could very well be an old soldier's knack for creating drama by magnifying his enemy's prowess, Tan nevertheless suggests that the entire Communist apparatus was more effective than the Nationalists. By way of comparison, he first denigrates the corruption of his own regime.

> I didn't worry too much about my parents. We were all living in a war zone so each person had to fend for himself. There was no way for them to get out, anyway. I, on the other hand, could join the army. That was my way of getting away. But I wasn't getting anywhere, really. At home, we hadn't had anything to eat. In the army, there was nothing to eat either. It wasn't that the army didn't have supplies. They did. It was just that the rations allotted for the soldiers were sent through the officers. The officers would skim some off the top, sell it, and send the money home to their relatives. It wasn't that the food was bad, it was just that we never got much of it.
>
> So when we went into communist areas we were starving. But we couldn't get a single bite of food. The Communists were really effective. They would come into an area and brainwash everyone in that area, children, adults, everyone. Even the kids were soldiers.

Many of Tan's friends were, as he spoke, in the process of moving to China, where living was cheaper and second or third wives could be had for a lower arrangement. They had begun to see China as a safe haven. Soon they started to look into their memories, readjust them, talk about times when the Communists were strong, when the Nationalists were weak. They began to put down, to complain about their lives. The promises made by the Nationalists never seemed to come through. Tan, who has a large family and lives in a tiny cupboard of an apartment, with books spilling out of one wall and debris piled up against another, no longer sees himself as the heir to a great social revolution, or even to a great killing machine. He repeatedly describes his life as *luan qi ba zao*—that is, utter chaos. His descriptions of the early Kuomintang military compared to the Communists convey a similar sense of shame.

> If eating was a problem, sleeping was even worse. We never had a chance to sleep. We were always moving. Finally, we developed a way to sleep while marching. The man in back would lean one arm on the shoulder of the man in front of him. If he leaned close enough, he could fall into a light doze even as his feet kept moving. The only problem was that when one person slipped or tripped on some rough ground, the whole file of us would fall down. No one would know what had happened. After twenty-four hours of marching like that, practically half of us would be missing our guns and most of our supplies.
>
> No one could beat the Communists. When we got to a major city or town, we could sleep a little. But when the Communists arrived at a destination, they didn't even let their soldiers sleep. No, their soldiers would have to attend thought-education classes, meetings, they would have to go through questioning, struggle sessions, face all sorts of logical questioning. That was the way the Communists did things. Let me put it this way, with an enemy like that, how do you ever have a chance?

Tan Hua-shen is only one of many mainland immigrants whose admiration of present-day Chinese Communist power spills over into his interpretation of the past. Twenty years of seeing China rise, as their own power in Taiwan decayed, have taught them that it is better to elevate the former enemy and begin to try to identify themselves with the rising regime in the mainland. All the travel across the Taiwan Strait undertaken in the last twenty years, the multitudinous gifts, the billions of dollars poured into China are yet further reasons to associate themselves with the mainland regime, an attempt that has largely failed.

At the same time is an appreciation of the difficulties in trying to unite China, which the Communists accomplished more or less. Such an appreciation is often full of humor. Here, the soldiers seem to have, at least partially, reached some level of having forgiven themselves for the great shame of "losing China." They can laugh at the difficulties contained in the task presented to them by their commanders: to unify all of China. Eighty-five-year-old Lin Ching-wu, who presented his stomach for viewing and touching, showing it to be hard and virile under a small deposit of fat, described a failed campaign, one that was doomed from the start, not by conditions in the field, but by his own ineptness with northern vernacular. How could he be expected to unite the country if he couldn't even talk to the local people? It happened during the Kuomintang's much-touted Northern Expedition in the 1920s. In the end, Chiang Kai-shek corralled a few of the warlords possessing middle and southern China over to his side, made flaky alliances with others, and generally left the northern ones alone—so long as they flew his flag. It was proclaimed a tremendous victory. In the memories of the soldiers who fought in northern forays, the desire to reunify China, this ideology, this great yearning of the time, nevertheless still lives on, indomitable, hopeless and constant. Amid failing campaigns, and the beginning of the all-out retreat to Taiwan, Lin describes an encounter that proclaims just how far apart northern and southern China were—and what a fool he was forever thinking they had anything important in common. He was from Fujian, an extreme southern, coastal province. The action took place in Shandong, in the far northern reaches.

> Southerners and northerners speak differently. But the commander wanted me to go and ask directions because we had to get over the pass. We had to go to save other troops. The place we were heading was very well known, a very important place. But it was easy to get lost. So they told me to go ask directions from a woman who was selling peanuts. I went. I said to her, "Madam, we want to go to such-and-such place, what road should we take?" She got down. Her feet were small, they were bound. "You are the madam! You are the madam!" she started yelling.
> "Hold on!" I said, "What are you talking about?" I didn't know what she was saying. I was so shaken up I thought to myself, at least I still have my knife, I even have a gun. Can you imagine? I was so startled and frightened I was actually thinking of ways I could defend myself against a small woman. Then I grew furious. How dare she act this way towards me? I just stood there.
> After a few moments, an older, local person came over and said, "What happened?"
> I said, "I just asked her, Madam, how do you get to so-and-so?"
> He said, "Oh, a misunderstanding, a misunderstanding. If you want to get there, you just head that way."
> So we kept going. After we had gone about twenty-five miles, I still wasn't comfortable. I felt it in my stomach. I had been humiliated. Our troop leader was riding a horse. He rode by and joked that I had harassed that young woman. I wasn't even twenty. I was really angry.

> Finally, another officer rode by. He asked me, "Lin Ching-wu, what were you trying to do back there?"
> I said, "I didn't do anything. I just asked that woman, 'Madam, if we want to get to such-and-such a place, which way should we go?' Then she got down and started yelling at me. And now the commander is saying I was harassing her." I was near tears.
> He said, "Ha, it's your own fault, kid. In this part of the country, 'Madam' means the head of a whore house. That's what 'Madam' means."

It was this memory that he took with him to Taiwan when the armies of the Kuomintang finally retreated in 1949. It was a memory involving the inconceivable vastness of China and the difficulties of uniting it under a deceptively common language. Lin couldn't even use the language to talk to a woman without calling her a whore. Yet it was this language that the Nationalist (Kuomintang) leaders would take with them too as they now attempted to unite a single island. The Communists achieved in actuality what the Kuomintang only dreamed. It makes sense, therefore, that someone like Lin, at a time when ideology along with pride had been stripped away, would later come to the realization of how far superior they were to the Kuomintang. Laid up, injured, shot in the foot, in a field tent in Nanjing, Lin learns through reading the newspapers and talking to a local boy of the vast prowess of his foes.

> I bought a lot of peanut butter every day. I got the kid who sold newspapers to do it for me. I bought a lot of newspapers so he was willing to help me. *The New China Press. The Save the Nation News. The Central News.* I bought every newspaper he had. Because I had to lie there, I couldn't move, I just ate peanut butter and read newspapers. I also learned something. The Communist newspapers were the best by far. Their propaganda was the best. Their organization was the best. The Communist commanders would brag that if their troops heard fighting someplace, they would all rush to get there. I learned this from the boy who sold newspapers. He was about eight or nine, a local.

These sentiments, this epiphany, are from a man who sixty years later still displays a Nationalist Party flag atop his television set. He had worked for the party, after his retirement from the army, as a party indoctrinator of students in Kuomintang ideology in Taiwan Normal University. His rush to acclaim the Communists as warriors, and to disclose his discovery of their greatness, like other former soldiers, followed a time of great sadness and anger, when he felt he had lost status in his own society and perhaps even safety. Alone, betrayed, wounded in their pride, many of the old mainland soldiers now began looking to their old foes for justice, for an imagined justice, even as they hated the new government in Taiwan with a hatred they had once felt for the Communists. Even his inability to govern his children has become a sign of the times, when locals from the middle and southern part of the island come roaring up to take over the universities and from there the halls of power. The first democratic election in Taiwan in 1996 elected the Kuomintang's frontrunner, Lee Teng-hui. But he, a local Taiwanese, later turned out to be interested in initiating even more reforms. When the opposition party actually succeeded in winning the election for president, in 2000, the stalwart mainland immigrants blamed Lee squarely for delivering the reins of power into their hands. On election night, a mob of them, armed with clubs, approached his home, only to be driven back by a mainland immigrant politician then serving as mayor of Taipei, Ma Ying-jeou.

Later, Ma would become president, as the mainlander party fought to resurrect itself. But by then it was too late. The mainlanders and the Kuomintang had already tasted defeat for the second time. They barely stood it once. Just that one time and still remained whole men, or at least men with the memory of what it was like to be whole. It was understandable that they were defeated by peasants in the mainland. Peasants had overthrown dynasties, and the Kuomintang knew they were superior, even if they had lost the war. They still had all the art works of ancient China. They still represented the land-owning and educated class. And they still somehow believed they might retake their home, until that dream faded away, too. For a while, at least, they still could believe in themselves. But to be defeated again, to be cast out of power again, on the island they had reshaped in their own image, by another party of essentially former farmers was too much. They recoiled. They renounced their past. They decided they couldn't even call themselves heroes anymore. Instead, they began to make up a new dream of themselves as part of a larger China, one led by their former enemies. They had looked into the mouth of defeat once again, and were no longer themselves, the selves they had known for most of their lives.

The frustration and sense of betrayal that led to this *recouchement*[3] Lin feels in recounting the collapse of authority. The authority of the party he fought for and nearly died for is gone, dead. Once the Kuomintang fell again, he says, Taiwan began to head into eventual collapse. Those in the middle and south of Taiwan that he refers to are the locals once ruled by the authoritarian Kuomintang. They are in control now. And their crass ways are going to further destroy the island.

> So Taiwan has now been through this kind of democratic election. Actually, it has destroyed our ethical and moral ideals. It has all been destroyed by these politicians. The young people in Taipei no longer have any morals. Hundreds of thousands of young people don't get married. This is because there are a lot of children from the middle and southern parts of the island who have done really well on their college entrance examinations. As a result, they get into a lot of the top universities. When they're finished, there's no way they would ever return home for some job in the countryside, so they stay in Taipei. They can't get married. There are too many of them. My son and daughter can't find partners either. They didn't go to top schools. So no one wants to marry them.
>
> So now Taiwan is turning into two separate countries. Those kids from the middle and the south who know how to study end up getting good jobs. But the kids who couldn't get out can't find anyone to marry either. So they go to the mainland or Thailand or get married with a foreigner. But they speak different languages there. And they don't always have a good level of education. Their children won't be able to find jobs either. You tell me, isn't that creating two countries? Now everyone yells and swears, no one has the basic understanding of how to be polite. This is the future of Taiwan, this is what it's going to look like. I try to convince my children to hurry up and get married, but I can't force them. I tell them that if you have children, I can help to look after them. Today in Taipei, you have to spend a fortune to get someone to look after your kids. At least, my son has a girlfriend. My daughter—I don't know. I have a lot of free time, I am very responsible. If they find a good partner, and want to get married, I won't oppose it.

So the changes in Taiwan even seem to threaten Lin's future familial line—his descendants. He thought he had found a safe place to have children. But now it looks like he was wrong.

He doesn't say it. But he almost feels like the whole thing wasn't worth it, the escape, the flight out of hell, the refuge he seemed to find on the island. They had left everything behind. They had had no choice. Following the devastation of the Japanese invasion and the war with the Communists, a whole regime was put in motion. Boatload after boatload of soldiers and families left the docks of Shanghai. Airplanes took off precipitously like swarms of insects, leaving Chongqing, the final capital of the Kuomintang government, heading for

Taiwan. Rage, embitterment, and loss pour through most memories. How else should they feel? But suddenly a different note reigns. That is humor. At no other place in all the exiles' memories, than in recounting their crossings from China to Taiwan, fifty years before, does humor shine forth so strongly. Strangely, at the moment when they knew without a doubt that they had lost everything—lands, family, country, pride, honor and history—when they made the jump across the Strait, they were finally able to laugh. Maybe not then. But now, thinking back over the crossing, they do laugh.

Remembering it, they become sarcastic, sardonic, even outright hilarious. One young opera singer, for instance, was tricked by her husband into believing that she was merely taking off for a brief honeymoon. "I packed nothing," she said. "But fortunately I had a towel that I could use to vomit into during the trip."

Suddenly, nothing is more important than the basic needs of their bodies. Needs to vomit, to defecate. They use humor to remember their sickness. Tan Hua-shen, the old soldier from Shandong who crushed out a cigarette in his bare fingers, summarized the massive retreat—including government officials, families and their loot—as a search for a place to shit.

> It was hell. I had just left home. I hadn't been a soldier long. Now suddenly I was in this kind of hell. Our retreat was absolute chaos. We started from Qingdao, took a ship to Hong Kong, then to Taiwan, then to Hainan Island, then back to Taiwan. A lot of people got sick, really sick, on the ship. Our ship was a landing craft. The bathroom was simply a hole in the ramp that you lower to land troops. But there was only room for one person. You had to release the ramp and lower it down over the sea for anyone to be able to go to the bathroom. If one guy wanted to take a crap, he would have to fight with four or five people to get over the hole. After a while, the whole ramp broke off and fell into the sea. A whole bunch of guys fighting for the hole fell into the ocean. But the boat just kept going. And we were in the middle of the Pacific Ocean.

Even with the ominous last two lines, the incident is generally told as a humorous one. On some level, the memory of the passage to Taiwan must have still represented the future, the unknown, perhaps even death, for this generation of seventy, eighty, and ninety-year-olds. As they faced into the unknown, leaving an entire life behind, they had no idea what was in store. They had to find themselves. They had to know what they were going to be. They weren't even sure who they had been pretending to be all along. In the case of Ku Chi, the Shanghai banker with a face vaguely resembling the steamed and wrinkled shell of a dumpling, his transition to Taiwan did not involve only physical and emotional distress. He had to forget who he was. His father, the doctor who fell down the stairs in an alcoholic stupor, had once made a promise to a wealthy but childless friend that he would give him one of his own children to raise as his own, enabling him to pass down his family name to posterity.

> My father had this good friend. A very good friend. So good that when he told my father he wanted a son of his own—he didn't have any children himself, this friend—he said to my father, "Give me one of your sons to carry on the Ku family line." Actually, people had been making this kind of arrangement for a long time. But then, the War of Resistance, against the Japanese, started. The man who was to be my future father, I'll call him my stepfather, went into the interior. He had to flee because of the war. He worked at a munitions plant that made weapons. Later, it was turned into a money-casting plant. It belonged to the Nationalists.

The promise was made when the child was eight. Then the Japanese invaded. By the time they retreated, he was seventeen and the promise had still not been fulfilled. The natural father, on his deathbed, regretted his idle words and told the mother to keep the boy by her side. But then another enemy force drew near. This time, the mother was weak. She dreamed of a brighter future for her son. He was now nineteen. Fearing for his safety, and knowing that the elder man was about to be transferred to Taiwan, along with his money-casting plant, she blindly flung her son out from her arms. He would accompany his new "father" to a new land, one of safety and plenty. He didn't see her again for fifty years.

> So that was how I became his son. When the War of Resistance was won, he came back. He brought the promise up again, with my mother. At that time, my father had already passed away. So he spoke to my mother. He said, "You promised to give the child to me a long time ago." I had already graduated from high school. I was already working. But he said, "Look, I'm going to Taiwan, to safety. Give your child to me, to go to Taiwan with me, and I promise he will live and have a new life there."
>
> At that time, I was working in Shanghai in a bank, in the Hsin-hua Bank. I told my mother to agree. I thought this was best for our family. I could send them money and bring them over later. I agreed to be an adopted son. I went with him. I went with the money-casting plant.

> Things were really bad; the Nationalists were about to be defeated. So when they retreated from Shanghai, they took my stepfather along with the plant. And he took me.

His name was now Ku Chi, rather than Wong Chi. He had cast aside his family name, his mother, sisters and his childhood home. His job in the bank was the result of a series of tedious exams, including the manipulation of an abacus. By the time of his adoption, at the age of nineteen, he had been helping to support his mother for several years. He was already a man. And he had a girlfriend.

> Of course, I worried about those left behind. But before we left, my stepfather had given my mother some money to help her out. He said, "You hold on to this money in case you need it." It would have been impossible to bring my mother along. My mother still had family there. She had a house in the foreign concession; it belonged to my uncle who had let us live there.
>
> I was also leaving behind my girlfriend. She was a classmate of mine. She was very pretty, beautiful even. She had short hair that just curled under her cheeks. Just like this. But I hadn't spent much time with her. There wasn't any time for that in those days. At most, sometimes, we would see each other for a few hours. In those days, if you had a girlfriend, you couldn't even hold hands. Not in public, at least. We would just meet and talk. Just talk. Nobody went to see movies, no way. We would just chat. My girlfriend—after I got to Taiwan, I lost track of her. It was decades before we could communicate with Shanghai again. There was no way I could find out what had happened to her.

Later, when he was an old man, he tried to find her. He figured he would just ask around among some of his friends from childhood. But what he heard didn't help him. She had married a soldier from the People's Liberation Army and moved to Shandong, a northern province near Korea.

> It wasn't until I went back, just a few years ago, that I learned that my girlfriend had married someone else, she had moved to another province, to Shandong. I found out that her husband was a soldier. In the People's Liberation Army. I never even tried to get in touch with her. It would have been impossible. Even if she hadn't been married, it would have been impossible to see her anyway. After all these years, she's probably dead, anyway, I guess.
>
> My classmates, friends, a lot of them . . . I did find. After I found them, I went back to hold a classmates' reunion every year. But I never

heard anything more about her. I don't think she even graduated. No, she couldn't have graduated. She only got about half way through her studies and dropped out. Of course, I missed her. She was the only girlfriend I've ever had besides my wife. There was a time when I first got to Taiwan, that I hoped that somehow she could make it out, but that was impossible, of course. We were the last ones out. It was impossible. Even just before I left, with my stepfather, we didn't even talk about it. We didn't want to think about it. We knew that, because of my stepfather's connections, I could get out. But my girlfriend and I weren't married yet. We just weren't ready. So I couldn't bring her. We hadn't gotten to that stage yet. We hadn't even talked about marriage. Not at all. It's not that I hadn't wanted to, though. She was the most beautiful girl I had ever seen.

At the time, of course, nineteen years old and on his way to Taiwan, Ku wasn't missing anyone. Not yet. In the telling, he remembers how good it felt to be free. He and his colleagues worked their way away from the crowded, throbbing stench of the cabins and slept on the decks. When they landed, at the port of Keelung, the importance of his new father's enterprise ensured they were met in cars by officials. From that moment on began a life of ease and pleasure, unknown to the young man before. So charmed is he by the memory, that he describes in intricate detail, with greater detail than any used before, his new life in Taiwan. The plant, which brought piece-meal from Shanghai, still had to be set up. And while engineers were working at that task, he and his young colleagues sported around post-war Taiwan in high style, drawing a full salary and spending it lavishly. His tone takes on an almost humorous quality as he recounts experiences still unbelievable for post-war China. His good fortune inspires him with wry mirth as he retells it.

> When we first got to Taiwan, we spent all our time just hanging around. We didn't have to do anything. The plant was still being set up. So we just collected our salaries and took it easy. It was a good time. We took the money and just spent it randomly. It was a lot for those days. We didn't know what we were doing. We were fools. Fools with a lot of money. We used to spend a lot of time trying out different kinds of Western food. There was this department store on Broad Compassion Road. We would go up to the fifth floor, to a restaurant where they served Western food, and spend hours there. It was pretty pathetic. We didn't even know how to use a knife and fork.
>
> I still remember it cost five dollars for a "first-class" meal. Our goal was to eat as many of these "first-class" meals as possible. We all went there

almost every day. On the other hand, sometimes we would just take off and explore the island. Generally speaking, we had a pretty good time until the plant was set up. Then we had to come back to Taipei and start work. We had been on vacation for about a half year. And we had spent a lot of money.

Even after we started working, we still had more money than we knew what to do with. We didn't think of saving. So if we had any free time, we would just take off. We went all over the place, to Sun Moon Lake, Lion's Head Rock, all over the place. We always took the train. That was a fun time. There still wasn't that much work to do. So we just waited for our salaries and then took off. We traveled around the whole island at least three or four times.

He just can't seem to stop remembering. His annual returns to Shanghai, to hold classmate reunions, every year without fail, are of far greater frequency than other mainland immigrants, who return every few years. He is still looking, among the paved streets and European-style buildings, for his adolescence. In Taipei, he lives in a small apartment with a wife who mumbles as he speaks, as if, speechless, she can only echo his words. She walks hunched over as if she were ready to tumble forward in a living room where the air throbs with dust and the apartment floor heaves under old newspapers and garbage. A tiny, airless room drenched with the stale smell of humidity and exhaust buries him amid heat and stuffiness, a reminder of his final resting place. His arrival on the island was only an interlude.

And that was the way it was supposed to be for his government—an interlude on the island. Not a long-term stay. This was the Kuomintang government under Chiang Kai-shek. The government took an active role in promoting a common culture, based not on the experiences of flight, but on the experience of its brief claim to represent all of China. The central government had been preparing for an exodus from the mainland for years. Even as early as 1945, at the end of World War II, when Taiwan was handed over to the Nationalist regime, the Kuomintang began setting up a base in Taiwan. According to civil servants such as Chang Ching-tan, a whole flock of Fujian men were trained to handle the retrocession. Yet Chiang Kai-shek feared, above all else, that the islanders had been "Nipponified," so swayed by fifty years of Japanese colonial rule, that they had lost their Chinese souls—a fear that had some basis in that many Taiwanese had already embraced Japanese modernity.[4] Still, it was a shallow reckoning of the Taiwanese. There was little emphasis, in Kuomintang ideology, on what the

Chinese in Taiwan had been *before* the Japanese occupation, and whether this foundation would contribute to Nationalist rule.

Prior to the Japanese fifty-year occupation, the island was a rugged outpost where life was brutal and virtual slave-like conditions reigned as Chinese overseers exacted harsh punishments to goad local farmers to supply sugar and rice to the southern provinces of Fujian and Guangdong. Merciless gangs, random violence, on both the local and the ruling sides, corporal abominations, low-level culture, and other afflictions scourged the population of Chinese settlers. The aborigines, driven off their land, killed and forced into mountainous regions, fared worse. This abomination of an island, that nevertheless supplied enormous amounts of rice to Fujian and Guangdong during the late Qing, was then tempered by half a century of Japanese colonization. The Japanese built roads, schools, telegraphs, railroads, and even fostered a few Taiwanese men to ascend to the heights of Imperial education. A very few Taiwanese, during those harsh but efficient fifty years, were even allowed to become doctors or lawyers.

Then the Nationalist Chinese armies began to arrive, starting in 1945. They brought with them a mixed breadbasket of goods and evils. On one hand, they brought mainland Chinese culture, memory, and tradition. On the other hand, poor Nationalist soldiers, often from rotting peasant huts in the interior, were so benighted and poorly trained that they immediately engaged in the worst kinds of pilfering, theft, corruption, and crime. Even the officers, emerging from a culture of corruption in the mainland, dismantled Japanese factories to ship them back to the mainland to sell for scrap metal. Rice, available if not plentiful under the Japanese, by 1947 was so scarce that there was public rationing. The Japanese-educated Taiwanese were disgusted.

Chiang Kai-shek was disgusted with them as well. In his fanatic and paranoid mind, he began to believe that every Taiwanese had been corrupted by Japanese ways. His experience in the mainland, fleeing and occasionally fighting the Japanese, had taught him that Japanese forces were the nonpareil of Asian warfare. His ragtag troops could not resist even a much-smaller contingent of Japanese forces. The conflagration beginning on February 28, 1947, in which Chiang ordered additional shiploads of Nationalist troops to the island to hunt down and butcher tens of thousands of locals, was motivated partly by this fear. Indeed, students trained under the Japanese fought off Nationalist soldiers successfully until overwhelmed by greater numbers and firepower.

But it was more than that. The Generalissimo had never thought that there would come men and women, scholars, after him who would see Taiwan in a new way. Eventually, after his rule had ended, a new generation of Taiwanese scholars gradually emerged. Eventually, they would come to revisit the identity of Taiwan before either the Japanese or the Nationalists arrived. Some scholars contend that Taiwan had over one thousand candidates for a high-level degree in the Qing imperial examinations before the two invasions. Such a record would put the island on par with the some of the wealthiest provinces in the lower Yangtze region.[5] Other historians have depicted Taiwan as a picturesque dale of flowing streams and wild horses.[6] Such accounts conflict sharply with the conception of the island popular in the West, in universities and in conference halls. That Taiwan during the Qing was a hellish, denuded, forced-labor camp where aborigines fought with locals and locals rebelled against mainland Chinese authorities who regularly mounted forays against them, chopping off heads, and torching villages.[7]

But at the time, when they first came over, the Nationalists saw themselves as saviors, saviors that would spread the divine influence of Chinese civilization. But they also felt an inferiority—not only to Japanese influence, as has commonly been described—but perhaps to a previous, deep inlay of Chinese culture. Just as other invaders found that it made more sense to negotiate with rich, complex regions, such as the lower Yangtze delta region, the Nationalists eventually realized that it would take more than massacre to occupy—and transform—Taiwan.

The Kuomintang had always set their sights on the biggest, richest, most comfortable cities. They had reduced Shanghai to ashes, squeezing businessmen, extorting money, running the economy into the ground until all that was left was paper money that wasn't even worth the paper it was printed on. Now it was Taipei. But this time they had learned some lessons, hard ones. They didn't so much occupy Taipei as transform it into something else, something bigger than themselves, something they could use to remember their loss. More than a monument to all of China, the city was transformed into a living temple to the lost mainland.[8] As the Nationalist forces lost more and more lands on China, its government sent a hurried batch of telegrams to the Taipei City Government and the Ministry of the Interior detailing how the new capital would be outfitted.[9] This included lavish road signs spelling out the names and provinces of the lost cities in the mainland. As their soldiers lost ground in the mainland, their officials recreated it, in miniature, in the road signs of Taipei. Northern parts of the city were plastered with street signs corresponding to the location of northern parts of the mainland. Southern streets were named after southern cities. The mainland was disappearing under them, as the Communists won increasingly more ground. But the government ordered it recreated, like a miniature world, across the Taiwan Strait, in Taipei. When the transformation was complete, the entire city of Taipei was renamed with little flags bearing the names of cities now lost. It was a map.

Then it became something else, something that its creators had perhaps never intended it to become. Feverish, detailed telegrams spelled out not only the names to be used for streets. They included, with a sort of feverish obsession, almost a hysteria, the exact height, width, material and other details easily left to local administrators. "Use only enamel for coating," instructs one, an expensive and time-consuming process usually used only for ceramics. The street signs were obviously for more than simply giving directions. They were given the highest priority. It was only after this batch of telegrams about such a seemingly irrelevant topic as street signs that the Kuomintang government in Nanjing turned to other topics, such as traitors, sewage and education.

The city was intended to not only remind the retreating soldiers and personnel of what they had lost, and hoped to regain. It was also meant to preserve a vision of what the Kuomintang believed they rightfully owned, a mimetic mirror of their identity, calculated by the lands they would someday possess, stretching from north to south. It was a static reminder of the furthest extent of their memory—even if that memory was not entirely true. Xizang Lu, "Tibet Road," for instance, snakes along the western part of Taipei, in a claim to a land that the Kuomintang government never truly owned. The city, in this sense, was a dream. It was also a crypt. By laying out in so static a representation the territories believed rightfully owned by the Nationalists, it soon became a reminder, not of what the Kuomintang possessed, but what they didn't possess. Newly-arrived Nationalist soldiers believed the rallying cry of "Retake the Mainland" for a matter of years. Then they stopped believing. When they looked at the gaudy street signs, adorning the streets of Taipei, each with the name of a city or province of China, they felt shame, perhaps even ridicule.

Soon the street signs themselves became almost an embarrassment. Taipei was a land of rice paddies stretching to the horizon. The occasional low, Japanese-style bungalow sprang up. Hu Yao-hen, a professor from Hunan, imagined that Taipei was refitted because in Chinese history generals often made maps of a territory that they were bent on conquering. But the city itself was a disaster of complex proportions. Japanese influence still hung over the higher quarters. News stories of the day often described unlicensed and debased scandal. One, for instance, revolved around a thirteen-year-old French prostitute, apparently working in the Japanese quarter. Her mother had cast her off and the court decided that such a move was justified. The mother no longer had to pay any support to her. Kuomintang news items always yearned for other cities, describing the "rebuilding of Changsha," even as the city fell to the Communists. Taipei was a city that was more like some kind of dream.[10]

The street signs were not only dreams. They were also arbiters of the fate of the Nationalists. They were reminders of the failure of the Kuomintang not only to win back China but to keep that hope alive. The street signs now became sad, heavy, tragic markers, markers of failure. Only a few years after the retreat, the city began to resemble a tomb. It was like the tomb of the first emperor of China, Qin Shi Huang, who adorned it with a great map of China, in some ways not dissimilar to the city that the Nationalists had remade.[11] The regime was already starting on its long deathfall. And it had built its own crypt for a capital.[12]

Hu Yao-hen came from a background bigger than he could ever hope to be. His father was the publisher of the Kuomintang Party newspaper in Hubei and rose to influence in the party through his work there. His grandfather was even more illustrious. He had passed the imperial examinations and reached the rank of *xiucai*. He was in a position to, and might even, become policy advisor to the emperor. Hu's family had moved to Hubei from the Jiangxi area as the Taiping armies drew near in the late 1850s. As a result of this move, Hu's father had a chance to go to Peking University—and eventually on to Kuomintang fame. Hu himself, now seventy-seven, with a wry sense of humor, dry voice, and a face that is always tilted back a little, looking down at his audience, would no doubt have followed in the family tradition if not for the Japanese invasion. By the end of two wars, against the Japanese and the Communists, the family's resources were shattered. As his ancestors had fled the utopian ideology and egalitarian-minded armies of the Taiping Rebellion in the middle of the nineteenth century, he eventually fled the utopian ideology and egalitarian-minded armies of the Communists. He began by trying to walk out of his home region during the Japanese invasion.

> There was no way to get out on a boat. The Japanese had a lot of planes bombing the coast and a lot of the boats were destroyed. We didn't own a car. The only choice we had was to walk. It was, shall we say, interesting. I was just a kid. I couldn't really walk. They put me in a bamboo basket and carried me. When I looked down one side of the road, there was a straight drop to a valley. On the other side was a mountain. I kept getting hit by branches of trees. Finally, I got down and walked. After a few days, I was able to keep up with everybody else. I call it my Long March. It took us about a month to get out.

Several times they met Japanese soldiers. But the soldiers, too, were on the run. Outside a large building, they ran into several soldiers. They had no idea that the Japanese, like them, were just looking for food—and that they most likely wouldn't be willing to take on a large crowd of Chinese.

> We were in a small town and when we heard about the Japanese coming, we tried to hide in a small alley. There were a lot of things, like clothing, all over the ground. We thought we were safe. But then we saw a lot of people hiding in there, too. And then a chicken ran in. There were a lot of Japanese soldiers chasing the chicken so when it ran into our alley, the Japanese soldiers came after it. When they saw us, maybe because there were so many of us, they didn't shoot. They just left. So we waited for a while, then we ran out of the alley. A lot of people were running out at the same time. The whole thing scared my mother so much that she turned around and took us back to our hometown. She was afraid of what would happen to her if the Japanese caught her alone.

So they were back where they had started. They spent the entire winter planning, selling whatever grain was left. Then they tried again. This time, they made it as far as Wuhan. Hu's father was there, working in the Nationalist government. He had been separated from them all this time. Every time they tried to escape it was his mother who had to plan it. She couldn't read or write, but she planned those expeditions as if she were a general.

Eventually, the family moved again, propelled by the Communist threat. Sometimes they were with the father, sometimes not. Sometimes his work would relocate the father, in an instant, to an outlying region. Then the family would follow. Other times, their father coordinated their flight together. As the Communists moved inward, Hu and his family reached, resided in briefly and then left Wuhan, Guangxi, and Chongqing. In Wuhan, they stayed three years, the longest. By the time they reached Chongqing, some inner sense—perhaps some instinct passed down from his ancestors—told the boy that his education was in disarray. He tried relying on his father for guidance. His father emphasized rote memorization, even though he had attended Peking University, where the "new thought" was taught.[13] It was this mixture of new thought and old forms of rote memorization that eventually got him into trouble.

> Our teacher had this idea that we should be ready for democracy. So he told each class to elect a representative. I, of course, wanted to be one. I told my father and he got so excited that he ended up writing the whole speech for me. I just had to memorize it. I remember I thought the beginning was just some sort of formula you would use at the beginning of speeches. It was something like: "That I may be here today to see you all, on the one hand I am delighted, yet on the other I am full of shame for my boldness." I got elected. But then when I got into junior high, I ran again. I thought that what my father had written was some sort of set, polite formula, so I used the same beginning again. The rest of it I actually wrote myself. But there was one kid who remembered my earlier speech. I had just said the beginning part, the part I thought was a polite formula, and he yelled out, "You're just using the same speech!" It was humiliating. I remember I said to myself, "From now on, I have to write all of my own speeches."

Soon the family moved on. Now without a school, Hu turned to other sources to advance his education. Because of the flight, he had left all his books behind him. He had nothing to read. There was no model. Then one day he found his attention diverted by another object, less literary but more available. Newspapers. He now had another model for his educational projects.

> The only thing I was interested in at that time was reading. But there were no books. In the hut where we lived, there were newspapers pasted over the walls to keep out flies. They were also there to cover up grime. Basically, someone had just taken a whole bunch of dirty old newspapers and stuck them up to cover dirty old walls, and I started reading all those old newspapers. I don't know why. I just wanted something to read, something, anything. I felt that studying would save me, somehow.

Long hours spent poring over those scrofulous newspapers, dirty and moldy, in a dank room led to a skin infection on the top of his head. His classmates in later schools, when they reached them, even called him names and imitated his terrific need to be continually scratching at the top of his head. Yet from deep in his mind now developed a new association—made clear by the newspapers. This was between literary achievements and power. He stopped minding the taunts of his peers. He began to retreat inside himself, to call up the images of the battles he read about, in the newspapers, and see himself, combining the literary attainments he dreamed about with the personification of glory he also read about. He now became fixated on the one figure in current newspaper reporting that was the very personification of pure, raw power. When he actually saw such a figure on the streets of Wuhan, he was barely able to contain himself.

> There was this one lieutenant posted in our town. I remember his uniform had a belt that went diagonally across his chest. He had a gun holster at his belt. He was my role model. If I saw him on the street, I felt a kind of pain, a kind of sweet pain. Even when I was studying, I would think about him. And when we had to memorize poems, it was worse. For example, one poem we had to learn was the "Yellow Crane Tower." The first line goes like this, "In those days there were men who rode on yellow cranes." The poem was interesting because it was written in Wuhan and we could even go to visit the Yellow Crane Tower. We were supposed to be in love with our Chinese culture especially now that it was in danger of being destroyed. But I was really only in love with the lieutenant.

So two figures now competed in the young boy's mind—the lieutenant and the Yellow Crane Tower, from a poem memorized by Chinese youngsters for a millennium. And yet the final apology suggests that the boy had already started to believe in pure power in and of itself, devoid of the gloss of literary gossamer. The "lieutenant" was now bigger than all education. Hu no longer even knew what the aim of education was. Education, the mastery of naming and knowing things, was no good without power now. There was no doubt. Beauty and antiquity? He could care less.

Such a value system was put to the test when the boy and his father arrived in Hong Kong as part of an army of refugees. The rest of the family had been left behind. His father believed that the fighting would soon be over. Then he would bring over the rest of the family. In the meantime, he and his eldest son would weather out the storm on the shores of Hong Kong. Yet living as refugees was not easy. Life was orderly but desperate.

> There was this bridge between Hong Kong and Guangdong. They never asked you for a passport or anything. They would just say, "Where do you live?" in Cantonese. I remember my father just handed them some gold. And they let us by. The Hong Kong government didn't know how to deal with all the refugees. We ended up living on the side of this mountain. Some of the refugees had cleared away some of the jungle. There were about three hundred people living there when we arrived. It got up to about three thousand after a few weeks. My mother had refused to go on and had stayed behind in Wuhan. I was just there with my father.

It is the last place on earth Hu wanted to be. The bridge is a reminder, the first of many future ones, of the act of losing his home ground, being separated from it. Future barriers will similarly be crossed in similar ways—just by giving money. As a narrator, Hu is talking now only of his experiences as a young man in a Hong Kong refugee camp. But at the same time he is talking about this loss as an older man, an older man who has come to realize that he is losing his home for the second time—Taiwan. Once again, he has become an outsider. Or he has simply been reminded once again that he has always been an outsider, ever since he left home as a child. By denying his status as one of the founders, saviors and rulers of Taiwan, the locals are in a broad sense forcing him to return to that refugee camp over and over again. Without a single friend except for his father, no home, not even knowing where he was going, he can only wait for liberation. He's got to go but there's no way out. His description of the temporary factory in which they lived, the routine of eating, defecating in the refugee camp, is eerie, as if he is some kind of ghost haunting the place where he died. They're trying to force him back there, the locals. He doesn't even know if he is thinking anymore about the past or the present. It's all real. The factory is obtained through the suicide-through-hanging of its owner, a Jew that went bankrupt. Hu didn't see any ghosts. But they rise up all around him as he talks so vividly. It is hot, so hot you could roast a chicken on the sidewalk. He just can't stop remembering. It's like the memories are more real than he is.

> So we lived on that mountainside. There was this old factory there and we heard it used to belong to a Jewish man. I think it made flour. But when the Japanese took over, the owner went bankrupt. He hanged himself from a

beam in the factory. So the factory was empty. So that was where we lived. We called it the "hanging factory." You know, in Chinese, the words for "hanging factory," have the same pronunciation as the words for "change of scenery." We joked that the owner had had a change of scenery. But so had we. If you go there now, it's a well-developed residential area.

There were only about twenty or thirty of us who lived in that factory at first. There weren't any houses. When more people came, we were pushed out and had to make our own houses. My father braced one piece of wood against another, to make an A frame. Then he added more pieces of wood to prop it up and put paper over it that had some oil on it. It was at least enough to keep us dry. But you could barely move inside. You had to keep bent over the whole time. This was basically how we lived. If you didn't move, you could fit five or six on the ground.

How did we support ourselves? We embroidered flowers. You had to do it one by one. Each flower took a really long time. People always wanted to buy these flowers, for weddings or funerals. So we were able to earn a little money. And later on, the Hong Kong government started giving us meal tickets, or as they were called, rice tickets. You would get one each month and every day you used it, they would punch one hole in it. It took about twenty minutes to walk down to the canteen from our camp. I was about eleven or twelve at the time. And after dinner, because of the bad food, I always had to go to the bathroom. The toilet was just a hole on a platform over the harbor. You just squatted over this hole. Usually for dinner they would give us rice and these small fish. But when I went to the toilet after dinner, I used to look down and see my shit and I'd also see those same small fish eating it. It was a very economical way to feed people. The people ate the fish that were fed with their own shit. The meal tickets cost ten Hong Kong dollars each.

As long as Hu can laugh, he's safe. He just can't stop laughing and it infects his whole apartment. He just can't stop talking either. The whole area, where he used to live, is now a developed "suburb," he says. Hu has survived the loss of Kuomintang ascendancy better than many of his cohort. A professor of Western drama living in a clean, upscale apartment in a university district, Hu seems untouched outwardly by the huge societal upheaval of the past twenty years. He still teaches. He's an emeritus professor now but he still goes down to the drama department. He has a book that's going to come out soon. His life suggests that the status of teacher, of university professor, at least in Taipei, is relatively immune from the ethnic shocks that are killing the idea of supremacy. At universities like National Chengchi University, for example, one of the top three universities on the island, entire departments are still full of mainland immigrants, or their children. National Chengchi University, more closely associated with the Kuomintang than others, nevertheless provides an example of how many northern Taiwanese universities provide an island within which mainland immigrants can retain status, prestige and someone to look out for them.

Hu and his father, living in the refugee camp, retained their own sense of status and prestige. Hu's father was still a leading Kuomintang organizer. They spent their evenings, when they were not embroidering flowers, making plans for the future. It was something they were used to. They had spent their flight out of the interior plotting how to reach the next destination. Now they planned to travel to Taiwan and have the rest of the family meet them there. When they eventually made the leap, and arrived on the island, Hu's dreams seemed to be coming true. People met them on the docks, waving flags. It seemed the door was finally open, that he had finally found a new home. But when he got to the city of Taipei, actually just a new staging ground for his government, he knew how far he was from his real home, or even from the other major cities they had traversed on their travel out. He didn't need anyone to tell him.

> Eventually, we were able to get on a ship to Taiwan. I remember I was sick and vomited the whole way. When I could finally stand up, I looked over the railing and saw an island off in the distance. It was mostly covered with jungle. There was a dock sticking out into the harbor. And there was a huge crowd of people standing on it waving flags. Somehow, after being sick for so long, I must have been a little out of it, so I got this strange idea that they were all there to welcome me personally. The dock was packed with people. And they all had flags. It seemed to make sense to me that because I had suffered so much, that they were all waving them for me, kind of like a celebration that I had finally made it.
>
> Later someone told me it was for my father. Apparently the party had organized it. After that, we took a train to Taipei. Now that was a different story. You want to talk about a mess? I remember we came into the city and I started to feel sick again. There were just old one-story houses. They looked like turtle shells that had turned brown from being left out in the sun to dry. Most of them were just crumbling. Some didn't even have roofs or walls. I thought, so this is our new home?

It was pure nothing, as dreams went, but a nothing like a rock hitting you in the head. He had moved so many times. His despair mirrored the official ideology of the Kuomintang that changed as the party realized their temporary flight had become a permanent exile. For the first decade, the government firmly promoted the idea of retaking the mainland. After that, the slogans were carted out and yelled through loudspeakers set up on islands closest to the mainland. The sound was supposed to reach clear across the Taiwan Strait. A good mile or more. If the Communists could hear it, it just didn't matter after a while. After a decade, there wasn't a single Kuomintang soldier who believed them, who believed anything the government promised about retaking the mainland. Soon it became absolutely clear to both sides that the Kuomintang in Taiwan would never "retake the mainland." Similarly, refugees like Hu soon realized they would not see their relatives left behind, perhaps ever again. Almost immediately, Hu realized the government was settling in for a long stay. He noticed the fancy, new street signs, each one painted with the name of a city or province hundreds and thousands of miles away.

> When we first got there, I thought the signs were mainly for the education of the local Taiwanese since the Japanese had controlled them for fifty years. I thought they were meant to familiarize them with China so they wouldn't forget their roots. But after a while, I realized they were there to remind us of what we had lost.

Shortly after his own arrival at Taiwan, the bulk of the Kuomintang armies and officials began arriving, and the street signs took on a different meaning. They now became proofs of a superior culture. They were one of many concrete objects brought or erected by the Kuomintang to bolster their claim for a superior culture—superior to the locals, superior to the Communists. They may have lost to the "land bandits" across the Strait. But they represented the real China—a myth to which the United States held on tight for decades. To the locals, the Kuomintang spread around the teaching that they had come to civilize to save the locals from fifty years of shame as Japanese slaves.

The Nationalists had brought with them all the art works they could carry—jades, vases, bronze sacrificial vessels from the earliest dynasty. They wanted to show that they had proof of their right to rule. They lost the war, but they were the real winners because they represented Chinese culture. The art works were proof. It was around the time of the Japanese invasion, in the 1930s, that the Nationalists had started to haul the art objects out of the imperial palace. The trains they got hold of were packed with cases of these treasures. They went to Shanghai then they carted them up to the mountains of Sichuan. That was about as far from the fighting as you could get. Under the direction of Curator Chuang Yen, a pipe-smoking patrician who wore long traditional gowns, the massive load of Song ceramics, Tang vases, and Qing calligraphic scrolls was transported by trucks into the mountains of Sichuan, stored in gigantic mountain caves, and eventually shipped down the Yangtze River and across the Taiwan Strait to Taiwan.

When they got to Taiwan, the Nationalist government built a replica of an imperial palace that you could see right in the hills outside of Taipei. That's where they put the art works. They were not only considered the spoils of war, but part of the proof of an old concept called The Mandate of Heaven. Whoever was bestowed with this "Mandate of Heaven" was considered the rightful ruler of China. So there was nothing more important for Chiang Kai-shek, the leader of the Kuomintang, to hold on to than those art works—the last proof that the mandate had descended on to his shoulders, just above the leather coat and cape Hitler had bestowed upon him as a friendship gift.[14] Chiang took the further step of renaming the major mountain to the north of his new capital after a Ming dynasty neo-Confucian philosopher, Wang Yangming, furthering his symbolic portfolio. Yet in the Generalissimo's own ignorance, he must not have realized that the actual philosophy of the ancient sage—operate directly from the heart even if it means violence—contradicted his claim to rule through transcendent moral governance.[15] Maybe that was what made him start off his time in Taiwan with destruction. The massacres and reign of White Terror that followed almost immediately after the landing of the Kuomintang were perhaps proofs that the Generalissimo was following the dictates of his token philosopher too strenuously.

But mainland immigrants pride themselves on their commitment to order, discipline, and most of all, politeness. This was, they felt, part of their refugee experience and part of their legacy. Most of the refugees interviewed came from large families with landlord status. Others came directly from a military background. Here, their interpretation of the past is often seen in military terms, as if they were disciplined above anything else. When Hu Yao-hen, the college professor, recounts his experience living in a warehouse in a refugee camp in Hong Kong, he does so with irony. When Wang Shu-chih, from a military background, does so, it is in the happiest of tones, as if suffering were part of their outlook.

To enter her house is to enter a large room cut off from the other rooms with bead curtains. She has a long face, strung down like a sheet on a laundry line, the kind of face a wife or a mother would have that had waited for her man to return from war, not ever really believing he would. She comes from Henan Province, one of the poorest areas of China before the Japanese invasion. Photographs of her, around the house, show her at seventeen to be a sullen beauty with heavy dark hair, a low brow and the most frightened eyes imaginable. When asked, she denies she is a member of an ethnic minority group although admits she is often asked that question. Both her father and her dead husband were soldiers. Her husband was higher up in the military establishment than most, more closely connected to the central government, so her flight from the enemy, whether Japanese or communist, was coordinated more intensely than that of civilians. While Hu fled chaotically around the region, sometimes with his father, sometimes not, Wang and her father were moved around China constantly, "towards the front," like chess pieces on a military strategy board. She is proud of the sacrifices she was asked to make.

> My family is a military family. Wherever there was fighting, that's where they would send us. I guess you could say we were all soldiers. That was our job. There was fighting all over the mainland. There were lots of little wars starting all over the place, small battles. We were always the first to the front. It was just like in all military families. The husband would be sent first, right to the front. His family stayed in the rear. They would set up a base camp there. For the most part, it was relatively safe, protected from the main fighting. But sometimes we could hear the fighting from the front. And then, it always happened, our troops would lose and have to pull back. It just kept happening and we kept retreating. So you can see how our life was different than the bureaucrats'. In a military family, you know the real taste of defeat.

When the final battle was lost, Wang and her family were transported to Taiwan. Her father, who stayed on the mainland, was thereafter killed in action. Wang's family now consisted of her mother, herself (she was ten), and her younger brother. The children were dubbed "Children of Revolutionary Martyrs" and were given a small stipend to cover educational expenses. Their mother went to a knitting factory to make up the extra. It was remarkable since she had been crippled by having her feet bound at a young age. A picture of her shows the face of a remarkably calm woman with only a pair of surprised eyebrows as if they were stuck there, on her forehead, when her feet were first bound and she felt the pain. Later in life, she went to work, hobbling on a cane, working in the factory. The small family was given a tiny corner of an old warehouse in which to live and study. The warehouse was divided by partitions of old pieces of tarp, creating relatively evenly-sized living spaces for each family. This was the home of the "Revolutionary Martyrs." Wang says that there was something about the place, a kind of eagerness or hope which they all shared that kept everyone not only happy but feeling like they belonged to a big family, bigger than their own. Or maybe that is really what she wants to believe, sixty years later, when there are no big families anymore, when her party and her government are no longer the tightly-knit organization they once were.

> So we finally got to Taiwan in 1949. They put us in a large warehouse in Taoyuan about fifty miles outside the capital. The warehouse had been built by the Japanese and then left empty when they left. It was some kind of storehouse, right near the railroad. They must have unloaded things right onto the trains. Well, the government divided it up so that they could get fifty families in there. It was just an old warehouse. But they tried to make it into a dormitory. It didn't matter how big your family was, you got the same amount of space. We lived that way for six years. I spent most of my childhood there. We got there when I was ten and we left when I was sixteen.
>
> Actually, it wasn't that bad. I guess we all felt like it was one big happy family. I had fifty mothers looking after me. There was no fighting. My mother was alone. My father was still back on the mainland. And she had two kids to look after. Out in the real world, we would have been a single-parent family. But not in that warehouse.
>
> Everyone watched out for us, everyone. I never felt alone or that I was disadvantaged in any way. As for my younger brother, that kind of hospitality probably saved his life. He was five years younger than I was, thin, weak, unhealthy. He just didn't want to eat much. And he was really picky. He refused to eat most kinds of food. But when the other families heard about this, they would stop by every evening, if they were cooking something special, and invite my brother to come eat with them. So he survived.
>
> Normally, however, we just ate rice. That was all we had. Once in a while, on Sunday, my mother bought some cheap meat. Most of the time,

she just cooked up a vegetable. We didn't even have vegetables all the time. And when we did, they weren't too good. I'm ashamed to talk about it now. But the way we would get vegetables is we'd walk over to where some local farmers were growing a bunch of vegetables, usually to sell. We'd stand outside their vegetable patch and wait for them to bundle up some of their vegetables. The farmers would cut off bits of the vegetables before taking them into market. Those bits were the bad parts, the rotten parts that nobody wanted. But we had no choice. We'd buy them from the farmers then pick them up from the ground. But we couldn't afford to buy those more than once a week. So mostly we ate rice, with a few scraps of vegetables thrown in.

Another thing, there were people from all over China with us. But we all had been floating around for so long that we all knew one another. Most of the families didn't have fathers with them. And most of them didn't know whether their fathers were still alive or not. We really envied those families that had fathers. There weren't many of them, maybe one or two, but we thought they were truly blessed. Now, after the mainland fell, some of those fathers did get out of there. Some of them just barely made it alive. Some got out through Hong Kong or Shanghai. Some of them got out on the last boat. After that, there were still about one-third of the families whose fathers hadn't gotten out.

Most of them were killed in battle. Some took the wrong route out and were killed that way. A few stayed on the mainland and managed to survive. But most of us didn't know where they were. Still don't. My father was killed in action.

After my father died, they set up a board on two benches. My mother told me I had to start studying. There was one light bulb hanging overhead. The warehouse was really high so there wasn't much light. But I just remember writing under that light on the board. For six years, I went to school and came home and did my homework on that board.

When Chiang Kai-shek first retreated to Taiwan, he told military families that the first year would involve regrouping, the second year preparation, and the third would be the actual striking back to recover the mainland. According to that plan, the makeshift quality of the homes where the military families lived wouldn't matter. It would only remind them that they had a common goal, and it strengthened their sense of purpose. Wang won't talk about what they all believed during those years. She won't say why. Maybe she felt cheated when all the plans just didn't work out. But she's not about to give up on the hope they felt during those years. For decades, mainland families lived in a bubble of eroding optimism, a bubble in which they waited for their present homes to be transformed into more spacious living quarters. Some of them, like Wang, achieved this. Others did not. A whole flood of poor squatter huts on Hsin Yi Road in Taipei was swept away by the building of the Ta An Forest Park in the late 1980s. By that time, used to the dirt and cramped living, the old soldiers inside had lost any sense of connection with anything outside their community. Their houses looked like turtle shells bunched together between four walls of tall, white buildings. It didn't take long before the old soldiers were driven out by business interests and changing policies.

Wang can never forget that it was the military that brought her out of the mainland. She figures she owes it her life, hers' and her children's. There's something about being part of the military that gives her a foundation, like she was part of something bigger than herself. She figures that she was critical because she belonged to a group that was about to save China. But what really happened was that their mission ended up isolating the very people it had once hoped to liberate—the mainlanders themselves. For decades, the military was a closed circle in which the preeminence of the mainland immigrants and their children was not just a fact, it was a religion. While the rest of society changed drastically, while the Kuomintang has filled up with locals, the military remained an isolated pool of mainland refugees. Officers, generals, and military leaders were almost entirely of mainland Chinese origin. While this has changed in recent years as the Democratic Progressive Party continued a process, begun under the Kuomintang, of elevating local soldiers to higher positions, Wang seems to draw life and hope and honor from the memory of her dead husband and the elite military he once served. Nearly every picture around her house contains a man in a uniform. Her wedding picture shows her and her husband, in uniform, looking off into the distance, almost as if planning to retake the mainland.

They lived in the warehouse and because they were all military families they worked together, helping each other, until they grew into a single family. That was the idea.

> We had to work our way out of poverty. So our relations were very strong. My mother had to go out to work every day, so I ended up taking care of my brother. I remember feeling that my mother was playing the role of the father and I was playing the mother and my younger brother was like our

child. And it was like that, in reality. Whatever I told my younger brother to do, he would do it. And I loved him as if he were my own child. I loved him with that kind of love. And we are still close. He comes to visit me here every Sunday. Hard times will nurture your family relationships. I guess it's because everyone was working for a single goal, to get out of poverty.

Her world inside the warehouse is in some ways parallel to her world today. The relationship of the government to the military is changing. Traditional, reliable structures are changing, breaking down, forcing her into new roles. Starting over the past few years, the Ministry of National Defense has ordered the destruction of the entire 888 remaining military housing complexes. The order includes a provision that the residents will be housed in newly-built high-rises. But only some have been constructed. As for the rest of the residents, the massive destruction seems like a betrayal of the most sacred of contracts: the military would look out for its own, would preserve the traditional world and order of its dependents. Just as, during the Qing dynasty, the Manchu rulers allotted each segment of its army, or banners, a circumscribed area of land for its dependents and farmers, so the military in Taiwan was, until recently, perceived as always taking care of its own, through housing especially. The old world of military villages is falling, just as the military itself is changing, becoming less dominated by the original mainland immigrants.

Wang, however, escaped her warehouse. For one thing, she tested into the island's premier girls' school, created for the daughters of the richest families. At the same time, her connections, acquired through a women's association to which she belonged at school, helped her family relocate. She was now playing an altogether new role for the family, no longer a young daughter, but a provider. They moved to a newly-built apartment complex in another military village, although this one was made of concrete and had running water, and had real walls, rather than the flimsy tarp she was used to in the warehouse. They had one bedroom, one bathroom, and a living room. It was paradise. "We were so happy," she says. They had escaped. And once again, the new military village—this one a real one, although the warehouse had, of course, been joyous as well—was also like one big happy family.

> All the doorways were so close you could smell what your neighbor was cooking. No one closed the door. All the sounds mingled in the courtyard.

> Babies crying. Mothers talking with children. It was like you could almost see them in the center of the courtyard. We also had a little more money because the government had more money by then. We could go to the market and buy vegetables. There was always a neighbor stopping by to borrow something. Onions or garlic. It was a great feeling. We were like one big happy family again. Sometimes I would even stay over at a neighbor's house. Even if their apartment was smaller, we would all crowd into one bed. This went on for eight years.

She just doesn't feel that the world is anything like a happy family anymore, with all the changes in society and the military. So it makes sense that she nostalgically emphasizes the past as a source of the happiness she is denied today: the emphasis on the happy family wherever their travels took them. They lived in the new apartment complex for eight years. Then there was a flood. These days, typhoons are weak. They come in off the ocean and dump a few inches of rain, then float back out, like a broom that has swept a bit of grass off the pavement. But even a decade ago, before the accumulation of pollution mitigated their force, typhoons were serious threats to life in Taiwan. It just took one person to hint that a typhoon might be coming, and farmers panicked, floodgate captains called for emergency aid, and families filled up bathtubs with a supply of clean water. When they struck, sometimes a whole river was diverted from its banks and scoured through the city with its clayey tongues, leaving a solid pack of brown water in its wake, breast-deep. The typhoon Wang describes was even worse. They had been living in the apartment for a decade, and no storm had ever come close to its intensity.

> Now, in 1963, there was a typhoon. It was really big—that one. It almost destroyed our entire village. When it hit, we went up to the roof. The rain just kept coming down, hard, like someone was throwing down bunches of stones. And the wind—it was coming in hard, too. We felt it like a man was pushing against you. We watched as the water below, it was a brown color, a deep brown, kept rising. We saw the water below kept rising. I was carrying my second child, a baby. He had only been born a few days earlier. He was crying and fretting. And there we were atop the roof in a storm like that. We were all there, all of the neighbors, and my kids. We just sat down and waited.
>
> Now, the water just kept rising and rising. We all watched the water, like it was a snake or a bear climbing up the side of our building. I kept thinking,

"What am I going to do, what am I going to do?" I knew I had to take care of my children. I had that baby and I had a daughter who was only three years old. I kept thinking, over and over, "We are going to die." So I said to my husband—he was my second husband. We had met in the military village. I yelled at him, "Think of something!" But he couldn't. He just sat there shivering. Then I thought of the water tanks. We didn't have running water then. All our water we got from tubs of water carried by hand. I said to my husband, "Look, you can swim. Go down and get a couple of those tubs." He did it. When he came back, I told him my plan. I thought, "We can at least put the children in the tubs. Maybe we can't make it, but they can float away, we might not know where they would float to, but we could at least give them a chance to live."

The water was getting really high now, almost to the roof. My husband started dumping out all the water from the water tubs. I said, "Wait until the water reaches the edge of the building, then put the children in and we'll push them away." I thought that, as for us, we could at least try to float on the water, near the water tubs, but when our strength gave out, I knew we would have to let go. At least the children would live.

Meantime, my younger brother just kept on reading. He didn't lift his head from his book. He was still in school. But after a while, he stopped and came and joined us where we were praying. It's not that we had any kind of religion. We just prayed. We said to ourselves, if the water stops rising, then we will believe in God. Some of us prayed to Jesus. There were some that believed in Buddha. They prayed to him. We all just wanted someone to come down and save us.

Finally, at around ten at night, the water stopped rising. At first we couldn't see anything because the water was black and there was no moon. Then the moon started inching up slowly from the corner of the sky and we saw the water. It had stopped, a foot below us. One big black curtain hung up below us. But it had stopped moving. It was the middle of August but we were shivering. Some said it was on account of our being saved, that we were so weak and dizzy with relief. Others said it was just that we were cold, given that we hadn't eaten any food all that day. Well, the water came up a little more during the night. We saw it. But by about dawn, it had gone down several feet. By the morning, around ten, we were actually able to go down to our apartments. It was gone.

When we got downstairs, everything was a mess. The flood had ripped out our clothes and stuff like it was ransacking our house, like it was looking for something or someone. Everything was wet and clayey. We couldn't get anything to eat. We adults were starving. But the children were so hungry they were almost sick. The baby was screaming but that was more from fright, because I had been breast feeding him. But the three-year-old, well, she hadn't had anything to eat in days. So I gave her the other breast to suck on. She didn't mind.

The utter aloneness of her and her family, as she makes decisions to save their lives is never mentioned. But she can't help feeling it now. At least, she says so, later. They are cut off from everything by the water. But still they feel part of a community, the few neighbors with them, their resourcefulness. Almost fifty years later, during a crisis much less severe, she can't help but feel trapped, almost as if she were right there surrounded by that flood water again. Her government, her leaders, and her military have all failed her. Now, sitting alone in her military dormitory, an old woman surrounded by photographs of men in uniforms, waiting for the order to move, she has come to feel isolated. As a mainland refugee, in a society that has turned upside down, denying them the privileges which they enjoyed for fifty years, she now for the first time has come to feel true discouragement deeper than even a catastrophic flood can bring.

Other refugees go back in time and hold on to other things from the past, trying to stop thinking about losing their present. As they recount their first years of moving to Taiwan, a number of the immigrants describe obsessions with tangible markers of their existence: clothing, shoes, and uniforms. Like Hu Yao-hen, who focused on the outward form of the lieutenant, these immigrants are, in a sense, repeating the Kuomintang government's drive to preserve its identity by throwing up markers to its borders: the street signs of Taipei. For Ko Jen-tao, the obsession is with his father's closet full of suits, each one of a different color, in the fading days of Kuomintang rule in Nanjing. The closet almost seems to sum up a world of lost chances. What could he, the youngster, have been, had he been able to stay behind in a promising world where he would have been able to fit into different identities as easily as he might have one day worn his father's suits? His father, Ko says, intended him to be a doctor. Just as his father seemed to progress from the old and outdated fashions to sleek Western suits, so Ko might have continued on the upward slope, transforming himself, taking on a whole new identity. Instead, he seems to be saying, he is stuck in a life of obsolescence.

> My father had dozens of suits in his closet. Dozens. When you walked in there, you could see them, hung neatly, in every color, black, white, blue,

red. For him, wearing suits was a sign of his success. It was also a sign of his education. He had gone to the university and he refused to wear those traditional robes. The suits for him were the stepping stones into a new world. And I always wanted to wear those suits. I would say to myself, "Some day I am going to have even more suits than he does." But it didn't turn out like that. I only have one suit now, and that's my police uniform. Before that, it was my navy uniform.

When he arrived in Taiwan in 1949, on a ship with his cousin, his mother having decided to send him ahead to safety, he decided to join the navy. His decision was not entirely for patriotic reasons, nor entirely for financial reasons, but for more characteristic reasons—he liked the uniforms.

The best thing about the navy was the uniforms. Actually, I had two uniforms then; one for the summer and one for the winter. In the summer, we wore white uniforms and in the winter, black ones. We always kept them real clean. Spotless. On our heads, we wore a sailor's cap and around our necks we wore a tie. It was spit-polish. I really liked the navy. But I almost didn't get in. I wasn't tall enough so I put leather pads in my shoes. Passing the test wasn't hard. I passed the first time I tried. Then they trained me, for a whole year.

Chang Ching-tan, the balding, freckled-head, eighty-two-year-old, originally from Fujian, is also haunted. From one look at his cluttered house, it is clear this obsession still reigns over his life. It is with shoes. Shoes are scattered around the floor. Up and down the banisters of the staircase, stuck in behind each railing, are pairs upon pairs of shoes. Chang admits how obsessed he was, as a child, with the most enduring kind of sports shoes made at the time. Why? Because they would last the longest. Here, the obsession may have something to do with preserving himself simply through flight, flight from warfare, flight from Japanese harassment with a dog. Or perhaps even—flight from his current predicament in Taiwan. His house, his memories, all point to one thing: escape.

When I was fleeing from the Japanese, I didn't even have a pair of shoes. Not many people did those days. Especially if you were a soldier. But later my father took me to buy a pair of leather shoes. They were the finest shoes available at that time. I thought they were awesome. They were. There was a shop in Fuzhou that had them. That was where we went. The shoes were made with German leather. That leather was really durable. It could withstand anything. You could walk for years in those shoes and they wouldn't wear out. And they were so light, you felt like you were practically flying. That was because the soles of those shoes were made with old airplane tires. They were thick and flexible. I wore them for the rest of the war until they finally wore out. That was the saddest day of my life—when I had to throw them out. I sure wish I could find another pair of shoes like that. They just don't make them that way anymore.

2
Mixing Memory and Desire

Ko Jen-tao thought he had come so far that the Communists couldn't get him as they must have gotten his family. He wore his naval uniform like it was a badge, a sign that he was safe. But he was too far from home now to even remember what it felt like to be safe. He actually didn't know what had happened to his mother and his brothers and sister. He only knew that the Communists had taken their city. He wore the uniform now not like one who was protecting his newfound country but rather as somebody who was trying to keep as far as possible from his old one. Or maybe he just found that living on a ship was the best way for a man to become a man without memories but only routine.

> I served in a big American ship. It was a leftover from when the Americans occupied the Philippines. They lent it to us so we could defend ourselves against the Communists. But it seemed more like a pleasure cruise to me. At first, at least. At first, I would look down at the ocean and think about my mother back in Nanjing. So I had to adjust. Anyway, we didn't have much time for being sad. We were patrolling through all the big islands between the mainland and Taiwan. Kinmen, Matsu, all of those. Sometimes we could even see the shore. We could see it, but we could never touch it, never go there. We went on like that for about a half year before returning to our home port in Taiwan. I have to say, it was hard work. But that was our job, to protect Taiwan. We had to prevent the Communists from attacking our base.

Patrolling the Taiwan Strait on an American-built naval ship may have been exciting, if monotonous. But Ko had to prove that he was ready and worthy. It was part of the time, when everyone had to show they were worthy, that they had earned their place. That the retreat itself was worthwhile, even if it was a retreat. So memories of arrival in Taiwan are mostly recounted as challenging but exciting, sad but grandiose. Over one million troops had crossed the Strait in disarray. The last boats were swamped with civilians and troops. Generalissimo Chiang Kai-shek had flown to Taipei, in defeat, yet vowing to recapture the mainland swiftly. It was a time of great chaos, and yet it is usually recounted, at least among this batch of interviewees, as a time of learning and, above all, freedom. Ko goes on to describe the luxury of serving in the navy, a nostalgia not only for youth and glory but fueled by the desire to escape the bonds of old age and frustration that keep him tied to his living room couch and his tiny apartment. One way he deals with all the changes in his life is with a sense of humor.

> Well, I had to admit that we had it pretty good on board, except for thinking about and missing our folks on the mainland. We ate well. They knew how to treat sailors well in those days. Our pay was good. But mainly it was the food. I remember I had a big iron tray. Then when noon came around, the captain would play a pipe into the microphone. It sort of sounded like this *tee ta tee ta*. Then after that we'd go and take our turn in line. They had all sorts of food. Duck, chicken, a big piece of beef. It was all fine food. And we had plenty of free time. All in all, it was a good life. That is, if you don't count the lice.
>
> In that respect, sleeping wasn't so great. You would think that, sleeping on a hammock made of rope, those lice couldn't get at you. But they'd lodge right in your hair and sort of squiggle around in there. They were trying to find a place to sleep, too. But it wasn't funny, because those lice, all they wanted was your blood, not just a place to sleep. Some of the men used to try to crush them in their fingertips, but that didn't work too well, because they had laid their eggs in your hair, anyway, so they'd just keep right on hatching. Finally, the captain got a big vat of pesticide from somewhere, and we had to bathe our heads in it. Well, I guess he thought he was doing good at the time. Some of the men got rid of their lice. Others had problems, though. A couple of men lost the vision in one of their eyes. Then, when that was all through, the lice just came right back. That was the only negative part of serving on that boat.

Ko can see his whole life behind him, see himself working on a ship, raising a family. His life culminates, expires actually, in the moment that the Kuomintang lost power in a presidential election. They're back in power now, but those eight years were the hardest that he had ever gone through as a man. It was as if society, his government had forgotten him. It was as if he had forgotten all that he had done because there was no longer anyone there to remind him of it. He thought that he was a hero. He knew from the start that someone would recognize it. And then suddenly there was nobody there to recognize him anymore. So for forty years he was able to live like other men, expecting like other men to find proof of his existence in something bigger than himself. Then it was gone. Suddenly. And he didn't know who he was anymore, even after his party clawed its way back to power. "I'll tell you, without the Kuomintang, there wouldn't be present-day Taiwan," he says, implying that his party and his group of immigrants were the ones to build up modern Taiwan.

What is more infuriating to mainland immigrants like Ko is that the Kuomintang of its own volition undertook the democratic reforms that eventually ended up with their being cast from power, even if only for eight years. It is as if, think many of the immigrants, the Kuomintang gave away too much power out of the goodness of its heart and a desire to be democratic—and now its members are paying the price for their liberality. No one is thanking them— there are no awards, no stipends, no recognition—for allowing the opposition party to take over. Now that they've taken power back, they realize that they haven't gotten over what happened to them. They could be hurt, hurt bad. And now they're ready to look someplace else for safety. Even if they have to look back across to their former enemies, they figure, anything could be better than this—this betrayal.

Perhaps he had fooled himself that everything was going to be alright. Back then, in the navy, he hadn't even had time to worry about who he was. He didn't have the luxury of thinking about women, not the new, cheap ones who lined the streets of Keelung nor the ones who had existed mostly in his imagination in the world of his past. Ko insists that his sex drive was non-existent—unlike now when it seems to embody the very source of his unhappiness and impotent rage. He says that he had no desire whatsoever at the age of eighteen. He watched foreign movies, catching some of the American perfume that wafted from the screen. It was a time when he could go to three movies a day, not like now when he is harassed and relatively impoverished, with no time or interest in luxury.

> There was this brothel on Kinmen Island that some of the sailors went to. Some of the women there were criminals and worked there so they wouldn't have to go to prison. But some of the women were just regular prostitutes and thought they could earn more money that way. Now I served on that ship for five years, and we stopped at Kinmen all the time, but I never went.

Actually, I didn't even want to. I was too homesick. I was still a teenager and I just wanted to get home some way. I think I thought that serving on that ship somehow would at least bring me closer to home than if I were in Taiwan.

There was another place in Taiwan itself, next to the Keelung dock, where the sailors would go to shoot darts or dance with local girls. They could buy sex there too. But, you know, I wasn't interested. Sometimes I would feel so homesick at the end of a voyage, that I could hardly drag myself off the boat. When I did have free time, I would go see movies. There was this movie theater in Keelung and sometimes I'd see three movies in a single day. They had all sorts of movies. But I liked the Hollywood movies the best. Now, my favorite was Elizabeth Taylor. I also liked Ingrid Bergman. They kept me company.

Watching those films was Ko's first experience of romance. He had never believed his life or the life of anyone else could ever mean anything more than simply getting through, surviving. The lives he watched up on the screen, the beautiful women, their intense and random loves, comforted him in a way the real world could not. When he left the navy and joined the police force, he carried those images with him, images of security and promise. "I would replay the movies in my mind over and over as I walked the street," he said. "I felt that those movies were real, more real than anything else."

He probably would have remained in that fog forever if he hadn't met a young woman who promised to help him. She was a local. She had a face like a shovel full of rocks, high at the top and flattening down to the blade. Cheekbones high, the size of rocks. And a mouth that was red with betel nuts. There was nothing Ko could do with a face like that, except follow it. He was like a man going down a hole, knowing where he was heading but allowing himself to drift along anyway. He believed that he loved her. He must have known what he was doing, or thought that he did. They were together for three months. When she left him, she took all the gold he had saved up for his family. All that she left him was a spurious belief in Catholicism—she was a convert, or said she was—and the fading possibility that there actually might have been something bigger than himself and his loss.

As two million immigrants spread out over an island roughly the size of a small American state, most were stationed with troops, either in Taipei, or in the central or southern parts of the island. Taipei, particularly, became a hub for civil servants and families of soldiers and other officials. Each had a movie playing in his or her head—of other lives, of promises made by their leaders, of impossible dreams. Each was living a dual life.

The city, which had been so meticulously labeled by the new government, shrugged off its new street names. Settling patterns completely resisted the mock map laid out by the Kuomintang. Instead, other factors determined where mainland immigrants would settle, such as proximity to military and central government forces. Dense farming areas, exclusively populated by locals who had lived in Taiwan for centuries, were shunned by the immigrants. The city today is, in fact, a map of the two styles of life, immigrant and local. Some of the boundaries have been obscured, but great divisions can still be roughly ascertained. No professional architectural or geographical survey has been taken along these lines—indeed, in the political atmosphere of the early twenty-first century, in which the entire population was trying to downplay such divisions, such a study would have been almost impossible. Even local police refuse to get involved.

Nevertheless, architecture gives clues. Areas where mainland immigrants predominate often fail to have any significant street life, such as night markets. In these areas, architecture usually lifts buildings away from the street, so that the sidewalk becomes merely a tool for transportation and not the lifeline for business and commerce it does in areas populated by locals. Take Neihu for an example. This is an area in the north of the city where aged lawmakers once lived. Elected on the mainland, they fled along with the rest of the exiles and pretended to represent all of China for decades until their deaths, sometimes in their nineties. Locals could predict the time of their deaths, almost down to the hour. This would come when their oxygen tanks and tubes no longer gave them enough corpuscles to support raising their arms to vote on bills and measures they no longer understood. Their wives and daughters still live in Neihu, steeped in Kuomintang and mainland refugee culture. There is a broad park with a lake with replications of imperial structures, bridges, viewing platforms and other grand sweeping architectural devices, as if the Manchu rulers of the Qing dynasty, with their eyes always on the distant horizon from where they had come, the grand scale of the steppes, had imagined the broad scale of the buildings. There are no night markets in Neihu. The chilly feel of the streets and sidewalks is due to the high enclosed buildings on either side of the streets.

At the opposite end of the city is Mucha, a suburb populated mostly by locals whose ancestors stretch back in some cases to Cheng Ch'eng-kung, the Ming dynasty rebel who made Taiwan a base. Less than a generation ago, the landscape was all fields and paddy farms stretching to the horizon. When developers came in, and whipped up cheap, serviceable cement barrack-like apartment blocks, they offered the farmers several floors in exchange for the land rights. The street culture in Mucha seems older, earthier, riper. Along the streets, one may buy fried fish. Motorcycles are disassembled. Markets with mounds of fresh oranges, bananas and other indigenous fruit occupy entire back streets. Children ride bicycles. Motorcycles squeeze through pedestrians. Massage shops advertise their wares. Educational cram schools advertise with slogans. Just one tiny block from the main street, cars stop, people stop, time stops, the market rules the street. This is an area where locals predominate.

Old time crouches in back alleys in Mucha. Under a brick roof crowded on either side with fiberglass, an old ancestral tablet glows. Signs advertise seeds of all kinds. Farmers live here. Dogs lie exhausted on the pavement outside. It is almost as if traces of something very old linger on here. In its transition from a centralized, military-ruled economy to a more open society, the Ming dynasty developed bustling local economies. The large infrastructure once used to convey official couriers was taken over by local merchants to transport their own wares. The local economies became paramount.[1] While most of the ancestors of the locals in Taiwan came over during the Qing dynasty, many came at the end of the Ming, especially those loyal to Cheng Ch'eng-kung. One might almost be tempted to assert that ways of life characteristic to older times, perhaps even the Ming dynasty, still exist in local communities in Taiwan, such as market-street life, commerce focused on the sidewalks. In that case, the mainland immigrants, amid their soaring architecture, might be said to still be living to some extent in Qing or post-Qing time. The locals, amid their bustling street life and decaying ancestral altars, might be said to be living still in Ming time. At least, this is one way to look at it.

Where to live was the first thing arriving mainland refugees had to think about. How to live hadn't yet become a problem. It soon would be. Even someone as well-connected as Shen Hsueh-yung had problems. There was something about her face, a face as wide as the moon, with a smile that seemed to promise that sunlight would come back after an eclipse, the kind of face that a man would never forget once seen. She sang Chinese opera but to look at her, as you can see by her photographs from those times, she might just as well have stood for everything that was beautiful and wholesome in Chinese culture, everything the Communists had destroyed. She tied her flowing black hair in a ponytail. She looked to be the kind of young woman who would just about be naïve enough to fall for the kind of trick her husband, a high-ranking military officer, played on her. With his kind of influence, it wasn't hard to arrange for a military plane for just the two of them. He told her it was just a quick honeymoon on the island of Taiwan, to get away from the warfare near Sichuan where she was studying. She brought nothing, except for a handkerchief she kept in her pocket. Her husband said she wouldn't even need that. Later, she used it on the plane flight to catch her vomit when the plane passed through rough spots. When they landed, he told her the truth. But he added one mitigating factor: he had brought several of her photo albums, and a few clothes, to lessen the shock that she would now be living on this island for some time.

They boarded with her brother. Owing to her family's influence, he had been made mayor of the eastern coastal city of Hualien. But he had not been given a large house. Worse, she, the daughter of a rich businessman, didn't even know how to light the stove.

> After we landed, I used the handkerchief to wipe the vomit off my clothes and face. Then we were taken to my brother's house. He didn't know we were coming. It was a disaster. He lived in a really small house. We found a spare bed but it took up the whole living room. I can't tell you how ashamed I was. Finally, my husband suggested that we sell all our wedding gifts. He had brought them with us. At that point, after flying all night, being sick all night, landing in a strange place, and now being told I had to give up my wedding gifts, I went into the bathroom, closed the door and sat down and cried. I remember thinking that I was selling my dreams, the only dreams I would ever have. I knew from that moment on that our marriage was doomed. We sold the gifts and actually got enough money to buy a small house that was outside the city, on some local's farm.
>
> It was tough living on that farm. I didn't even know how to start a fire in the stove. No one had ever taught me. Life was hard. You see, I had gotten married right out of college, so I didn't know how to do anything like that. Our life was very simple and hard. I remember working from when I first got up until I went to bed.

Like many refugees, even in the military, there was no place for them to work. Her husband eventually found work as a liaison officer for the Ministry of National Defense, meaning he helped them communicate with Americans. His English was superb and he later wrote a manual translating military terms for aircraft and weapons into English. She found work teaching music at a nearby high school.

Shen, who has now clipped her hair as short as a man's, has lived for sixty years on the idea that mainlanders brought culture to Taiwan. She is like a candle flame whose wick, her own beauty, has been consumed with this idea, this flame, that the mainlanders had a duty to preserve Chinese culture by bringing it to this island. She describes years of persevering on the mainland, even during Japanese air raids, to perfect her singing. Her classmates, for want of a piano, drew keys on a wooden board and went through the motions of accompanying her as she sang while bombs fell around them. It didn't stop when she came to Taiwan. She was teaching in a high school, teaching her students what she described as a whole range of Chinese songs they had never learned. Her belief that she was distributing a higher culture was unquestioned. She was even relieved to have this role to play.

> I walked into that classroom and the first thing I did was ask the students to sing a Taiwanese song for me. They didn't know a single song. When I asked again, a couple of students sang one or two short folk songs. But they were quite simple. I was actually happy. It was like walking into a field of grass carrying hundreds of seeds for different flowers in your hands. It was like bringing culture to a native tribe. They did know some Japanese songs and some Taiwanese folk songs but they didn't know any kind of cultured, or artistic, songs.
>
> I had brought copies of hundreds of old Chinese songs. Some of them were from books I had gotten from other immigrants. Some of them I had written out from memory. I remember thinking that these songs were the only treasure I had escaped with. Fortunately, the Taiwanese students also saw these as treasures. In fact, years later, some of the manuscripts of these songs were put in a local museum. They don't have any record of songs like this in the mainland because the communists destroyed this kind of stuff during the Cultural Revolution. But recently, they've started bringing some of these songs back to China. In Taiwan, they've been around now for fifty years.

Today, Shen lives in a spacious, dim apartment and walks around it in long, loose gowns, like the purveyor of culture she makes herself out to be. Whether her students are the Taiwanese of the past, the locals that ripped away power and status from her and her party, or the mainland Chinese of today, all can benefit from the superior storehouse of traditional music she has amassed. Her role as purveyor of classic Chinese culture transcends time. And, in that respect, it also resembles the ideology put forth by Generalissimo Chiang Kai-shek during his fading years, that his government represented the true China, that it somehow had moral authority and a cultural mandate to speak for China in the United Nations.[2]

They just didn't know what they were getting themselves into. Was it a dream? Was it of their own making? They would have liked to have thought so, at least. To the settlers, it made sense that Taiwan would have appeared something of a frontier. They brought with them the chaos of the war years, the memory of pain and of loss. But what they found was something they hadn't quite expected. As Shen found to her delight, the crumbling peripheries of the Japanese empire still contained significant possibilities for cultural advancement. The fading lines of Japanese civilization also meant she had opportunities for fame that her lesser training and talents would have denied her in the well-established music halls of mainland China.

> I wanted to continue studying music in Taipei. So I found out there was a national philharmonic orchestra being formed. I had some friends introduce me to the director of the chorus. He said that he was actually being coached by a music teacher from Japan. So I got his name, too. I couldn't speak Japanese, but I thought that that wouldn't matter because the language of music is international and besides he could judge me by my singing and acting. So the chorus director took me to meet his teacher, the Japanese. He heard me sing one aria and asked me to star in *Madame Butterfly*. The chorus director, who could speak Japanese, translated for us. Later, when the performance went on the road to Japan, in 1951, I went with it. It all started from that one performance I had given him.

For most of the next decade, the Kuomintang government groaned under its vanishing dream of retaking the mainland. Shen became something of an international diva. The conditions that had destroyed two empires—the late Chinese republic and the Japanese—created an international zone of moneyed refugees, beautiful and sophisticated, who posed as purveyors of dying cultures. Shen appeared around the globe, on yachts, famously dressed as an Indian woman, swaying to her own vocal accompaniment, in furs, giving concerts in Japan, her long, beautiful face with its perfectly symmetrical nose reaching down to the depths of gaiety amid misery, or misery amid gaiety, as she smiled and sang for select audiences. Gradually, however, as conditions changed in Taiwan, she was no longer the svelte singer from the heartland of China—demand for that role had abated. Taiwan's ruling establishment stopped calling for older Chinese songs to be performed in concert halls and at formal dinners.

It was no longer the same establishment. As democratic reforms took place, and the locals swarmed to power, a new generation of performers and singers now occupied the national concert hall and most outlying theaters as well. Groups such as U-Theater, an acrobatic and drumming group, epitomized a new distribution of power in Taiwan. The performances were no longer of Chinese "artistic" songs, but of native Buddhist dances, with half-naked dancers, sheathed with sweat, cartwheeling over each other's bodies to the incessant tattoo of huge drums.

> One thing that this new generation doesn't understand is that the Chinese people are the accumulation of many, many, many years of culture. You can't just destroy that in a single day. What they don't understand is that we need to tap into our heritage and only then can we do things better than others. When I was in Japan, the Japanese said I sang Japanese songs better than the Japanese themselves. I think what most impressed them was that a foreign woman could sing their songs so well. Actually, it was mostly because I had a foundation in Chinese music. Every time I would sing a Japanese song, I would think about a Chinese song I knew that had a similar theme. It would add a richness and maybe even sadness to my performance. Or maybe it was because many of their songs are based on ours.
>
> We must never forget our ancestors. As long as we don't do that, then our talents and our wisdom will come out naturally. Obviously, you need food and clothing before you can have any culture, but without culture and art, there's no meaning to life.

Even in her eighties, Shen is still living out the role of the cultural sophisticate, purveying advice and apothegms. Only in the end, does one get a sense of the frustration that must have beset her all along, from her first triumphant moment of fame in a production of *Madame Butterfly* on a Taiwan beset with the stench and dust of armies of retreating soldiers. As her government gradually lost respectability over the decades and she continued to perform—perhaps it was the cantatas of Chinese "artistic" songs—how isolated must she have felt, wondering if anyone important was still listening. As if in recognition that her time has already come and gone, her son, a well-known photographer, recently held an exhibition, in Taipei and Paris, simply titled, *Mother*. In it, photos from a half century ago show a beautiful woman with a long ponytail and a wholesome smile, so wholesome it makes a man happy just to see it, lifts him out of whatever else he has on his mind. It is the kind of face and smile that in another time, another place, might have inspired a nation to win a war. Other photos show Shen in a train station, in some unknown but obviously European city. Another photo shows her in her famous Indian apparel, hands laid palm to palm above her head, swaying. The exhibit, by a second-generation mainland immigrant, is a tribute not only to his mother's past, but to an ideology that worships the past.[3]

Her son had taken thousands of photos of her. But the only photos he really ended up using were the photos of her before he was born. In one she is leaning against a fence, among leaves, her head turned back, a smile flickering like a fire eating up everything else in the photograph, sucking in trees and light and sky. The early pictures, the ones that dominated his exhibition, might have been the photos of a Midwestern American farm girl, outside of the grip of tragedy and famine. The scene is rustic; the woman is young and attractive. It could be anywhere. But for her son, it captures a moment lost, a world that no longer exists. Were he to go back to Hunan, where the photo was taken, he would instead find cement factories and gutter water laced with pollution, landscapes devoid of birds and wildlife.

Now, there is only a veneer of fatigue that was not there before. There are few photos in his exhibition of his mother as she is now. In this way, he has inherited something from her: the need to only remember the past. If he can only catch it on film, if he can only display the photos of how beautiful his mother once was then perhaps people will believe that her life was justified. People will believe that she is not getting old. He wasn't born when most of the photos of her were taken. So in showing his exhibition he is, in a sense, removing himself from the equation. Perhaps that is why his mother is so beautiful, he seems to be saying: he had not been born yet to sully her beauty.

Shen Hsueh-yung didn't talk much about her parents. But others did. Many of those who came to Taiwan did so at the expense of those left behind, those who had made a sacrifice for them, so that they would survive. Now those survivors couldn't face up to the guilt they carried with them like dead corpses, like the corpses of those they left behind, those they imagined now rotting in Communist jails or starving in work camps. Ko Jen-tao, as he was living on American-made ships, had no idea if his mother was alive or dead. Later, when he was a police officer, he would come home on Sundays and drink whiskey until he was finally able to cry for her, something he couldn't easily do during the week, when he had to keep his guard up. Usually, he would simply cry himself to sleep, sleep the whole day of his one day off, wake up with a hangover and head back to another week of chasing down criminals while the real criminals got away free. Yin Tsai-chun was also one of those who did not know whether her relatives, particularly her father, were alive or dead. For forty years, starting in 1949, nearly all communications were cut between the warring sides. It was not possible to write a letter. Word of the Cultural Revolution, starting in the mid-1960s, leaked out to Taiwan, but only piecemeal. Yin Tsai-chun is an attractive woman in her early seventies whose loose, open shirt reveals a swathe of red flesh—perhaps from allergies or the sun. She has that kind of petite, pretty face, like a bell waiting for a piece of wind to hit it, which goes with her origins in Nanjing. She is eager and each sentence she speaks is followed with a simple sound made in her throat, "ungh," expressing her agreement or enthusiasm. What seems to be bothering her most is that she was unable to get her father out of the mainland before the Communists took over.

She describes her childhood with her father as one of both promise—her father was open and talked to her as if she were a boy—and failure; he had failed in his career as a painter and chosen to become a bureaucrat instead. Nothing could ever bring back that lost chance for her father. And she just couldn't get over the fact that he had lost his chance a second time, to escape with her. She tries to joke about it. But the pain comes through, like an old wound that's just started oozing again, after forty years of wearing a bandage.

> My father got into the Hangzhou Art Institute. He had potential. Anyone who studies painting went there. But in all the time he was there, I don't think he produced a single painting. It was a violent and chaotic time. He

couldn't concentrate on his work. He was worried about stability. In order to paint, you need the right environment. You need space. He didn't have that. It's hard to produce art during wartime. He had to find something more stable. But for him, I guess, that was okay. He actually felt he was a very humble artist.

So my father ended up using his talent in different ways. He used to design clothing. But it was so outlandish that no one could actually wear it. It wasn't traditional enough. He believed people should dress freely and openly. For example, in school, girls had to wrap a cotton cloth around their breasts as tight as possible. This way, men wouldn't be distracted. When my father found out, he went to school personally and talked to our teachers. He said that girls need to develop naturally. The next day I refused to go to school. I was so embarrassed.

But if I can say one thing for him, he never looked down on me or treated me like a girl. Whenever he came back from his office in the city, he would take me and my younger sister on a walk. He would ask us questions like, "What is the effect of the sun's radiation on people?" I had no idea how to answer. I just knew that the way he would talk to us was not like the way an average father would talk to his children. He was a unique father.

He would say things like, girls should not have to stay at home and learn sewing or cooking from their mothers. He said that, in the future, all that would be done by machines. They would free us from slavery. He said we should spend our times exploring and playing. His influence on me was immeasurable. He was a man who was entirely different from the men of his time.

Now that she has retired—she worked in a newspaper for most of her life—Yin is holding a painting exhibition. She admits she has never been a painter. Writing has always been her salvation. By painting, she believes she can finally atone for escaping while her father stayed behind. She believes she can fulfill his desire for a painting show, even if he is already dead. She wants to take over where he failed, pick up the past like it is a painting brush and erase all the time that she was apart from him. What she's really doing, though, is keeping that pain alive, with every stroke of the brush, remembering her father and his failed chances. She knows that most of the people who come to her exhibit do so simply because she is a famous writer. They don't expect much from her paintings. But she keeps up a good front. She won't allow this to discourage her from trying to pay back a debt she never really owed in the first place.

My father's whole life was unfulfilled. He wanted to be a painter but he was never able to sit down and complete a single painting. He had too much work to do for the government. I think this was because the war made everything chaotic. He used to say he felt like time was passing too fast. Then he would try to get us interested in nature, in the kinds of things he wanted to paint. He would say if he couldn't paint it, at least he would take his children to see it.

His philosophy was that our lives should not be limited by what we saw inside our house or school. He would say, open your eyes, and look at the mountains, the sun, the earth. Sometimes, he'd get depressed. But I could understand that. Now, sixty years later, I am trying to help him fulfill his dream. On the other hand, maybe my desire to paint has more to do with my own genes. I mean, I'm sure I inherited some of that desire from him. That would be another reason for my desire to paint. I'm not merely carrying on his unfinished projects. My dream was also to be a painter. That is my dream, not his.

No longer a newspaper columnist, she didn't have anything to fall back on when her party lost power. She spent those eight years, when the Democratic Progressive Party (hereafter DPP) took power, trying to pretend that the past was still alive, that it was as easy for her to become a painter, like her father, as it was for her party to take back its past. If the past, any past, can be brought back to life again, then it is still possible to delete the trauma left by that past—whether her father's failed career or the disruption of the political sway held by her class. If she could achieve what her father failed to do his entire life, then perhaps he never really failed after all.

As she describes it, the end of her childhood marked the beginning of another series of traumas, those that would consume her for the rest of her life. Affected by her father's radical teachings, she was eager to help her country during its dying years. She joined a special group of young idealistic women under the tutelage of a female Kuomintang leader. She passed a test in Nanjing and was admitted. Young women were needed to promote the morale of the troops, like cheerleaders at a football game.

> We had heard that there was a lot of good food in Taiwan. They supposedly even had bananas, which we had never even seen. We didn't join up because we were patriotic. We just wanted to have a good time. We thought that, in maybe two or three months, we could come home. If someone had told

us then that it would be sixty years before we could come home, or that we could never come back, we wouldn't have believed him. So I took a test and was accepted. It was just like applying to a school or a university. It was considered difficult to get in.

The government was recruiting a group of young women to come to Taiwan—to keep up the soldiers' morale and to teach the illiterate ones. We were first sent to Nanjing and then to Shanghai. I got really sick on the ship going over to Taiwan. I had never been on such a large ship before. In general, mainlanders rarely went out onto the ocean, unless they lived on the coast. When we got to Taiwan, they began training us. We were called the United Women's Work Team.

In Taiwan, the young women lived together and were indoctrinated in the Three Principles of the People, the ideological base of the Nationalists (Kuomintang), a mix of Western democratic principles and traditional Chinese thought. They studied some academic subjects to be ready to assist the soldiers in the classroom, if so assigned. Then they were sent off to their duties. She was sent to an island just off the coast of the mainland that was still controlled by the Kuomintang. It was the frontline, a military base within striking distance of the Communists. Each one of her team lived in a different unit. When Yin got to her regiment, she found that most of the men were illiterate, uneducated and wanted nothing more than simply to escape or die a quick death.

A lot of the soldiers we were supposed to teach were illiterate. So we taught them to sing songs. We would also try to teach them about the Three Principles of the People. Some of the soldiers could write a little and we helped them to write letters. For the illiterate ones, we would ask them to tell us what they wanted to say and we would write it down for them. It required a lot of patience. That was why the government hired young women to teach them. As women, we had more patience than men.

As time went on, her chief duty became just that: helping the soldiers write letters home. The process was simple. A soldier, perhaps from a farm in inner China, told her what to write, watched the black ink forming characters under her small fingers, then told her the address or rough location. She sealed the letter and the soldier slept more soundly that night, knowing word from him would reach his family sometime in the future. She, the pretty young girl from Nanjing, with a face as dainty as a bell just starting to tinkle, would take care of it.

She wrote. She wrote hundreds, perhaps thousands of letters, each soldier reciting the same endearments, the same lies, the same requests for money or for some other material help. Some soldiers cried. She wrote down all the words. She even wrote down words that they were too tired, too scared or too ashamed to write down. She guessed what they wanted to say. And she wrote it. Then she dumped all the letters into the ocean.

> We lived in one big room in a barracks made of wood. The wind would come in at night under the door. We each had our own bed. A lot of the houses on Kinmen were made of stone, so they were really hot. But we were relatively cool. After classes, we would all come in and talk about what our families were doing at that moment on the mainland. Everyone knew exactly what each member of her family was doing at that precise moment.
>
> On weekends, we would go to the bunkers along the shore and look at the mainland through giant telescopes. It didn't seem far away. After the Communists took over, however, we would stand in the bunkers and yell through loudspeakers across the water, "Comrades, China must be reunited according to the Three Principles." We honestly thought we could brainwash them by yelling slogans.

At first, it was only an adventure, something you could take on for a day, maybe a week at most, and then be safe at home. For a youngster, stationed on one of the few islands still held by the Kuomintang just off the coast of mainland China, it must have seemed almost a dream. Even the island, a flattened rock surrounded by barbed wire and garrisoned with Taiwan's finest troops, earnestly believing they might be called upon to retake the mainland, was daring. It was like she had stepped out of her history books and into the real world. This world was called Kinmen, or Quemoy. When she climbed with the soldiers mounting watch towers, within shouting distance of the mainland, and yelled slogans through a megaphone, she was too young to realize she might have been shouting for her father, now lost perhaps forever in the depths of the mainland. Perhaps she realized it in a different way. By the time she was sent to Kinmen, in early 1949, there was absolutely no contact with the Chinese Communists, except for the occasional artillery shell hurled from island to shore and back again. There was no mail because there probably wasn't anyone to write a letter back on the mainland. They had either been killed or rounded up. So when she wrote the letters for the soldiers, she felt somehow perplexed. She knew she could never mail the letters. Yet those letters brought solid comfort to the men. So when she had to dispose of them afterwards, she must have felt she was involved in a tremendous betrayal. She knew, as well as anyone, what a letter meant. Even with the ability to write her own, there was still no way it could reach that loved one somewhere in China. Letters could also be used by the enemy.

The worst of it was that her father didn't even know that she had come to Taiwan. She hadn't told him. She was afraid he would try to prevent it. She knew they were fighting for the same thing, the same ideals, and she wanted to make him proud. So she had simply taken herself off, in secret, to join the women's patriotic organization without letting him know. And she had taken her younger sister along, too. Now both of them were stranded outside enemy lines. She knew it was too late. She knew that the end was near for her government, that the "land bandits" were approaching, that they would soon win the final battle. So just before the entire mainland fell to the Communists, she wrote a letter to her father explaining why she had run off. Her father never received it.

> After we arrived at Kinmen, I wrote a letter back to my father telling him where we were. My father only knew vaguely what had happened to us. We didn't tell him we were headed for Taiwan, just that we were members of the women's organization. I wrote him a letter but it never reached him. Eventually, I lost any hope of having any contact with my father. And I was right. It wouldn't be for another half a century, think of it, half a century, that I would have any contact with him again.

At first, it wasn't hard for her to destroy the letters written by the men. If she could not reach her father, why should any of the others expect to reach their families? But as time passed, as she stayed on Kinmen and as the volleys of artillery increased and the island eventually lost all its trees, cut down by the rain of bombs, she began to regret her mission. All those letters written and disposed of haunted her as she finally was sent back to Taiwan and to begin a new life. All those letters she had written for poor soldiers, asking her to, "tell my mother I'm fine," or other sentiments, now rotting in a garbage bin on Kinmen, or floating to the bottom of the ocean, were a sign, or direction, for her future. She worked first at a girl's junior high school in Taipei as a military instructor. But after a time, the work was too much like her life on Kinmen. Then she found a job at the Kuomintang's major newspaper as a columnist answering letters. She had been unable to write a single letter to her father in the mainland, or read one from him. Now she began reading thousands from strangers, responding to several each day, in her own letters, and building fame as the "Ann Landers of Taiwan." Her column took off. She was earnest and sincere. But she did more than offer gracious platitudes or sympathy. She was repeating, to some extent, her experience on Kinmen, except this time she was able to take action, to make sure all the letters she dealt with were not only sent, but answered. She brought in experts who responded to letters sent to her, and she published their advice in her column. She linked up letter writers seeking help with government officials or with experts in new and daunting fields. The letters now became her gods, her idols.

I wrote in the *United Daily News*. And the *United Daily News* had a wide circulation. But I never considered myself a literary person. I just wrote letters. But I think because of my interaction with so many people, through letters, that I have a good understanding of that period, starting from around 1963 and up until the late eighties. I just wrote one column each day. I can't say it changed people's lives, but it did have an impact. I felt I was fighting for justice, against anything that was unfair. If a reader would write in and tell me about something unjust going on, then I would write about it in the newspaper. I remember one case. There was a college girl who was raped behind one of the universities by a taxi driver. And she was humiliated in court. I wrote several columns about it and got justice for the girl.

Yesterday, there was an older gentleman, about seventy years old, who came to see me. He said he was really grateful to me. He said at one time I wrote a column that helped him a lot. He had had some kind of trouble getting certified as a teacher in a middle school. He didn't have enough money to take the necessary test. He said that after I wrote the article about him, the government allowed him to take the test for free. In those days, the media could still have an impact on people's lives.

I think the greatest injustice I wrote about was about women. In those days, there was a lot of discrimination against women. For example, if a woman got married, she wasn't allowed to have a job, especially in banks or government offices. A lot of women were unhappy about this but didn't know how to get their voices heard. So I wrote about it, in a number of columns. As a result, the laws were changed, to some extent. In those days, a large newspaper still had some influence on society.

Family issues were another big area that people wrote in about. Let's say your husband was having an affair. You would be so humiliated that you wouldn't want to even tell your friends about it. But if you wrote me, it was safe because I didn't know you personally, and you would know that

I would keep your name anonymous. So people would write in. I would then get in touch with a well-known psychologist and ask him to answer the letter in my column. Individual people didn't see psychologists back then so people were really interested in my columns.

People didn't know where to seek help. That was their biggest problem. Every day I got a lot of letters from unhappy lovers, from lonely grandparents, from every kind of person you can imagine. A lot of them would pour their hearts out in their letters. Others would just be stuck about how to solve a problem. I acted as a bridge. I would get some expert, like a Dr. Wu, to respond to questions about love. Or if someone didn't know which government department to talk to, I would consult the government and write about it in my column. I would tell them who they should talk to. I was basically a bridge.

She had never thought, that with one blow, her entire past would be called into question. Her pride, her sense of mission, her status, were all blown away like a leaf when the opposition party took over. Perhaps she had once seemed like a savior of sorts, if not to herself, then to the people she helped, wrote to. But, in a flash, all that was gone. The opposition party no longer had much need for columns like hers. It was a time of wild, uncertain questioning for the mainlanders. If the new regime was here to stay, how would history judge them now—a history now to be rewritten by native Taiwanese they once enslaved? Would their decades of contribution, as police officers, as singers, as writers, as bankers, be swept away with a new world order? Would the new government recognize their lives at all or simply cast them aside, as villains from a defunct and dangerous regime? These were the poisonous and savage questions that were troubling people like Yin, who suddenly found themselves no longer celebrities but almost closer to war criminals. Perhaps her painting exhibition had less to do with her father. Perhaps it was more about proving to the new Taiwan that she could change, that she still had value.

It's almost as if the mainlanders expect it, though. They expect to be punished for their failure in the past to hold onto their homeland. They know that they've lost something valuable, the only thing valuable, and now it's as if they are cursed for it. That's why they need a government, a party, to tell them that it's okay, that there are other ways to carry on, other ways to earn pride and honor. They wait, eternally, for the propaganda they know must come from their leaders that they have for most of their lives only half believed, if that, telling them of a future destiny. That's why when it doesn't come, when they are suddenly seen as enemies of the new order, it is so hard for them to take it. They are no longer a protected people, but a people that now must cling to the idea of protection, to hope for it, to enamel it onto their stories, as if their honor, pride and achievement were all something definite, certain, preordained and not at all accidental.

Ko Jen-tao's memories have taken to him the moment when he joined the police force, after leaving the navy. He had been in Taiwan for several years and was starting a new career. He was lucky enough to meet his wife while the whole police station was vying for her, he explains. He was a handsome young man with smooth, copper flesh and something jaded in his face, as if he had memorized his father's expression as a Kuomintang official. He was not smug, but serene. As he tells his story, he contrasts those years of seamless good fortune with the moment when it seems that his good luck ran out; all those years of hard work wasted, or rather destroyed, by those who had somehow gone against the natural and right order of things.

> It was around that time that I was transferred from an outlying station to the Renai station, which was in the heart of the city. One day I was riding a bicycle through the market and this young woman runs into me from the side. She was carrying a lot of fruit and vegetables in one hand and steering with the other. Well, when she hit me, all of it fell down onto the ground. I got off to help her pick it up and we looked at each other for a moment. It was just a moment but something passed between us. I was a mainlander and she was Taiwanese. But it didn't matter at that moment. I found out she worked in the market making alterations to clothes.
>
> Then, a few months later, I was coming back from patrol and walked into the station and she was standing there. At first I didn't recognize her. She looked completely different. Her hair was shorter and she seemed more—shy. But when she looked at me, I remembered everything. Now, she was working as a janitor and office girl. She had just got the job. She was in charge of cooking and cleaning and delivering documents around the station. I thought it was destiny that had brought her to my station.
>
> There were a lot of other officers who were interested in her. But she was only interested in me. I was younger. I remember I wrote her a note apologizing for bumping into her in the market, even though she had been the one who bumped into me. She wrote back saying that she'd be fortunate to have me as a friend. She was bold when she wanted to be. So I asked her to a movie. Movies were still my great escape. We took a rickshaw. First, we had

dinner, then we saw the movie. After that, we went to see a movie together every week. It was hard because I didn't have much time off.

She agreed to marry me after her younger brother got into a motorcycle accident. She had six brothers, but she was closest to him. He worked for the post office delivering express mail. So he was always on his motorcycle. One day, he got hit by a truck and his skull got a crack in it. He had been taken to National Taiwan University Hospital but the hospital was full and his bed was sitting in the lobby. She came to me saying, "Oh my god, oh my god, my brother is going to die." So I took her and we rushed over to the hospital. Now that hospital was not in my district. But I knew a few people who worked in the station in that district. So I called them and they called up the hospital and the hospital gave him a room immediately. By the time all of her relatives got to the hospital, he was already being treated. I heard them saying, in Taiwanese, "Eh, this mainlander is not a bad guy."

After her brother got out of the hospital and returned home, she took some time off and went home to ask for permission to get married. I couldn't get any days off to go with her. Her family is from Bamboo Mountain, in Nantou County. It's a small village where the villagers harvest tea. When she got home, her family told her they opposed the marriage. Despite the fact that I had saved her brother's life, they all opposed it. Her parents said that marrying a mainlander would be a big mistake. The Taiwanese really discriminated against us in those days. They thought that we were uncultured and violent. The whole family opposed it. But fortunately, while she was there, her younger brother who had been in the accident recovered enough so that he could support her. He basically shamed the rest of the family into supporting her marriage to me—an outsider.

It wasn't easy for Ko to win over the native Taiwanese from Bamboo Mountain. When the settlers came, they met with the kind of resistance they thought they had left behind on the mainland. They thought they had come to Chinese lands, to an island of Chinese people. They knew that Japan had ruled there for fifty years and tried to turn the people into loyal Japanese citizens. But they hadn't figured on how much the locals would resist them. When Ko first visited Bamboo Mountain, it was unlike anything he had ever seen before. Up in the mountains, the tea bushes twist and snag along the road. There are giant banana trees that tower over a man's head. And the locals fish the streams with wires strung to car batteries, shocking the tiny ribbons of fish into stillness then scooping them up out of the water. Some of the Chinese settlers, the poor troops, had never even seen a car battery before.

But the story is not just about Ko. It encompasses the entire saga of the mainland immigrants coming to Taiwan, as they would later tell it. Ko maintained order as a police officer. This was the role he had laid out for himself. He brought safety and security to Taiwan. When necessary, he went out on a limb, by calling in favors, and then bestowed health and life, much as Shen Hsueh-yung had bestowed culture. Places such as Bamboo Mountain resisted the coming of the mainland immigrants, he believed, simply because people in these places did not know the true character of the mainland immigrants and the true Chinese civilization they represented. When Ko visited the mountain, he would watch the long walls of bamboo and behind them the farmers snipping off tea leaves with razors taped to their fingers. And he would smell the endless odor of DDT and burning trash lazily listing around and through the banana trees and he would think how far he had come from his home in Nanjing. Smoke rolled through brick houses, through doors that never closed, into hallways and sitting rooms that always contained slow-moving farmers waiting for nothing. To Ko Jen-tao, these people, who spoke an unintelligible dialect, were refugees of an earlier Chinese civilization. But to his superiors, they were seen as people sitting in darkness, resisting the sheltering embrace of the superior civilization and its emissaries that had come across the sea. Or, worse, they were seen as the corrupted blood of the Japanese empire.[4]

Soon Ko's memories begin to betray a sense of uneasiness, as if they'd run out of steam, or he had run out of reasons for going on talking. As he talks, he begins to find fault, though subtly, with his government. It was his government that had brought him to Taiwan, saved him, created the conditions for his marriage, and even allowed him to find a new role for himself, as a healer of the injured. But it eventually betrayed him—by being unable to resist the tide of demands for democratic reform that would eventually unseat his entire class, even if only for a short while. No matter how you look at it, he was a man already cheated out of a better life, out of a life that could have belonged to him if he had only stayed on the mainland and his party had won the war. As it was, the life he had built in Taiwan should have been stable and secure. No one should have been allowed to take it away.

> We got married when I was twenty-seven and she was twenty-one. I was supposed to provide for her. But I couldn't. I had nothing, no relatives,

no savings, absolutely nothing. I did have a colleague in the police station who was well-off. He had just bought a house in the western district but he wasn't using it. He and his family were living in an apartment uptown. He offered it to us, free of charge. I didn't want to accept it at first. But I had no choice, really. I didn't feel like a man. It was for her.

I had a cousin, the one who brought me over in the ship from Shanghai. He had just retired and he and his wife came to visit us. I had no way to refuse them. He had saved my life. So I let them live with us even though the place was really small. We were all sleeping in the same room and had to take turns cooking in the kitchen; it was so small. Fortunately, the district chief was aware of how hard I was working. He always told me I wrote beautiful calligraphy. He had always praised my bravery. Because I *was* brave. I didn't even need to use handcuffs in those days. No criminal would dare to run off from me. He knew I would jump on him if he tried to get away. I was also good at handling household registration. When the district chief heard I had just gotten married, he assigned me a place in the station dormitory. So we could get out from under the noses of my cousin and his wife.

We got a room on the third floor of the dormitory. It was just a single room and my wife was pregnant at the time. After she gave birth, we had two kids. They were twins. I was happy to be living in our own place. It was small but it was our own. The only problem was that it didn't have a window. Well, it actually did have a window, but you could never open it. It was sealed up with plaster. That was because the dormitory was right across from the Central Police Command. No one living near that building was allowed to open a window. It was a military institute, a secret institute. It was where the government put spies and anyone who was trying to destroy our republic. During the time we lived there, we all got colds all the time. My two sons, my wife, and I always had colds. There was no ventilation, so as soon as one of us got sick, we all did.

This took place during the years of White Terror. It was a dream spun out by Chiang Kai-shek in which thousands, perhaps tens of thousands, of mostly locals were arrested and tried in secret and often shot. And if not shot, then transferred to distant islands to spend half of their lives in prison. One of the resources of the Terror was the Central Police Command, stationed next door to the new room given to Ko and his family. No matter how much his superiors respected his work, they couldn't protect his children from the demands of the White Terror. Even the most loyal servants of the party were touched. The health of his children was still threatened. Half a century later, these massive security arrangements still ultimately had not been able to hold back the tide of change.

All that he really had to prove himself was his uniform and a couple of awards he picked up along the way. The uniform was khaki-colored, like earth. It was not as swaggering, perhaps, as his naval uniforms. It was more like the uniform of a soldier or a cadet, not the kind of uniform a man would wear if he were simply keeping the peace. Maybe the uniform couldn't make up for the loss of his mother or father. Maybe it couldn't make up for his past and for the loss of his home. But it was at least a symbol that he could count on now, something bigger than himself to which he could belong. That is, until it was taken away from him in recent years. In photos from his early years, he is always the shortest in a line-up of police officers receiving awards. That might have been one reason: his fury at his height, at how it set him at a disadvantage not only with the crooks he was paid to apprehend, but also with the brother officers whose awards he should have been getting. The relentlessness with which he pursued felons appeared to be fury, but it was in fact outrage over his own unfair allotment. His work kept him at the police station, on duty, six days a week. He even slept there. His family saw him briefly, on Sundays, when he returned home to drink and then sleep most of the day. He came home and went straight to the liquor cabinet, a sort of tall, glass box of shelves with a glass door and liquor inside. His wife said how he would drink and cry, not about his life in Taiwan, but about his mother and his family that he had left behind on the mainland, as if he had had any other option but to flee by himself, as if he, a grown, hale man, could have found a way to go back in time to that moment when he stepped on the boat, and haul his whole family along with him. What he didn't realize was that, by spending so much time living in the past, crying for it, he was leaving the present, the family he had raised in the present, somewhere in the past as well. He was as isolated as he had been all along.

Yet he believed he was a new man. His wardrobe was filled with khaki police uniforms. He pasted photos of himself, in the uniforms, his hair held down with heavy oil, as he received awards. He was able to pay for private schooling, as he advanced in rank, for his two, then three, then four children. Trophies of his successes lined the dining-room shelves and stood behind glass, on shelves, in the living room. The liquor collection was now no longer simply bottles of whiskey and gin. There were now plastic containers of liquor, shaped like cars or airplanes, models of the Eiffel Tower, also filled with alcohol, perhaps mimicking some idealized room or study glimpsed in a foreign movie. A giant fish tank took up an entire wall of the living room. The fish was a Red Dragon, the most costly fish in Taiwan. Most of the time, he and his wife didn't talk much when they were angry. But when they did, when they fought outright, she would threaten to fry the fish up for dinner while he was away. When he was home, on Sundays, he would emerge from the bedroom in his undershirt and boxer shorts and stare at the fish from time to time. He liked to listen to opera or classical music that was heavy and maudlin. He had the luxury of melancholy.

    His sense of failure has kept him isolated his whole life. First, from his family in Taiwan. Later, from his mainland wife. He figures that no one will remember him, that when he dies, he will be more isolated than ever, if he isn't outright dead already. When his party loses its hold on the government, he takes the first step down towards a hell of shame, shame that has just burst like an abscess malingering for decades below the surface. When his new wife refuses to sleep with him, he whines like a baby. It is pure shame, thinned out like baby food for an old man with few teeth left, whining out of him as he watches his wife's body move around the room. He can never understand that it is also her own sense of shame, for leaving her son behind, which drives her. She thinks she has made a deal for his future, marrying a man from Taiwan. But what she doesn't realize is that she loves her husband and is afraid she will lose him as he drowns in his past. For now, Liu Rong, the new mainland wife, spends her days flitting around the apartment like a trapped bee, fanning herself, sitting for a moment listening to him complain, then retreating to the kitchen, from which suddenly bursts forth the sound of pots and pans striking each other like hammers driving in nails. Soon, though, she figures out a way to beat herself at her own game. She takes on a job as nurse's aide in a hospital where she pulls off catheters and changes bed pans eighteen hours a day. Husband and wife, each swimming their own shame, are like two opposing figures on a chessboard: her hard, white body, in a blue flowered dress, and her white legs exposed every time she sits down and her dress flies up. He like her shadow, the shadow of what she will look like when she gets old, sagging, decrepit, sinking into the couch. He sits on the couch in an old tank-top T-shirt, his stomach like that of a pregnant woman's, his grey hair mottling a little at the side of his head where the dye has washed away. About the only thing he wants to think about is the glory of his police days.

I got my awards because I had guts. I wasn't afraid of anything. If I had been back on the mainland, I might have been afraid, maybe of the Communists. But here in Taiwan, I wasn't afraid. I'll give you an example. We heard that there was this wanted felon who was in a shop eating a plate of fruit and ice. Everyone else kept saying, "We've got to get our guns. We've got to get our vests on." But I wasn't afraid. That's how I got to be deputy chief. I just walked right into that shop. The guy took one look at me and didn't even get up. He just sat there waiting for me to come over. He saw that I meant business. He saw it in my face. I wasn't going to take anything from a criminal. I didn't even have to use handcuffs. That was how I got my first award.

I was living solely on my guts. If I had the guts to do my job, I would get promoted. I did get promoted. I was in that station for a total of eight years. Most guys get transferred out after one or two years only. That was because it was the most important district in the city. All the big hotels, the Taipei Hospital, the basketball stadium, the baseball stadium, the richest district in the city were all part of my jurisdiction. I was busy all the time, guarding those areas. If I didn't have the guts to do my job, I would have been out of there.

Actually, my whole purpose in being out there was to serve the people. That was what I thought about all the time. There were times when a kid would get involved in a car accident, for instance. Since there was no national health insurance at that time, a lot of these kids from a poor family would be taken to the hospital and have no way to pay. The doctors would say they couldn't treat anyone who couldn't pay. Taiwan was not such a rich country then. So if the kid couldn't pay the admittance fee, I would pay it out of my own pocket. Then the hospital would ask for a guarantor. You had to have someone guarantee payment in order for them to do any kind of treatment. I would be the guarantor in a lot of cases. I would be the one who signed my name on the form.

Eventually, there were so many patients like this, who couldn't pay, that the hospital sued me. The judge asked me in court, how could you take responsibility for so many people? I answered by saying that I was a police officer and my sworn duty was to serve and protect. How could I do nothing when some kid was lying there dying? Eventually, the court let it go and the hospital stopped calling me.

Ko believes he has failed to take care of his mother in her old age. She was in Nanjing, he in Taipei. He believes he has lost the chance, the one precious, irremediable chance to show his duty to her. Every time he speaks of this, tears fill his throat and desperation overflows as he speaks. "Ah, I never had the chance to even talk to my mother," he says. It is the same panic he felt as the boat pulled out from the shores of Shanghai, the same panic that he was not allowed to feel then, because he was in flight from the enemy, although he may not have fully understood it then. Now he is attempting, as an old man, to feel, to speak about what he could not speak about then. Parting. "She took care of me as a child," he says. He calls himself "false." So when he recounts a case he handled as a police officer, in which the tie between parents and a child are broken, he finds hope again, his guilt becomes outrage and he speaks as if it was easy to solve the problem. The case, involving a neglected and abused boy, hit him hard. Suddenly, he was that boy. It was no longer a case of him leaving behind his mother, but of his mother abandoning him. He tells the story as if it had just happened, with a kind of eagerness and forcefulness, as if someone listening might not believe him. The story also has something to do with his party's recent defeat in the presidential elections, although it is hard to say what it is. Perhaps shame. He thought that when he was an old man he would be honored as a savior of Taiwan, not an enemy. It doesn't matter to him that the Kuomintang has come back into power. His idols have fallen and been cast in the dust.

> One day someone came in to report a crime. It wasn't an ordinary crime. The report was that some neighbors had been complaining about an abused child. The report was that the kid had been beaten up. So I took a car and went over to the address listed on the complaint form. An old woman let me in. As soon as I saw the kid, I was sick. Really sick. There were bruises up and down his arms, his legs, even on his face. He was thin, really thin. When I examined him more closely, I could tell that he had been beaten with a stick. The stick had left black marks in the middle of each bruise. The mother and father were not at home. And the kid wouldn't say a word. He was about eight or nine, but he refused to talk to me.
>
> So I went and investigated. I went from door to door, talking to the neighbors. Many of them were Taiwanese and didn't want to talk to me because I was a mainlander. But I could speak a little Taiwanese because of my wife. So some of them opened up to me. Some of them were mainlanders, too. I found out that the kid's father worked in some big company. He and his wife were divorced and she was long gone. The father had remarried and so the kid had a stepmother. I also found out that she worked for China Airlines, which meant she was a mainlander. I thought to myself, how can this be? They both are well-educated people with good positions? I ordered the neighbors, "When either of them comes home, call me."

That night around seven, a call came in. The father had come home. So I hopped in the police car and sped over there. When the child saw me, his face dropped. I said,

"I represent the police in this city. Would you be so kind as to tell me what is the relationship of this boy to you?"

"My son."

"So you can still identify him with all those bruises on him?"

He didn't answer; he just stood there, his head hanging down. Finally, I said, "I demand to know who did this to him?"

He just kept looking down.

"Go ahead," I said. "You're going to have to explain it to the judge."

He looked up. He had this sort of sick grin on his face, as if he wanted to defy me.

"I beat him," he said.

"And why did you beat him, if you would be so kind as to answer me?"

"He doesn't do as he's told."

"So you tell him what to do by beating him up?"

"It's not what I want to do. Look, his mother and I had a terrible marriage. She is a very sick person. After she left, the child started acting out. Now he threatens my new wife with physical violence. We've both had it with him."

"Where is your wife?"

"She's on her way home."

After his wife got home, I asked her the same questions.

"He threatens me. What can I do?" she said.

"You work at China Airlines, right?" I said. "Tomorrow, I'm going to go down to your office and have a little talk with your boss, tell him what goes on here, that a China Airlines flight attendant is beating her stepson. Do you think those air force generals who run the company are going to like this?"

"I'm also going to contact some reporters I know to have the case written up. It'll be on the front page tomorrow."

The father knelt down in front of me. He touched his forehead to the ground.

"If you do this, we'll lose our jobs. And we'll never be able to find any others."

"So, what are you going to do?"

"We won't beat him anymore. I give you my word. I will do everything I can to make sure he has a good life."

"The child is innocent of whatever happened between you and your ex-wife. He should not be punished for what happened between you," I said.

>The next day, they came down to the station and signed a contract with me, agreeing that if they ever hit the kid again they would go to jail.
>The neighbors said I saved that kid's life.

Despite the glory, Ko wishes he had been a doctor. He believes it was the war which had cheated him that and his father's early death. He feels, secretly, that he's part of the cultured class represented by the flight attendant. The flight attendant worked for the Kuomintang Party airline, China Airlines. She was chosen by top party officials for the job. Ko says that he was surprised at her behavior. How could someone with a background like hers behave so immorally? She was supposed to represent culture, Chinese culture, to the world. Ko never even went to college. He never even attended a junior high school. He just never had the chance to live up to what his father wanted for him. His father, on the other hand, was a student at Peking University. Ko just can't seem to get his mind around this outrage to culture—to education and training—by those who should have a higher level of morality.

Ko's response is to try to do better than those in authority, to be more moral than they are, to always carry out his duty, not only regularly, but zealously and passionately. He is willing to risk his life without a moment's hesitation. He wants to shame those around him. He has been abandoned by those above him and his only response is to conform to the rules with even greater passion.

>I am willing to risk my life for the people. One time, we got a phone call. There was some guy with a gun hiding out in a movie theater. Actually, it was a movie theater just down the block. I was just getting my gear together when my wife showed up. She said, "You haven't even put on your bullet proof vest, what do you think you're doing? Do you want to die?" I said, "I'm not afraid of dying. I'm only afraid of not being able to live up to my family."
>
>I meant my family left behind in Nanjing, actually. But she thought I was talking about her and our children. It's not that I didn't love them. I was always a good father. It's just that I had left my heart and soul behind me. I was enraged that I went after criminals here in Taiwan while the biggest criminals of all were in charge of the mainland. Well, we searched the movie theater and the surrounding neighborhood and turned up nothing. He had gotten away.

Ko's first marriage helped him to learn that he could survive what he believed were his failures. He was looking for someone who would believe in him. She was never one to give way on anything. She didn't always trust him. But she was proud of him, of his bravery. Ko was able to raise a family and, even though he was hundreds of miles away from his mother, prove to her also that he was filial, that he was a good son. He couldn't see her but he could he could do the single most important thing a Chinese man can do: raise children. Photographs from the time of his active duty show him grinning, in sweaters, youthful-looking, his wife tight-lipped and awkward in front of the camera. Despite the problems they faced—sexual, cultural, poor communication—he admired her for her thriftiness and relied on her support for his continued work as a police officer. It was during this period that he made some of his most lucrative real estate deals, buying apartments in out-of-the-way areas then selling them, ten years later, for ten times the amount. Eventually, he accumulated enough wealth to buy a large apartment in the center of town—at least what was then the center of town— behind the Kuomintang Party newspaper, the *United Daily News*, an apartment with a long spacious wooden floor and a swimming pool. The family rented it out while living in a smaller, tenement-like apartment on the east side of town, near the old dusty train station, in an area swarming with garbage and cockroaches.

In the apartment, the cockroaches were so big that they looked like snakes climbing right up the walls of the bathroom. A child would have to be pretty brave to watch those slimy things crawling up a crack in the tile as he brushed his teeth before going to bed. They had four children, two boys and two girls. The wife had always felt like sex was a "duty." Now she would go in the back and sleep with the kids when they had a fight. Ko Mama, as she was known, had skin as brown as molasses and breasts as smooth as egg shells that you could see when she bent over in her nightgown to shuck corn or peel lychees. Ko just couldn't get enough of her. But he was just too ashamed of himself to speak out. So he just never stopped working. She started to work in a factory, making televisions. And the whole time they were investing in real estate. The family fortunes continued to mount. When they finally got together enough money to buy what looked like a European villa in the hills outside of Taipei they still spent weekends working together to clean it. They would be standing side by side, their pants rolled up, shooting garden hoses at the walls and scrubbing them down with brushes and soap. You could almost say that they built modern Taiwan together. He was just an orphan from a war who kept himself going by clinging onto the belief that he was a little better than she. She was from a people that had their own belief in their superiority. The Japanese after fifty years had made them a little better than the rest of the Chinese. She was willing to work as hard as any fool who came in from the mainland. Why they stayed together, who can tell?

For men like Ko, marrying a local was as high as they could hope to climb. Usually, it was the richest mainlanders, the generals, the bankers that married among themselves. So while Ko was settling down to build a family, he was also confirming his status as one of the defeated. Defeated not just by the war, but by his failed hopes and dreams. If he had been a doctor, as his father meant him to be, he might have married another mainlander. Now he was stuck with a local. Still, in Chinese, the character for safety is a woman under a roof. So he was safe, committed. His world had begun to shift, at least in part, to Taiwan. Other settlers felt the same. They decided to get married because they felt rejected by the mainlander establishment; they had been rejected by their commanding officer or, maybe, by the bureaucracy. They felt that they had nothing to lose. But then they discovered that most Taiwanese families didn't want their daughters to marry mainlanders. The families remembered when the mainlanders first started arriving in 1945, the officers who stole whatever they could lay their hands on and the soldiers, mostly peasants, who took whatever they wanted, whether it was bicycles, clothes, or women. The families also remembered February and March of 1947 when the Kuomintang army killed tens of thousands of Taiwanese because a few had protested against their rule. So for the mainlanders, marriage with a local often meant a retreat from their own world, which had rejected them, into another world that didn't want them either. One could also say that it meant a fusion of the northern capital with the middle and southern parts of the islands, where most of the locals lived.

Ku Chi got married after he was laid off. After working at the casting plant for two years under the direction of his new father, the plant ran out of gold and silver. "There was nothing left to cast," he says. Originally, the plant had been set up in Taiwan to supply gold and silver dollars to soldiers still fighting on the mainland. Now that there were no more territories being fought over on the mainland, the central authorities stopped supplying gold and silver. Ku underwent a renewed period of wandering. His stepfather ensured that all laid-off employees enjoyed a sixty-percent continuation of their salary. But it wasn't enough to live on. Ku found work at a cement plant. The work was tough. On his time off, he continued his wandering habits. He ended up in the middle of the island, playing in a basketball tournament of rival knitting factories. This was just outside of Taichung, in Fengyuan County, in the center of Taiwan. By this point, he had more or less decided to forego the cement factory and play basketball instead, just living off the sixty-percent salary from the casting plant, just barely scraping by, but free to wander. A member of one of the opposing teams, taking a liking to him, invited Ku to come and work for their knitting factory, in the accounting division.

> I was playing basketball in a league in the center of the island. Almost anyone could play in it but it was mostly made up of members of knitting factories. At the end of one game, the boss of one of the factories came up to me and said, "You're pretty good. You're from the mainland, aren't you?" I said I was. He guessed I was from Shanghai by the way I spoke. He said something like, "Well, if you want to get a job, you're going to have to beat me in one-on-one." I had nothing to lose. I was a lot shorter than he was. He had long fingernails and they kept scratching me. But I beat him by one point. He had to take me on. I worked there for a while, as an accountant. But then the factory went bankrupt. I should've known that would happen from the start by the way the manager acted. He thought everything was some kind of game.
>
> So I went with some other guys to Taichung. That was the biggest city in the central part of the island. There weren't many jobs. But there was an opening in a middle school. They needed an assistant principal who would mostly be in charge of discipline. It didn't sound so hard, so I exaggerated a little about my work experience. They did like that I had worked in a bank. And I got the job. You know what? It was the hardest job I had ever done. We had to fine any student who spoke Taiwanese, so I had to be on guard constantly. There were all sorts of discipline issues. Fighting, swearing, you name it. Finally, one day, I just up and left.

Mainland refugees were flooding the countryside. Their business enterprises were often failing, due to corruption or simply post-war chaos. Ku met his future wife on the factory floor of the knitting factory where he worked. But as soon as locals in the surrounding townships learned of their romance, and his intention to ask her to marry, they often cursed Ku as he walked by, as well as the local girl. So ingrained was hatred and mistrust of mainland refugees that it became necessary to not only get another local as "guarantor" that the marriage would be profitable for both of them, but to get the most senior local available.

Between the two of us, we were earning more than her father could have earned in a year. I was still getting my sixty percent from the casting plant. On top of that, I had a job in the knitting factory. And my wife had a job in the knitting factory. Her father was just a farmer. Do you know why he opposed our marriage? Because I was a mainlander. They thought all mainlanders were dirty and uneducated. They didn't know what it meant that I had come from Shanghai. Yes, her father opposed it. Bitterly. He said he would rather see his daughter dead than marry a mainlander. The fact that I had a stable income in an uncertain time meant nothing to him. I was making more than he could ever have dreamed of.

But it wasn't against the law to marry a mainlander. So I got the foreman from the factory—he was a local Taiwanese—to go and talk to her father. The foreman was well respected in the community. The man went to her father's house and said, "What reason do you have for opposing this marriage? Just speak it publicly, then we can respond to it." He was smart. He had brought a bunch of workers with him. Well, her father was too ashamed to say anything outright. So he had no choice but to agree to the marriage. Her father did lay down some conditions. But he agreed to it. He had no choice. I don't think, though, that I've ever forgotten how he treated me at first. After all these years, I still don't know how to make things better, to feel better about it.

We set a date. I bought the food for the wedding. Her father showed up. I toasted him and my wife toasted him but in my heart I hadn't forgiven him. Even when we went on our honeymoon, I couldn't stop thinking how he had snubbed me. Who was he? A Taiwanese farmer. We were planning to go to a place called Stone Lion Mountain. It was one of the places I had gone to when I first arrived on the island. But when we got there, there was no way to get from the railroad to the hotel. I had forgotten that my friends and I had walked the whole twelve miles before. Now that I was married, and had suitcases and things, there was no way we could walk that far. So we simply waited in the train station for the next train back. And the whole time I blamed her father. He had made me forget. He had flustered me so I couldn't think straight. That was our honeymoon.

These locals didn't believe the Kuomintang myth that they were bringing Chinese culture and civilization to Taiwan. Local families felt the reverse. They knew that most of the mainlanders were poor, that they had no land. On the contrary, mainland men started seeing local woman as cheap and easy, like whores.[5] Local families feared their daughters would fall into the hands of mainlanders—and become just that. There was no way out except through the kind of negotiation that Ku Chi went through. And even then, wealthy local families, by and large, would not allow their daughters to marry mainland immigrants, no matter how high their rank or position was.

Many mainlanders who did marry local women never really let go of their resentments. They buried them deep, so deep that they never really burst out again until the party of the locals took power. Even before then, refugees like Ko Jen-tao would learn to speak just enough local Taiwanese to grunt a few greetings at his in-laws, but never develop an easy facility with the language that allowed deep communication. Visits to the local in-laws, by mainland immigrants, were often short and infrequent, even as recently as the first part of this century, when the children of such marriages had reached middle age. But it wasn't until the Kuomintang lost to the local party that this resentment burst through, like something struggling inside a burlap sack, screaming and ripping its way out. It was as if the mainlanders had been rejected once again. The first time was on the mainland. The second was by the families of Taiwanese. And now the third and last time was by the Taiwanese voters. Lin Ching-wu, the former soldier whose baseboard-hard stomach shows how much basketball he still plays describes locals as overrunning Taipei and destroying the future of Taiwan. All the disappointments in his life reverberate through his narrative. His children's failure to get married, the lowering quality of life in Taiwan, his leaving his parents behind on the mainland, even his failure to become an officer, all—all of them—are linked like spokes to the hub of a circle—to the local Taiwanese.

> Is it because I left my father behind that my children speak disrespectfully to me? We Chinese believe in respect for parents above all else. I sometimes feel I am cursed. Now my son doesn't even listen to me. He talks back and sometimes even shouts at me. This is actually because what the local Taiwanese politicians have done. They have changed the island. This so-called democratic election has destroyed any ethical or moral ideas these people might have had. They have no respect for the past.
>
> Taiwan is turning into two separate countries. Here in the north, we mainlanders mostly hold on to our past traditions. We feel guilt about leaving our parents behind, so we hold onto the traditions they taught us. But in the middle and southern parts of Taiwan, there are a lot of local kids who have their whole families with them and so all they care about is making money or they have the time and money to put a lot of resources into preparing for the college entrance exams. So they all get good scores.

The result is that my kids can't get into college. And now the north is getting taken over by these young kids from the south. Most of them are men. They bring with them their lack of morals. And they leave behind them all the local girls. So now that they're here, and they are getting into the good universities and getting the good jobs, our girls are starting to marry them. Our boys, like my son, are unable to get a girlfriend and can't carry on the line. This is all because I have been cursed. Or you could say it's the fault of those politicians. Maybe both are true.

Now those mainland boys who can't find a wife, some of them are even going back to China or to places like Thailand to try to find a wife. But the women there are uneducated. The result is that the children of this kind of marriage don't get a good grounding in tradition. They end up rude and uncultured and without any sense of direction. I try to warn my kids to hurry up and get married, but what can I do? I can't force them. Taiwan is now democratic and they have grown up here so they don't respect me. They think they have a right to decide their own future. Well, let them. When I was in the army, I used to put on a lot of shows, plays, for the other soldiers. I was popular. I had a lot of hope about the future. I was the one who told everyone to have hope about our future.

Unlike many of his fellow mainlanders, Lin did not marry a local woman. Thus, it is not as easy for him to blame Taiwanese for the failures of his life. Or perhaps it is simply more complicated. When he did marry, it was also after a defeat in his career. He expected to advance, but was shunted aside. Then, when he thought with horror about his future prospects, a mounting sense of failure seized him. It was then he decided to let down his guard and marry. It came about that he was able to marry as close to home as possible, thus hiding his failure in a sense of geography. At a dinner arranged by a matchmaker, he met a woman who, like him, was from Fujian. She had the same accent, was even from the same small area. He was thus able to hide with a woman of the same background. It was as if he hadn't ever really left home. Even today, his apartment has the feel of an enclave, of something preserved behind closed windows for a long time. So does he. "I have the same amount of teeth I've always had," he says, smiling a ferocious, toothy grin, pulling up his shirt again to show off his hard stomach. Behind him, on the wall, is a decorous photo of his children, as if they too are preserved in the motionless air. They appear stupefied, their lower lips hanging, their eyelids drooping, as if they were still posing for the photo and would go on posing until they died, their faces already ghostly white from waiting, from lack of blood.

Atop a television set, which occupies most of the small living room, two tiny flags are crossed. One is the Kuomintang party flag—a white sun in a blue field. The other is the flag of the republic. Ferocious in their stillness, like toy flags left by children, they seem to shout out through the dust-driven air something about preserving the past, through defeat. Something that the local Taiwanese, outside in the car exhaust and deteriorating environment, can't understand, something that stays in this small apartment for now.

> On the other hand, following tradition is not always fair. In 1967, I was placed in a student dormitory as a military instructor. After a year, my students had the best records in military training of anywhere in Taipei. But there were twenty-eight other instructors in the universities around Taipei. None of them had as good a record as I did. But they were older. So the commander said to me, "You're still young, you have plenty of time ahead of you to be promoted. The older instructors don't." So I wasn't promoted. I should have been promoted. I should have been made an officer. But the commander was thinking in traditional ways. So I never became an officer.
>
> After that, I was so disappointed, I decided to get married. I thought, if I can't rise in rank at least I can create a family. One of my students introduced me to my wife. He took me to a restaurant and when we started speaking I could tell by her accent she was also from Fujian. Tears came to my eyes. It was like I was going home. Later, I realized that it wasn't that I wanted to get married so much. It was more that I just wanted to go home.

Immigrants like Lin, who have preserved a room full of memories and aspirations, like breath that has been breathed and rebreathed in a small space, easily feel trapped. From the window of his small apartment, he can see street signs named after mainland Chinese cities. He does not know how much longer they will remain that way. The local party tried to change the names of major streets near and in Taipei. Its greatest success was with the international airport, which is now simply called "Taoyuan Airport," for the city that surrounds it, rather than "The Chiang Kai-shek International Airport," as it was known during the Kuomintang rule. The postal system, similarly, is no longer called the "China" postal system, but the "Taiwan" postal system. As these changes were taking place, the mainland immigrants were going over and over in their minds activities they took part in—that at the time seemed to bestow upon them identities—and were now examining them, questioning them—as if they were under attack. No longer the ruling party, they wondered about the value of their efforts.

Ku Chi, the Shanghai banker with the shriveled skin, began to wonder about the value of the calligraphy he had been taught as a child and which had helped him find a job. After he got married, his father found for him a position with the Central Bank. The only requirement for the job was the ability to write a perfect hand. The reason was the president of the bank had to write reports for Generalissimo Chiang Kai-shek. The Generalissimo believed he could resurrect the past, when he had been the hope of all China to get rid of the foreigners, the Japanese and the warlords, by proving that he was a sort of modern-day sage. He believed that even something as mundane as financial reports from a bank ought to be presented in ancient calligraphy. Ku had been trained as a child. But his attitude towards calligraphy was ironic. The calligraphy which Chiang wanted was a kind that had been used in the last dynasty. It was almost as if, through the calligraphy, Chiang felt he could recreate the grandeur of past dynasties. It was as if he were trying to align his regime with all the dynasties that had come before it. In fact, historians working for the Kuomintang drew a chart of all the dynasties, from the first to the last. Each one was represented by a little circle, like a soap bubble. And all the soap bubbles were falling down in a straight line, and each one was connected to the one above it with a tiny line, like a string, as if the soap bubbles were beads, all strung together, hanging straight down as if they were hanging from a single hook at the top, which was attached to the first dynasty, the first bead. At the bottom of the string of beads was a larger bead, a larger soap bubble, twice the size of the other beads, hanging down as if it were the weight that kept the string taught. In it were printed the words, "The Republic of China." The chart showed that it was just another bead on a long thread, perhaps the bead that all the other beads were building up to.

> Later, my father, that is, my stepfather, got to be really close with the secretary general of the Central Bank, good friends, because he was from the money casting plant, and the other was from the Central Bank so the two of them had business relations. The Central Casting Plant was a subsidiary of the Central Bank. So the secretary general of the Central Bank, wanted me to work for him. Why did they want me to go to the Central Bank to work? Because the Central Bank had a president, that is a head, he needed to write in calligraphy, he needed a person to write in calligraphy.
>
> That was because he needed to give reports to the president. At that time, it was Chiang Kai-shek. He had this habit. The official documents that you gave to him had to be written in calligraphy. Also, you had to write it in

zhengkai, the formal square style. You couldn't write it in grass loose style. So he asked my father, saying, "I heard your son can write calligraphy really well. Write something for me and I'll give it to the president to look at. How about you write just one document?" So I wrote something.

Now this is funny. He just told me to write something, anything. So I just took something from the Chinese classics, without paying any attention to the content, and just copied it word for word, not even paying any attention to what I was writing, just concentrating on the strokes of the characters. Later, I realized it was a funerary notice. A funerary notice is written immediately after someone dies to inform relatives and friends about the death and get them to start mourning. I sent it to the secretarial division. They wrote back, saying, "Ah, do you think you could have written something else?" Actually, it wasn't funny. People had lost their jobs or even been put in jail for that kind of thing. The president might have thought I was giving him some kind of a hint. But they fortunately just sent it back to me and told me to choose something else.

So after that I chose some characters from the *Peach Blossom Journey*. It was really a beautiful tract. I sent it off and they kept it for some time. Then eventually they told me I would no longer be receiving sixty percent of my salary from the casting plant. I would have to come to the Central Bank and start work. My days of loafing were at an end. But what choice did I have?

I started in the personnel division around 1960. I was lucky to have a secure job. There were a lot of people looking for work in those days. I stayed in that position until I retired. But I was never asked to write calligraphy again.

Through the 1970s, the Kuomintang government ran a brutal literary inquisition that touched the lives of both its own mainlanders and locals as well. A well-known writer, Bo Yang, who had come over from the mainland, drew a cartoon of Popeye that some censors within the party apparatus said was meant to resemble Chiang Kai-shek. Bo was shipped off to a prison on Green Island, a short distance off the coast of Taiwan. Ku was lucky. And he believed in his luck for half a century until his party lost the election and its power. Then he began to see his past in a new light. He stopped talking about his calligraphy as if it were part of some giant joke or comedy. Instead, he began to long for his childhood, when calligraphy actually meant something more than the whims of the generalissimo or a relic of the past.

My father was a doctor. But during the Japanese invasion, he didn't have many patients. He would spend his last money on calligraphy paper and brushes for me. Then, in the evenings, he would sit down with me and tell me to write. I was usually tired. I had been at school all day and didn't understand why I had to keep writing the same characters over and over. My father would simply say, "You've got to carry on." I didn't know what I was carrying on. I just knew that if I got lazy or was distracted and didn't write the characters properly, my father would circle them with a red pen. If I had too many circles, he would hit my knuckles with a stick. If I didn't have any red circles at all, he would give me some peanuts. Peanuts were really hard to get at the time.

I don't know if the document I wrote for the president ever really got through to him. Later, I wondered if all the time my father forced me to practice had really made a difference in my life. I suppose it taught me to persevere. But up until this day, I still bear some hatred towards my father. What did he want me to carry on? Cruelty?

He just couldn't believe that his father was wrong. In the first place, it wasn't calligraphy that had gotten him his job. After all those years of training, Ku learned that he had been brought into the bank not so much for his calligraphy, but simply for the sake of connections—his foster father who brought him over arranged it. Then, when he finally had a chance to use it, it was just to make the bank look good in the eyes of Chiang Kai-shek. His childhood training turns out to be unrelated to the rest of his life. It doesn't really matter to anyone. He has learned all that calligraphy for nothing. He does not teach it to his children.

If only he had lived in a different time, his childhood training in calligraphy might have shown people that he was a scholar. Good calligraphy is the mark of a scholar, of generations of scholars stretching back on the mainland for thousands of years. It takes some time, but with the DPP in power, he starts to feel some connection with those mainland Chinese scholars, with mainland China. One of the most important developments, affecting the identities of mainland refugees in Taiwan, is the massive rise of China economically. Many refugees have either moved back to China or invested in business there. It has not only seemed a sound economic policy, but a way to boost their identity. In other words, they are from China originally, and so ought to be associated with the rise of China now. They take pride in it. This is another aspect of the calligraphy story—it represents him as Chinese. It is not surprising that he organizes classmate reunions every single year in Shanghai. It is almost as if he is trying to become Chinese again. For decades he imagined himself an exile, now he is re-imagining himself as Chinese, but part of a new China that is defined by China's economic might and not by its political ideology.

He was ready when the chance came to return. It was in the late 1980s, when Taiwan lifted the restrictions on visiting family members left behind. He could go home now. Suddenly, a pack of mainland immigrants, absent from their native towns for half a century, were applying to travel back. Theoretically, it wasn't that far. But they still had to fly through Hong Kong and then to the mainland. They brought expensive presents, envelopes full of money, and trusted shady con-men in Hong Kong who would buy their tickets or send messages for them and who half the time robbed them blind. They had not been back to China for so long that they expected things to be different. But they were disappointed. There was still the same rubble strewn around brick houses where old mothers and brothers and sisters still lived. They had heard about the Cultural Revolution, but no one really thought his own family members would be tortured or killed all because they had a relative in Taiwan. Chang Ching-tan, the freckle-headed civil servant who stocked his house with shoes, was one of the first ones to go back.

> I go back every year. Even if I don't have the money. I am already in debt more than I could ever have imagined. Every year since the opening, I have gone back to see my older brother and his family. It's not just guilt. I was genuinely curious to find out what had happened to our family's antiques and property. It turned out that my brother sold them almost immediately after the Communists took over. Later, he was labeled a landlord. He never talks to me about what happened. But I know his wife hates me for having gotten away. What can I ever say to them? All I can do is offer money, even when I don't have any left myself. But I'll never let them know that.
>
> My parents, I know, died during the Cultural Revolution. The Red Guards came to their house and wanted to smash everything up. But my mother was really smart. She put a strip that said, "Long Live Chairman Mao," across our oldest porcelain vase. The Red Guards were afraid to smash it. But they sent my mother down to the countryside for reeducation. I heard this from a classmate of mine from primary school. She was sent down to the countryside and because she had a son in Taiwan—that was me—they gave her the job of spreading human feces over the vegetable plots. My classmate said that even after she came in at the end of the day and washed her hands, she could never get the smell of shit off them. He

said my father told him that the day she died, she died smelling the shit on her hands.

Chang had thought Taiwan was a safe place. When he heard how his mother had died, he said he was thankful that he and his family were in a place where that kind of thing would never happen. He wouldn't talk more about his mother. When the DPP took over and started putting down the mainlanders, he started feeling that maybe Taiwan wasn't as safe a place as he thought it had been. There could be a Cultural Revolution in Taiwan, he thought. He had come all this way, lived all these years, spent his life working for the government, and now here he was in the same fix again. Someone was preparing to take his land away. He might even end up in jail or in a work camp, like his mother. Of course, this was all conjecture, fear. But there was no doubt that it had happened once. It could happen again, he said.

Lin Ching-wu, the old soldier who played basketball to keep in shape, said that he felt betrayed by the whole experience when he tried to make contact with his relatives on China. The first thing he did, kind of paving the way for a good reception when he himself would head back, was to send his relatives some gold. But he was unlucky. That gold was stolen by a travel agent in Hong Kong. Then, when he finally goes himself, the first thing he learns is that his father starved to death. It wasn't that he was poor or didn't have enough to eat. It was the Communists that had done it. They had rounded up the neighbors, villagers that his father had helped, had taken care of, and threatened them with death if they brought food to the old man. Then they locked him up in his house to die. And Lin found out that it was all because he had a son who was in Taiwan, who had been a soldier in the Kuomintang army. But the funny thing was that rather than just get mad, Lin ended up admiring the Communists even more, in the way a man might admire Stalin or Hitler, not for what he had done or the number of people he had killed but for his willingness to shed all trappings of decency and morality. "The Communists were strong," he said, repeating what he had said when he was laid up in a tent after being wounded. A man can only hear so much about the sufferings of his family, suffering that he caused, indirectly, before the guilt becomes so strong that it turns into something else, like shame or anger or even respect for the enemy that had started the whole thing. The Communists were strong. And the death of his father was the proof.

At one point, I tried to send some gold jewelry to my father, so he would have something to bargain with. A Taiwanese friend of mine found an intermediary in Hong Kong who was supposed to have it delivered to him. But the intermediary was a crook and just disappeared with it. Unfortunately, I had also written a letter to my father. And this the intermediary in Hong Kong sent on. Perhaps he felt guilty about stealing the jewelry. Perhaps it was simply easier to send it than to worry about what to do with it. When my father received that letter, the Communists accused him of being a spy. I think I had written I worked for the government. Much later, a cousin of mine told me what happened. This was years later, after cross-strait travel was permitted. I had to give my cousin two bottles of liquor from Taiwan. He was some kind of low-level party official. But he knew the whole story. My father starved. The Communists set a guard outside his house and didn't allow a single person to come in. He stayed in there until he died. I remember thinking to myself, when I heard this, how my father had come back from business trips and brought food and candy for everyone. And now not a single person would dare to try to get him food. I guess the Communists were too strong, too powerful.

Table 2
Fate of relatives of mainland immigrants to Taiwan

Mainland Immigrant	Fate of Relatives on Mainland
Chang Ching-tan (civil servant; Fujian)	Mother sent to countryside; assigned work with human feces
Lin Ching-wu (soldier-educator; Fujian)	Father starved to death
Hu Yao-hen (professor; Hubei)	Mother beaten to death
Weiwei Furen (Yin Tsai-chun; newspaper columnist; Nanjing)	Father suffered, survived by abandoning old career early and becoming a Chinese medicine doctor
Ko Jen-tao (police chief; Nanjing)	Relatives sent to countryside before Cultural Revolution
Ku Chi (banker; Shanghai)	Mother died from "respiratory disease" during Cultural Revolution

Table 2 shows just how much the relatives of mainlanders suffered on the mainland during the Cultural Revolution. This was all news to the returning mainlanders. And what's more, their relatives kept demanding more money, more presents, more gold each time they returned. Some of the mainlanders went through their entire pensions trying to show their relatives that they had made good in Taiwan and now were back to take care of those who had suffered on their account. Through all the sacrifices, the men expected to be rewarded or at the very least recognized for their generosity. As long as the Kuomintang was in power, this was easy. Their return visits were covered on television; the newspapers wrote about them. The whole society seemed to congratulate them on their devotion. Ko, the former police chief, gave up the opportunity for a second career so that he could go home and see his mother. Now if he were a local, his life would be much easier, he says. Then all his relatives would be in Taiwan and he could just stay on the island. Why, if he were a local, he says, he could have kept his career and seen his mother and not have to choose between the two.

Even after restrictions on travel to China were lifted in the late 1980s, civil servants and police officers were not allowed to go. The government was afraid that they would leak some of the island's secrets, or be forced into revealing them. Ko wouldn't stand for it. He had a choice to make. So he quit his job.

> When I was assistant chief of the station, there was a big hotel down the road, called the Tsung-tai Hotel. It was across from the Tai-An Hospital. They had the largest disco in Taipei. Sometimes there would be gangs in there selling drugs. The owner would call me immediately. I would go down there single-handedly and kick them out. He was really grateful. Now when I got to be fifty-nine, I realized I couldn't wait another six years, when I should have retired, to go see my mother. Who knows how long she would live? So I told my superiors I was retiring early. They all did everything they could to get me to stay. My boss said I was too young to retire, that I still had a lot of good years left. But I thought in my heart, "No way. My mother comes first." This is what the Chinese call filial piety. So I quit my job. Now when the owner of the hotel heard about it he offered me a job. He called me every day for four or five days and finally I agreed to meet him at a coffee shop.
>
> He was there waiting when I arrived. I thought that if I took this job I could not only have the kind of job I had dreamed of—I didn't have any education to speak of—but I could also travel to the mainland to visit my mother. The first thing he said was, "Chief." They all called me "Chief" even though I was only the second in command. He said, "Chief, do you know how many people have applied for this opening? Do you know how hard it is to get a position as head of personnel in a five-star hotel? And you don't even return my phone calls."

I felt ashamed. I said to him, "Thank you so much, but I'm afraid I can't handle it. As a police officer, I always worked on the streets. This is an administrative job, working in an office. I've never done that kind of work before. What if I make mistakes?"

He said, "You won't make any mistakes, don't worry. Every time I've gone into the station, I've seen you behind a desk, writing." It was true. Every morning I spent filing reports. So he said, "So what exactly is the problem? You shouldn't have any problems."

"There is one big problem," I said.

"What is it? Tell me."

I remember I could hardly get it out. I was sort of choked up. Finally, I said, "Look, my mother is now eighty-five years old. I haven't seen her face for over forty years. As a police officer, I couldn't go back to see her. The whole reason I retired was to go back and see her."

The boss said, "Look, if you want to go home, I don't have any problem with you taking a few days off."

I didn't say anything. I was torn between the kind of job I never thought I could have, that only an educated person could get, and the need to see my mother before she died. For the first time in my life, I thought maybe I could have both.

"Okay, how many days do you want?" he finally asked.

"At least two weeks. That's not much to ask after forty years."

He just said, "Ah." And I knew I wouldn't get the job.

This was because the head of personnel had to be in the hotel almost all the time. There were over five hundred employees in that hotel. There were always transfers going on. The employees were rotated on a regular basis. There was no national health insurance at the time, so the head of personnel had to be in charge of all their medical bills. You had to keep an eye on a lot of things. There were different kinds of insurance the employees could take out. If you were away for more than a few days, things would fall apart. That's why I didn't get the job. I knew the boss was disappointed.

He didn't get the job, after all. But the way the boss courted him made him feel proud. He felt like a man who for the first time in his life was being shown a way back to his past to make everything right. He felt that even at that late date, he could still have a shot at what he had lost out on as a kid: to live like a scholar, an official, someone of a higher class. His colleagues at the station couldn't stop asking him about the hotel boss, saying that in most instances a man like that would never be interested in hiring a police officer who on top of that only had a primary school education. At long last, Ko was finally living the life his father had planned for him. But he wasn't really living it. In fact, he had just given it up.

> After a police officer retires, nobody wants him. He's worthless. But after I retired, after only a few days, word got out, and the hotel boss had asked me to work for him. When my former colleagues found out, they started talking among themselves and said, "Hey, Ko Jen-tao thinks he's a big shot now." They were jealous because none of them would ever be offered a job like that. And then when they found out I had turned the job down, they couldn't believe it. One of them even came by my place and said, "Are you crazy? Do you know how hard it is to get a job like that?" I just said, "There's no other choice I can make. My mother is waiting for me."

He just couldn't wait any longer. Even before his travel papers came through, he sent an American friend over to Nanjing with enough gifts and money to prove to them that he was as successful as they had possibly imagined. He sent over jewelry, watches, at least twenty gold rings, foreign cosmetics and other presents. And he put over ten thousand dollars in cash inside a money belt that his friend wore. When his friend reached Nanjing, he used an old letter that had somehow gotten through to Taiwan from Hong Kong with the family's address to track down the family. It was snowing hard and the city was frozen under a sheet of hard ice. When the family opened the duffel bag that Ko's friend was carrying and saw all those presents and the cash, they seemed nervous but not surprised. Ko had found a way to call them just before his friend arrived.

When he heard about the visit, Ko just couldn't wait any longer. His permission to travel still hadn't come through so he decided to go secretly, not letting anyone know he was going any farther than Hong Kong. When he got there, he took a train instead of a plane into the interior. He figured it would be harder to track him on a train. But he was still afraid as he would have to rely on his government pension for the rest of his life and he didn't want to lose it.

> After I quit my job, I found out that I still had to file a report to the government asking permission. I had quit my job, given up the opportunity of a lifetime, and now I still had to file a report. It was because I had been a police officer. So I lied. I said that I wanted to go on a trip to Southeast Asia. I said I had worked for forty years and I deserved a vacation. Well, they granted it. On my itinerary I had written that I would start out from Hong

Kong and then go on to Malaysia and Indonesia. Well, I did start out from Hong Kong.

I took a plane to Hong Kong and then booked a ticket for the train to Canton. I decided not to fly directly to Nanjing because I thought they might have a computer link with Taiwan, in Hong Kong. At the border, there was no problem. I boarded the train and after a couple of hours we arrived at Guangzhou. But when I went to the airport to take a plane to Nanjing, the police searched me. They took everything out from my suitcase, even my dental floss. One of the guards actually took apart my dental floss. They found a scrapbook I was bringing of pictures of my family in Taiwan. But then the chief came out. He had a mustache and was wearing a leather jacket. I could tell he was in charge. He looked at me and said, "Where are you heading?" I didn't lie. I said, "Nanjing." He said, "What business do you have there?" I looked at him and tears started to come to my eyes and I said, "My mother." He understood immediately. "Let him through," he said. And so I was on my flight to my home.

Fortunately, they hadn't gotten to my carry-on bag. That was where I kept the gold jewelry I planned to give to my relatives. They also didn't go through my wallet or money belt. I had 10,000 US dollars with me. That was a lot of money for China. My older brother, who had been left behind with my mother, earned about 300 renminbi a month. One television set in China cost more than a year's salary for him. I bought four of them for my family. I bought three video players, Japanese ones, and four video cameras. I cleaned out the stock in the biggest store in Nanjing.

Some of the old soldiers were once poor peasants from the inner part of China. They knew how hard the life is in their home villages. So they borrowed money, pledging their pensions, putting themselves heavily into debt. Wang Shu-chih, the woman who lived through a flood, knows lots of old soldiers in her neighborhood, which is a community for ex-military officers and families. Unlike Ko, who had resources to draw upon—from real estate and savings—these old soldiers ended up borrowing from lending associations, like neighborhood banks, and ruined their lives.

Many of these old soldiers who go back looking for their families fall into a bind. The first time they go back, their families are really grateful to them. An old soldier returning for the first time might bring back as much as thousands of US dollars. So the family on the mainland starts to build up expectations and an image of what their lives must be like back in Taiwan. But actually, as China has gotten richer, the lives of those old soldiers in Taiwan are actually only a little bit richer than their relatives in China. But they don't want to admit it. They go into debt to keep bringing money back to their Chinese relatives. They join lending associations, which is like owing money to the mob. Well, maybe not that bad, actually it's owing money to your neighbors.

Then things start to change with their families on the mainland. The old soldiers or civil servants or whatever start bringing back less and less each visit. Eventually they can only bring a few red envelopes filled with a little cash. And their relatives in China start to resent them. And then the mainlanders from Taiwan, who keep going back, they develop resentments too. Right after the Cultural Revolution, the Chinese were really poor and Taiwan was rich. But now the lifestyles are becoming similar. So the mainlanders who return to China sometimes find their relatives investing the money they brought back on the first visit and now they live in nicer houses than they, the mainlanders, have back at home in Taiwan. Some of them end up having arguments and even break off relations. They reestablished their relations after half a century. Then they break them off again. Then the mainlanders in Taiwan don't have any family left. They don't even have the dream they once had that they did have a family. All they have left is the wife and children they have in Taiwan. Their past is gone.

Wang feels no desire to visit her home. Perhaps she once intended to visit, proudly, as the daughter of Kuomintang military heroes who had conquered Taiwan and China, if not militarily then economically. If it had been twenty years ago, when Taiwan's economy still surpassed China's, she might have felt some pride in going back. She was proud of her party. The Kuomintang were making the island rich. But a flip-flop has occurred, not only across the Strait, but in Taiwan itself. By looking at her face, one might even imagine that it showed the strain of this transition. Compared with the photos she keeps around the house, her face appears to have lengthened, and her gob of thick black hair she had in her twenties is now a cylinder of steel-grey. Her eyes droop as if she is lost in reflection. She has traveled and has visited China, but when she finally stepped foot in the province where she lived as a child, she refused to go home.

> I did take a tour to Henan, which is where I was born. But I never left the tour group to go into the countryside and see my relatives. I have one uncle there who is eighty-three. He wrote me and said you better come see me or we'll never see each other again. But I thought if I had to travel alone across country as a woman in China, it just wasn't worth it. China is too

complicated. I know my uncle has kids and other relatives and I do have memories of him although they are vague. But I just felt it was too far and too much of a risk. So I stayed with the tour group, visited the major sights and went back to Taiwan. I didn't even tell my uncle I was coming back. I was only ten miles from his village. But it just wasn't worth it.

Yin Tsai-chun, the newspaper columnist, never stopped hoping she could see her father again. She became famous, which increased her confidence. The newspaper gave her a new name. She was now known as Weiwei Furen (Madame Wei Wei). After twenty years of writing columns, of responding to letters, she was more well-known around Taiwan than anyone else in the newspaper business. When the US wanted to promote good relations with Taiwan, they chose her out of a dozen celebrities. She was invited to Washington, DC, to meet with Ann Landers. And the US press even started calling her "the Chinese Ann Landers." She toured Europe for months at a time and the United States, often on her own, even when she could not speak the language. Secretly, though, she attributed her success, her independence to the way her father raised her, taught her new ways of thinking, that women didn't have to bind their breasts or that they could talk about things that were beyond their own lives, like life on other planets. She never forgot how she and her sister had run away to join that women's mission and got stranded in Taiwan. It was as if, in trying to live up to her father's teachings, she had separated herself from him forever. Then the restrictions on travel between Taiwan and China were suddenly lifted.

Even before travel opened up, my father was able to get some letters out. He had a family friend who had escaped to Hong Kong. He sent them, by friends, to Hong Kong, to our friend. Of course, there was still no way to get him out. But then it turned out, through my column, I met a friend whose husband was an American. Now he started to work on the case. He wrote letters to the American embassy and to his congressman. Eventually, they were able to put pressure on the communist government. The Communists weren't afraid of much, but at that time they were afraid of the American government. So they let him go. He got to Hong Kong and then got on a plane to Taiwan.

After my father came here, he spent most of his time in the living room staring at the TV. He wasn't really watching the shows; he was simply staring at the set. He wouldn't tell us what had happened to him in China during the Cultural Revolution. I guessed he must have suffered a lot, but it wasn't until much later I took a trip back and met my nephew who told me that he suffered a lot, although it still wasn't clear exactly what had happened to him. We weren't landlords but my father did have overseas connections, that is to say, my sister and me, so I'm sure they mistreated him. He just wouldn't talk about it at all.

My nephew and my relatives said the worst experience they had was when we sent a jar of pig oil, via our friend in Hong Kong, to them. He said the authorities said it proved that they had overseas connections and that my father might have been a spy for the Kuomintang and the Americans. Can you imagine? A jar of pig oil?

My father came to live with us ten years ago. At first, he seemed happy. I had to work every day so I had hired a young woman to take care of him. She would go with him on a walk every day. But later he started to ask questions like, "How come there's never anyone at home?" One thing about the mainland is because they were poor, there were always a lot of relatives hanging around. They would sit around, in front of the television, or on the doorstep just chatting. In Taiwan, all the neighbors were out working. In the end, my father just withdrew to his room. He started spending more and more time there and he would go to sleep earlier and earlier.

He had changed a lot. It was almost like the shock of bringing him out was too much for him to handle. When we first met him in Hong Kong and brought him to Taiwan, the first thing he did when he saw our flag in the airport was to say, "At last I can see our country's flag again." He didn't seem to know me that well, at first, but he remembered the flag of the Republic of China that the Communists had overthrown. He actually started crying when he saw the flag. That was the first and last sign of emotion I ever saw in him.

After he came out of his period of isolation in his room, he gradually started asking me questions like, "Is this house our house?" Or he'd see my car and say, "Is this our car?" I think he thought I was some kind of high-level Communist Party official. He was still living in that world. He couldn't understand he had actually escaped. And then he wanted to eat only one kind of food. It was a mainland Chinese dish. Braised beef. He ate it every day, three times a day. I was worried about it so I asked the doctor, who was also a mainland refugee. The doctor said, "He's been through so much, why not let him eat it?" I felt like the doctor, too, had given up on him.

My father had given up, too. He stopped talking to me and my sister. He watched television but I knew he couldn't understand the shows, they were so different from what was on in China, even though the language was the same, or almost the same. He spent his last years in loneliness.

What had she achieved? Her father's loneliness, as he came to the promised land of Taiwan, where he had been dreaming of living, with its freedom and its flag? He was lonelier now than he had ever been when he still had the dream of her to sustain him. And she, too, was disappointed that she could not create a home for him, the kind that she had remembered he had created for her. After he died, she felt humiliated that her whole class of mainlanders, many of whom had gone through the same thing, trying to save lost relatives, were now shamed by the local populace. She did not see it coming, had not seen the loss coming, when Chiang Ching-kuo, Chiang Kai-shek's son, ended martial law and a half-century of authoritarian rule in 1987, promising a new era of democratic reforms to modernize the island's political system. She and the other mainlanders probably did not see that, ultimately, this would mean the toppling of the ruling Kuomintang, their party, which in their eyes had been the driving force building the island up from barbarism and fifty years of Japanese brainwashing—"Nipponification." They did not see that the Kuomintang would ultimately be left bankrupt, forced to sell their party headquarters, and that their status as the ruling class would be shattered. They did not see that as cable television spread and the media diversified that they would now be described not as the saviors of Taiwan but as the animals that fed on it. Ultimately, her father's disappointment was almost a foreshadow of her own disappointment as the island's political system took her to a new place, to a place where she just didn't matter as much anymore—thus, she fled again. She fled into the dream her father had once failed to achieve. She achieved his liberation by holding the painting exhibition he never had a chance, because of war and flight, to have. Except these were her paintings.

Later, when the Kuomintang finally fought its way back to power, and the president from the other party was in prison on charges of corruption, Madame Wei Wei bought a house in the coastal city of Tamsui, an hour's drive outside of Taipei. Now she looks out her window and sees the flat river crawling up to the mountains and the unmoving ships standing in the water. She says her place is a mess. But she still paints and she likes to listen to classical music. "I have some friends who listen to Mahler," she says. "But they say it's the kind of music that makes you want to jump off your roof."

Just by turning his head a little he can see the photograph from where he sits on the couch. It's a picture of an old woman with a face that looks like it has finally taken a break from worrying after a long time. Her grey hair is wild, almost as if she hasn't combed it for all that time either. She's leaning back in a blue suit that looks like it had once belonged to a factory worker, a son perhaps. Ko Jen-tao has kept the photograph on his ancestral altar during the whole time the opposition was in power. "Devotion," he says, "devotion to one's parents is what we Chinese value the most."

After the DPP took power, no one seemed very much interested in Ko's devotion to his mother. The native Taiwanese weren't. They had all their family on the island. Their government wasn't. The DPP was always on the verge of declaring independence. What that meant was that they would somehow tell the world that they were an independent country that could never be ruled by China. But they weren't really going to do that. They just said that to get votes. The Chinese said they would bomb or invade the island instead. And they could do it. By the time that Ko went back home to see his family, the Communists already had hundreds of missiles pointing right at Taiwan.

So the DPP started to attack the mainlanders in other ways. Lots of mainlanders had gone back to China, as soon as travel opened up, and married women from their home towns or nearby. But soon reports started coming out in the papers of how most of these marriages had failed. Old men from Taiwan married teenagers from China who, when they came over to the island, started working as prostitutes instead. The local government implied it was a sign that Taiwan and China could never unite or, worse, that the mainlanders didn't even belong to Taiwan, since some of them had to go back home to get a wife, either after the first one died or if they had never gotten married in the first place. That was the kind of thing the DPP had been saying all along.

For Ko Jen-tao, his first marriage, with a local woman, was all about raising a family, making money and finding a certain amount of empathy and encouragement. In a sense, it was all about building up Taiwan. After getting married, he and his wife moved from apartment to apartment, moving every ten years or so, each time doubling their money in Taiwan's fast-growing economy. His wife, Yeh Chan-chuan, was a constant presence around the apartment, cooking, cleaning, yelling at children. Like Taiwan, she became obsessed with buying and selling stocks and she would walk around the apartment—cursing her eldest daughter who was scouring the wooden floor with a rag—her head shaking like an opium addict's as she listened on an earphone to the fluctuations of stock prices. In the early days of the marriage, she was willing to work at almost anything to increase their savings. She cared for their neighbors' children while her husband was at work. She worked in a factory assembling televisions. But as the family got richer, she became bolder. One of the last things she did, before she got cancer and had to go into the hospital, was to find a new way to protest against her husband's decisions when he didn't consult her. In this case, he ordered an aquarium, half the size of the living room. And when the aquarium boys brought it in, one glass pane at a time, she stood in the middle of the floor, in her pajamas, her arms crossed and a toothbrush sticking out of the corner of her mouth like a cigar. She didn't say anything for a while. She waited until her husband came in. He was bowing and smiling, ready to explain how it would look good for guests or that he had talked with shop owner about the problem of humidity which she had brought up before. She didn't even look at him. She just stood there, waiting until the tank was finally assembled and one of the boys went down to the car to get the Honglong, the long red and silver fish with a jaw the size of a large pair of scissors, waiting for her husband to tell her again how much the fish was worth, how rare it was and how hard it was to get. Finally, she struck. "If it's that good, I'll just have to wait until you aren't around, which is most days, and fry it up for dinner for myself."

She didn't look so powerful after she got cancer and was lying in a hospital bed with her head shaved and her face worried and focused on her Buddhist scriptures. Like many Chinese who have relatives in the hospital, Ko brought a fold-out cot to the room and slept there every night. His hair was long and unwashed, greasy like ropes that had been dipped in tar or oil. His face was long and haggard. But his children had somehow found out that he might have arranged to meet a woman from mainland China after his wife died. In any case, Ko, as he talks about those days in the hospital, focuses on how devoted he was, since that's about the only way he knows how to be when he is losing the most important woman in his life, first his mother, now his wife. Is it somehow his fault? Did he lose his mother? Did she send him away because he was unworthy? Was the same thing happening with his wife? He had to show he could take care of her, that he wasn't to blame, that it wasn't his fault.

> I was by her side every moment of every single day while she was in the hospital. Even when she was sent to intensive care, I brought my cot in there

and slept there, too. One of the nurses said to my wife, "You are a very lucky woman." My wife was in acute pain. The cancer had already spread into her bone marrow. So it made sense that someone said something like that. She listened to Buddhist tapes every day, but she was still angry. She said, "Lucky? Are you kidding?" The nurse said, "It's true, many patients with cancer feel like you do. But sometimes it takes a situation like this to see what kind of love those around you have for you. Your husband has been by your side twenty-four hours a day. He even sleeps on a cot by your bed. Think about the other patients. When they yell or cry in the middle of the night, there is no one with them to hear. There's no one with them."

She died and they held a large funeral. They brought her out in a see-through coffin so that everyone could see her face one last time. Her sister, who was visiting from Bamboo Mountain, flung herself on the coffin and wailed. She later asked Ko to help pay for fixing her rotten teeth. Ko had other things to think about. He already had feelers out for a second wife. He said that the way they met was completely accidental.

> I used to run a lot. Every day, I would head out to the Sun Yat-sen Memorial at five o'clock in the morning. I would do a circle around the monument then head out into the city. I was usually the fastest runner out there. By six or seven, a lot of the other retired police officers would be out there running, too. Sometimes one or two of them would run with me, but usually we'd just nod to each other or something.
>
> I'd usually see one of my colleagues out there almost every morning. He wasn't actually a runner. He would do a kind of qigong called Wai Dan Gong. I never knew him that well in the first place because he was the station chief of another station in my district.
>
> One day, when I was finished with my run, and stretching, he came over and said, "Jen-tao, I heard about your wife and I'm sorry." I nodded. I didn't look at him. I just kept looking at this longyan tree in the courtyard of the memorial. Almost all of the fruit had fallen on the ground. "Have you ever thought of getting married again?" he said, "What? Do you know how old I am? I'm almost sixty." "That's not old. You look like a forty year old."
>
> He had this sister who hadn't gotten out and was still living in China. She lived in Qingdao, in the north. She had a daughter, he said, who had just gotten divorced. He said her husband hadn't been good to her and she was still young. Actually, she was twenty years younger than I was. He said when he heard that my wife had died, he immediately thought of me. He

said, "What's twenty years to a man like you? Men can still father children in their eighties." Later, he showed me her picture. We started writing each other. Her name was Liu Rong. At the time, I was grieving. I was just interested in her appearance. Who can blame me?

He had worked his whole life as a police officer, then vice chief. He had been a dutiful son, as much as possible while his mother was locked away in China somewhere. And when he had been allowed to visit, he had lavished gifts and dollars upon her. Hadn't he proved himself dutiful, filial? His life had been a pattern for the Kuomintang occupation of Taiwan—at least as the party liked to portray its history. He had defended the island from the communists in the navy, secured the peace as a police officer, built up a family and several homes and now, when his wife died, was finally going to have his reward, well-earned and well-deserved. He had made no mistakes. The moment came when his eldest brother got sick in Nanjing. He immediately jumped on a plane. Except the ticket's final destination was not Nanjing, but Beijing—and ultimately Qingdao.

> Then something happened. One of my brothers in Nanjing got colon cancer. I couldn't believe it. One of my other brothers called and told me about it. I was sitting in the living room on the sofa when I got the call. I had a letter from Liu Rong out on the coffee table and I was looking at it the whole time I was talking on the phone. By the time I hung up, I had made up my mind. I decided to go to Nanjing, to see my brother. Then I would go to Qingdao to meet my future wife. Cancer had brought us together the first time. Now it would bring us together for good.
>
> So I met her. Apparently she had a good impression of me. Her mother, her father, her two sisters, even her ex-husband liked me. I made a good impression on all of them. They all said I was a nice man. I stayed in Qingdao for a few days then I returned to Taiwan. The only thing I was afraid of was that my children would be against the marriage. It was not just that I had met her so soon after their mother's death. It was also because she already had a child, from her previous marriage. A few days after I got back, her uncle called me. I think he knew what I was worrying about. He said, "How do your children feel about it?" I hadn't told them anything. But I said, "No problem."

The children didn't like her. They didn't trust mainland Chinese women. They knew that she was after their father's money; that was all. Why would anyone be interested in someone from their family if it weren't for money? Perhaps the sense of unworthiness that Ko had felt, being sent away from his home, had passed down to his children. A younger son broke a window in an argument. The rest of the family just couldn't leave Ko alone with their complaints and questioning. The eldest son's wife spoke in loud whispers then stopped suddenly when Ko approached. Always devoted, if not to his wife then to his children, Ko began to divide up all his assets, to prove to his children that they would not lose anything by his marriage. He bought one apartment for each of his children. With the remainder, he bought a house on the mainland, in Qingdao, for his new wife, and took out a loan to buy an apartment in northern Taipei for the two of them to live together when she was allowed to visit—which at first was only six months a year, according to government regulations. When the children still complained that she was breaking the family apart or that she really just wanted his money, he became furious. As a family whose father had been torn away from home by war, both the children and their father were probably just afraid of losing each other. That was where the anger really came from.

> Their father slaved his entire life. I came over here as a boy, practically as an orphan, and had to work every single day of my life, first in the navy then as a police officer, every single day, sleeping at the police station, only being able to come home one day a week. I never really had a family, either here or in Nanjing. I never knew what it was really like to enjoy the comfort of a home. And now, now, after a life of slavery, I retired, hoping to find some peace. Then my wife died. Do they think I wanted that to happen? I didn't ask for my wife to die. I had never planned to get married again. They won't even grant me that. They think I somehow planned it. They also think because I'm old I don't have the right to get married again. They all have children now. Am I supposed to go live with them? I'd be a burden. What right do they have to oppose my marriage?

Then he resorted to the same tactic he had used before: an appeal to his own scrupulousness. When he had returned to Nanjing for the first time in half a century, he had been scrupulous in meting out more than a fair share of his wealth to his mother. Now he made it clear to his children, and to his new wife, Liu Rong, that her share of his wealth would include nothing that had come from the labor of his former wife. At first, this tactic seemed to work. A cessation of hostilities took place as both sides waited to see what would happen. But there was a new element now. That was the woman from China.

The family in Taiwan went through the motions of accepting her. The daughters-in-laws left their children with her during the day. The sons exchanged pleasantries with them. Ko's idea of dividing his wealth into five apartments, four for each of the children and one for himself and Liu Rong, seemed to be working. According to government regulations, she had to stay half the time in mainland China, so Ko went over there, too, and lived with her in the house he had bought for her.

But new problems emerged. On one visit, Ko flew to Qingdao and Liu Rong asked him if he wouldn't mind for the time being staying in the apartment that her father and mother shared with several sisters. Ko had forgotten that he had agreed to let Liu Rong rent out the house he had bought for her, a Swiss chateau molded out of concrete, overlooking the ocean, with a fountain in front. It was already being rented to a Japanese businessman. She needed the money for her teenage son. Her son, from her former marriage, wasn't doing well in school, and she was planning on saving up enough to send him overseas to New Zealand to study. Perhaps Ko wasn't entirely clear what she was going to do with the money from the house he had bought for her. But when he found out it was for her son, it added fuel to the bonfire that was already burning. When Liu Rong stayed in Taipei, for six months out of the year, she worked as a nurse's aide in a hospital, earning additional money for her son. She had found the job fairly easily after first arriving. Then when she was back in Qingdao, with Ko, she encouraged—it seemed to him—the bad habits of her son. Ko grew to hate the boy, who was not only much taller than Ko but was also a student in college. Ko had barely finished primary school. There were many times when Ko tried to discipline him, yelling at him and trying to shame him, almost as if he were one of his subordinates at the police station. But, to tell the truth, Ko yelled at his own kids in the same way.

> All that he does all day is just play on his computer. Or he listens to the radio or CDs. He doesn't do any homework. But when he has a test, he always writes out the answers on little pieces of paper. Then he puts them in his pocket so he can cheat. He says that's just the way he studies. It's a lie. It's not like I haven't been in school myself. When I was a student, you just read the textbook and made a few notes in the margins. No one wrote out the answers to a test in advance and hid them in their pocket. So I told his mother.

Of course, she backed him up. She said all the kids study that way. She's a pushover when it comes to him. I had the last laugh, however, because even though he cheated, he didn't pass a single subject. He took the entrance exam for college and his score was about 300. Maybe 320. On the mainland, you need at least 520 to get into college.

One time the son just walked out of his college and came home. This was the kind of thing that would drive Ko nearly insane. He and Liu Rong had lavished bribes on the school principal and on government officials so that the boy could attend college despite his low test scores. The son said he just couldn't take it any longer, that the water was so polluted even boiling it wouldn't make it drinkable and the air was equally bad since the school was in the heart of an industrial district. So he just walked away. Ko couldn't believe he had ever seen anything like the ungratefulness of the boy. Ko had been through a lot as a boy, he told his wife and her son. He expected the boy to be grateful for what he had. And he felt shame that the boy was not only better educated than he was, but that he could disregard his wishes in front of his mother.

I never wanted to pay for that school, but what do I do? His mother threatened to leave me. Well, I sent him there. And after only four days, four days, he was back in Qingdao. Boy, was I angry. I said, "What are you doing here?" He said, "Oh, I've already taken all the classes they offer there." Four of his classmates had come with him. They were just having some kind of party.

The real reason they came back, was to see off one of their classmates who was going to Japan. The classmate's father was a prosecutor in the Qingdao municipal court. So he had the money to send his son to Japan. So they got a four-day leave to come and see him off. What was I paying that school for? To give out four-day leaves? I was so angry I almost couldn't see clearly for a while.

The boy was eighteen. He was tall, taller than any of Ko's children, who usually cowered down when he yelled at them. The boy defended himself. He argued back. This was new.

He said that the air around the school was really bad, that it was an industrial area with a lot of factories, that the factories polluted the air. He said the water was polluted too; it had salt and sewage in it. He complained that the toilets at the school were all disgusting. He even complained about the other students. He said they were all from farmers' families and were ignorant and rude. He refused to go back.

His mother had given him money to rent an apartment off campus. That was from money I had given her for herself, for her own needs. There were over 10,000 students in that school, and he was probably the only one with his own apartment.

Now her son wants to go to New Zealand. One of his classmates went to New Zealand to go to graduate school so he's gotten it into his own head that that's what he wants to do, too. And his mother of course supports him. She can't say no to anything he wants. So now that she's come to Taiwan, instead of being with me, she works all day. She asked me for the money first, but I said I can't do it. I don't have that kind of money. So she went to work. She worked in a restaurant then she worked in a laundry, now she's working in a hospital. No matter what I say, she's going to send her son to New Zealand.

I'm actually quite miserable. I say to her, "When you're at work, I'm alone by myself. You leave early and get home at eight or nine at night. I spend the whole day by myself. I wash my own clothes. I cook every meal for myself. You only care about your son. He graduated from college, didn't he? Why does he have to go to graduate school? And why in New Zealand? Don't you know that New Zealand was a colony founded by the British? Don't you know they discriminate against Chinese there? Don't you know it's impossible for a foreigner to get a job there? Your son will still have to come back to Qingdao to get a job." And then she said that we could all immigrate to New Zealand. But I said, "What would I want to go to New Zealand for? My children are all here in Taiwan. I don't have any friends or relatives in New Zealand."

What she really wanted was to sell the house I bought for her in Qingdao. She has the idea that then she could move to New Zealand and buy a house there. Then her son wouldn't have to go back to mainland China.

Ko Jen-tao believes he has been faithful to everyone and everything that ever mattered to him in his whole life. That includes the Republic of China in Taiwan, the Kuomintang, his police colleagues, and his family. He believes that he has been loyal to his wife and his mother, even though he was parted from his mother for more than half his lifetime. Didn't he return home after all that time and just shower her with gold? He believes that he has been faithful, perhaps most of all, to his children. He took all the money and property that he spent his whole life earning and he divided up, fairly, for anyone to see, between them. The fact that he kept enough for a house in Qingdao for his new wife and for an apartment for the two of them, when in Taiwan, doesn't seem to matter to his kids. "I'm an old man. I've worked my entire life, don't I deserve the chance to enjoy myself?" he said.

 Ko was thinking that returning to China and his home would round out his life, complete something that was only half understood in the first place. Even before he married Liu Rong, he invested a large portion of his personal savings in a factory that made electric switches for machinery on the mainland. The factory had been recently constructed in Xian and was run by one of his younger brothers, who worked for the state electricity bureau. When all the electric switches had been completed and were ready to ship, the factory asked for payment, but the buyer refused to pay until the merchandise had been delivered. After they delivered it, the buyer went missing, with the switches. Ko lost his whole investment. He thought he would be more careful next time. After he met Liu Rong, she encouraged him to invest in a tree farm that would grow a special kind of tree that could absorb pollution that they could then sell to Beijing before the Olympic Games. In the end, though, the Communist government changed their mind and went with different trees. If you add on all the money he gave to his relatives in Nanjing, Ko spent in mainland China more than most people had ever earned in their life in Taiwan. The worst part of it was when the opposition party came to power and suddenly made it seem like these sacrifices were in vain, that there was no reason for going to China anymore.

 What was more, his Chinese wife, Liu Rong, was now spending eighteen hours a day working, to pay for her son's education. Other immigrants were complaining, too. Some of them said that the Chinese they had come back to seemed to care only about money. Ku Chi, the former banker from Shanghai, said, "Their value system is power and money only. They don't think of anything else. Everything else is a sham. The mainlanders have no sense of accountability at all."

 But that didn't seem to matter anymore after the DPP came to power. Mainland immigrants, shattered by their fall from power during the first decade of this century, have held fast onto some association with China. They have come from China, they reason, so they must ultimately have some connection with China. The Communists' achievements, whether on the battlefield or, more recently, economically, are a source of pride, a pride that the local Taiwanese cannot share. Perhaps, even more fundamentally, mainland immigrants for most of their lives have felt like orphans. They and their families have been isolated from their ancestral line. Now that they can travel back to their childhood homes, some have gone looking for ancestral tablets or other signs of their lineage.

When they reconnected with their mainland heritage, through business, relatives or marriage, the mainland immigrants from Taiwan felt a great burden placed upon them: What had they to show after all this time? What had they to show to ancestors who were so illustrious? A sense of failure is part of their legacy. This is the reason, for instance, that Ko is so upset about his stepson's education. Ko's father, after all, went to the finest university on the mainland, Peking University. In facing down his Chinese stepson, he is setting himself up as an authority on education.

These days, Ko Jen-tao and his wife don't fight as much. They live in their villa three months out of the year in Qingdao. But they can't see the ocean. Businessmen from Shanghai and Guangdong have built even bigger, classier apartments closer to the water. Ko takes the bus with his wife around the city like any other Chinese. Since the mainlanders have begun to return home, China's growth in big cities like Qingdao has made Taiwan look small, cheap, and poor. The island's new president, Ma Ying-jeou, won the office back from the DPP and opened up tourism, business, and study between the two sides. But China has gotten so much richer in its big cities that no one really knows which side is getting the most benefit from the arrangements. When Ko visits his sister's house in Nanjing, he just can't get over how clean and fancy the place is. The electronic equipment alone, the television and the stereo system, are worth more than several months of his pension.

Table 3
Of ancestors, parents and refugees: Status, wealth and distinguishing marks[a]

Ko Jen-tao (Nanjing)		
Ancestors	Father	Refugee
grandfather: morphine addict; sold off lands	Peking University graduate	primary school graduate
	top official in Republic	vice police chief
	2 houses	6 apartments
	wanted son to be doctor	

Mixing Memory and Desire

Chang Ching-tan (Fujian)		
Ancestors	Father	Refugee
ancestor was *xiucai*	college graduate in engineering	junior high
head of private bank under Qing dynasty	worked in electricity bureau	civil servant
large home	large, traditional home; 2 gates, 2 living rooms servants	tiny, cluttered apartment

Lin Ching-wu (Fujian)		
Ancestors	Father	Refugee
traveled in SE Asia	father traveled in SE Asia, gave largesse to neighbors, hid money around house	junior high school
		stipend from military
		small apartment
		was military instructor in local college, kicked out in 1990s with reforms

Shen Hsueh-yung (Sichuan)		
Ancestors	Father	Refugee
moved from Hubei to Sichuan fleeing	Peking University graduate in economics	junior high; music institute
successful businessman	business teacher in Sichuan University	
	large traditional House around courtyard	lives in spacious apartment high above street level

Hu Yao-hen (Hubei)		
Ancestors	Father	Refugee
moved from Jiangxi to Hubei fleeing	graduate of Beijing Normal University	PhD from Indiana University
Taiping	leadership in provincial KMT; publisher of Hubei Party newspaper	professor of Western drama
	later taught in Taiwan	

Yin Tsai-chun (Weiwei Furen) (Nanjing)		
Ancestors	Father	Refugee
landlords	Hangzhou Art Institute	high school
	big house in Anhui with big redwood beds	newspaper columnist
	civil servant/bureaucrat	

Wang Shu-chih (Henan)		
Ancestors	Father	Refugee
ancestor was prime minister under Qing	military officer; disbursed salaries	top middle school in Taiwan
		civil servant/bureaucrat

Ku Chi (Shanghai)		
Ancestors	Father	Refugee
	attended medical school in Japan	high school
	father: doctor; stepfather: engineer	stipend from bank
	house in foreign concessions in Shanghai: 3-story, 3 courtyards	tiny apartment

a. For the most part, there seems to be a pattern that war has led to refugees having lower attainments than the previous generation, that a decline has taken place. This further augments the feeling of bitterness experienced by the refugee.

Photo 1

Hu Yao-hen with American wife, 1965. After surviving a refugee camp in Hong Kong, he obtained his PhD from Indiana University.

Photo 2

Meishu, daughter of Ko Chen-tsang and aborigine wife, Hsiao Sheng-tsun. Pictured in Taipei.

Photo 3

Colonel Tan Hua-shen after retirement in Taipei. His motto: "If the enemy is bigger than you, run! If he's smaller, fight!"

Photo 4

Hsiao Sheng-tsun, aborigine wife of Ko Chen-tsang. Pictured on wedding day.

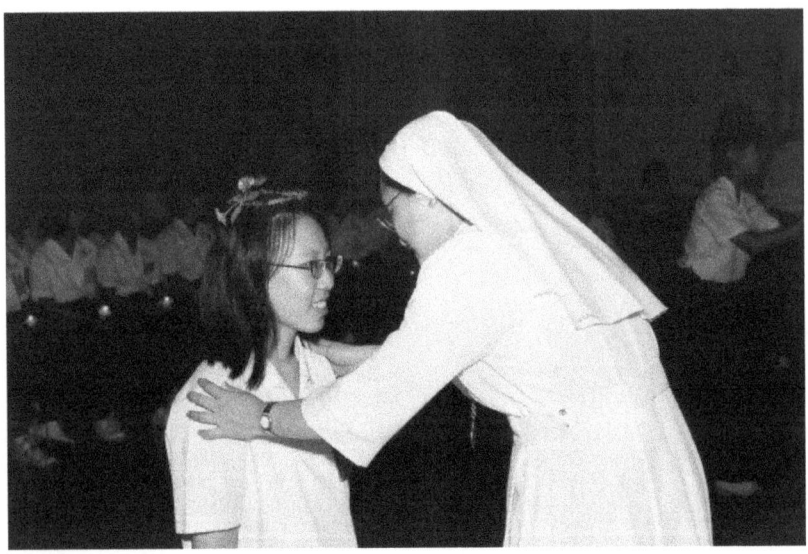

Photo 5

Mini Hu, third-generation mainlander. Christianity as a way of retaking the mainland.

Photos 6–7

Ko Chen-tsang, son of Ko Jen-tao. Top: taken outside of Taipei around the time he married his aboriginal wife in opposition to his parents' wishes; bottom: pictured at boot camp, Ko is in the back row to the far right, wearing glasses.

Photo 8

Ko Yuan, daughter of Ko Jen-tao. Pictured by an artist friend after her mother died.

Photos 9–12

Ko Jen-tao. Clockwise from top: as a young man in the Nationalist navy; as a young police officer in post-war Taipei; wedding portrait with second wife Liu Rong; with first wife, Taiwanese "Ko Mama," from Bamboo Mountain in central Taiwan.

Photos 13–14

Weiwei Furen, newspaper columnist. Left: as a young girl on the mainland; right: after having succeeded in bringing her father to Taiwan.

Photos 15–16

Liu Rong, second wife of Ko Jen-tao from Qingdao. Left: as a young girl in Qingdao; right: pictured shortly before her first marriage, shown here dancing in front of a friend.

Photos 17–18

Chang Ching-tan. Left: as a young man in Fuzhou before being captured by the Japanese; right: after escaping the Japanese and coming to Taiwan.

Photo 19

Chou Chih-shui with his wife and father shortly before he was killed by a local truck driver who was never brought to justice.

Photos 20–23

Lin Ching-wu. Clockwise from top: after being wounded during fighting on the mainland, Lin has played basketball in Taiwan through his eighties; after surviving the retreat to Taiwan; marching with Nationalist troops on the mainland; Lin's hospital papers. While he was convalescing, he learned about the communists' superior abilities.

Photos 24–27

Shen Hsueh-yung. Clockwise from top: as a young woman on the mainland just starting out as a singer before the retreat to Taiwan; shortly after arriving in Taipei, as an artist, she felt that she had a duty to bring Chinese culture to Taiwan; in Taiwan with her son, Quo Ying Sheng, later to become a famous photographer; in Taipei, growing to new heights of fame after the fall of the mainland.

3
Low Lie the Shattered Towers

In late August, a radiant blue sky occasionally swoops down over Taipei like a giant tablecloth dropped from heaven. These days are rare. Usually they come when a strong breeze shoots over from mainland China. On other days, the sky seeps grey from its pores like a tree saturated with ants. This is pollution, a wall of it, seeping over from China, where thousands of factories belch noxious air into the stratosphere night and day. The orange cloud crosses the Taiwan Strait, picks up humidity from the ocean, and turns the color of a dead piece of cheese: maggot-grey. On some days Taiwan is swathed in this rhythmic shroud. Like its weather, Taiwan's culture is now ending a long period of frigid isolation. Its children are increasingly influenced by mainland Chinese culture. This includes the second and third generations of mainlanders. The flow of people between China and Taiwan, begun in 1987 when Taiwan first lifted prohibitions on travel to the mainland, rockets strange eddies of recent Chinese culture into the island, carried by mainland Chinese come to settle in Taiwan, in many cases as wives of the first or second-generation mainland immigrants or, more recently by Chinese tourists and the one million Taiwanese now living on the mainland.

Today, it is raining in Taipei. The morning shivered apart with loud groans of thunder. Then a torrential rain lumbered over the trees and grey pavements, swishing like a broom, clearing away debris and pollution. After the rain lifted, cars waded through the pavement water, sending out sighs like the sound of tearing silk. The island's trees and foliage had begun to breathe again, sucking in the rain, driving away the cloud of pollution that built up during the day, and creating, if only for a moment a space of sticky clean air and humid vapors, through which sound could travel long distances, horns of cars be heard miles off. Then the pollution gradually damped down again.

When Ko Jen-tao looks out from his apartment in Neihu, the rain has already passed. He can almost see the butterflies shooting along the breezes that waft through the hills. There's a lake not far from where he lives, at the foot of the hills. It's got bridges built in the ancient dynastic style. They rise up, like the tops of Ferris Wheels and sink down onto the other side of the lake. When they first built that lake, when the mainlanders first started settling in that part of town, the water must have been clear and pure. Today, it has sunken down to a puddle filled with muck. Weeds grow up along the banks. And the city has put up rusty metal walls around it. People still jog around it and walk up into the hills. But it's no longer a sign of the splendor of an august Chinese past. The younger generation, in fact, no longer even uses the lake. They swim in a large complex that a private company has built alongside the lake. There's a swimming pool that contains almost as much water as the lake does now. But it's crystal clear and the bottom of the pool is blue and shimmering with the jagged lines of light passing through the water. It's almost as if there was never any need for that lake. Compared to the giant swimming pool complex, the lake and its ornate but muddy bridges and ornamental walkways now look a little like a movie set that was used once and after that just left to fade away in the weather.

The second generation

Table 4
List of second-generation mainlanders providing oral history and their relationship to first generation

Name	Description
Ko Yuan	44; daughter of Jen-tao; teacher of Chinese classic, *The Book of Changes*
Chou Hau-yi	48; son of Kuomintang air force pilot; beef noodle shop owner
Chou Chih-sui	43; son of Wang Shu-chih; psychiatrist at Taipei Veterans' General Hospital
Ko Chen-tsang	42; son of Ko Jen-tao; salesman; married aboriginal woman in defiance of parents
Lin Ju-lin	39; son of Lin Ching-wu; television engineer; raced cars illegally and dangerously
Daniel Hu	37; half-American son of Hu Yao-hen; writing PhD dissertation on Aeschylus

Low lie the shattered towers

After he left the navy and joined the police force, Ko Jen-tao had four children with his Taiwanese wife: two girls and twin boys. The younger of the girls was special. She wasn't as smart in school as her older sister but she was intuitive. She could intuit her mother's moods. This wasn't all she could do. She is tall, wand-like, with pale skin, long stringy hair, and a smirky smile that plays over the feverishly thin skin on her face like a finger in a glass of warm milk, skimming along the top. She has the high cheekbones and flat face of her mother, the native Taiwanese, and the long nose and flat, staring eyes of her father, who came from Nanjing. She now teaches the Confucian classic, *the Book of Changes*, at a university in northern Taipei, but when she talks about her earliest memories she emphasizes her Taiwanese side. Of course, she is talking at a time when the government belonged to the Taiwanese party and was trying to put down anything that had to do with the mainlanders. So it is possible she was just being fashionable. But she was a person always slightly confused about her identity. The only grandparents she had ever known were Taiwanese and lived in the country, on Bamboo Mountain. She hadn't even heard very much about her father's side of the family, since they were still in China. So between her mother's yelling and her father's being gone from home all the time, she never could really be a child except on Bamboo Mountain.

> When we visited my grandmother's house in the country, I sometimes acted in a strange way. I would spend a lot of time staring at my reflection in a big pot of water. In the country, they get water from streams and then boil it in a pot. If you wanted a drink, you would use a big ladle to get water from the pot. I used to climb on a bamboo chair and look down into the water. It was really clear and black. For some reason, I really liked to look at my reflection. It wasn't that I didn't like to play with the other kids. It was just I was amazed that I could see myself so clearly.
>
> Then one day I fell in. I just wasn't being careful. I had climbed up to get a really good look and was leaning over the pot and slipped. My head went in and my legs were sticking up. I now realize I could have died. When she heard the noise, my grandmother came running. I felt myself being pulled out by my legs and then my grandmother started hitting me on the rear end. Then my grandfather came and he started hitting me, too. My grandmother said, "Beat her to death. Beat her to death."

She believed that Bamboo Mountain was a home. But she also believed that she was more than that. Her father's side of the family, the mainlander culture, would teach her that she was from a better, a brighter, a more culturally rich place. Her mother's side would discipline her, thus laying their own claim to her allegiance. It's almost as if she knew what was coming, staring at herself in that pot. If she had been older, one might even say she was trying to figure out who she was. Bamboo Mountain was the only real place she had ever set foot on that she could call home. Among the tea bushes and banana trees and all the Taiwanese women swathed in shrouds and hats to keep out the sun as they collected tea leaves, among the eroding concrete and brick buildings, the uncles who spoke Japanese and downed rice wine, the insects the size of a man's fist, and the incessant mangled language of Taiwanese which was like little fingers clawing at her throat (until she learned to speak it), she thought she had found a home. So when the Democratic Progressive Party (DPP) took power and the government encouraged the establishment of a dominant Taiwanese identity for the island, as an independent country rather than as a memory of Kuomintang glory, it seemed to fit right in with her ideas about herself. She doesn't have any memories on the other side, the side of the mainlanders, to draw from. Without that Taiwanese side, she would be just as much an orphan as her father.

The problem was that, generally speaking, most of these second-generation mainlanders, the children of the settlers, never really felt accepted by the local Taiwanese.

Take Chou Hau-yi as an example. The fiery forty-eight-year-old man who has that kind of bland, impassive, handsome face that newscasters have runs a noodle shop along a busy street in a district of Taipei filled mostly with local Taiwanese. His father came to Taiwan as a refugee air force pilot like the ones in Wang's military settlement. He sits outside his noodle shop, propped back on a plastic chair in the heat, and describes the battles that went on outside these military villages, long after the Kuomintang had already been beaten on the mainland. When he was a kid, he would leave the village with his friends every morning and walk to school. And it happened every morning that a pack of local kids would throw stones at them.

> Our encampment was our home. It was like a cave. We knew we had some safety there and outside it was dangerous. We always tried to stay there,

in the village. Once we got outside, we were in the realm of the locals, the Taiwanese. They didn't like us very much. We were intruders.

Whenever we went outside, they would come up out of nowhere with rocks and start throwing them at us. Some of us would run back to the village. I always held my ground. Those Taiwanese would yell at us. They'd yell things like, "Mainland pigs. Go home. Get the fuck back to the mainland." We were only children. They were only children too. But they had probably heard their parents calling us that or saying those things. So they just imitated them.

But they were just stupid farmers. We had the better strategy. We would wait until they had thrown all their rocks. Then we would rush them, run at them as quickly as we could until we went into closer range, then we would throw our rocks. We could almost always hit someone. The older we got, the more accurate we got. They, of course, picked up on our strategy and would throw and then retreat. It went back and forth like that.

Both sides got injured really seriously. We were always bleeding. Sometimes, someone would get hit in the head. Sometimes, there were kids who got hit in the eyes. I got several broken bones. But we never gave up. Neither did they. They felt they were defending their home. We felt we were defending our right to be there.

Several times our fights spilled over into school. Normally, the teachers watched us really carefully. But after some of the worst battles in the street, we would also fight in the school courtyard. There weren't many rocks so maybe someone would throw one rock, then all of us would go charging over. They always outnumbered us. About twenty or thirty of us would fight at once. I was a good fighter. I was good with my hands. I could knock kids out with a single punch. They were good fighters too.

Our fights would always end when some parents came out, or teachers pulled us apart. Even then, they didn't stop yelling, "You mainland pigs, go the fuck home, go the fuck home." Of course, we couldn't go home. We didn't have any home anymore.

But they couldn't say anything back. They couldn't tell the local boys to go back someplace else because the local kids were already home. The mainland boys didn't know it, but they were in a situation similar to the ones their parents had been in. Their parents, some of them at least, had spent the last part of the war with the Communists, moving from location to location with their parents. They ended up in a new school, a new city every few months or years. It was in those days that they first got the name of *waisheng ren,* meaning people who were from a different province, in other words, strangers. But the second generation, at least in Chou's case, doesn't really have the same kind of dreams and sense of destiny to sustain them. They never thought of trying to win back an entire continent. Chou has already failed in several business ventures. He opened up the noodle shop several years ago and he and his wife spend their days wiping down the tables and carrying bowls to customers. His father was an air force hero who ended up raising his family in a military village and now lives in Canada with a second wife. Chou doesn't talk much about him while he watches television in his shop or talks out on the sidewalk with other mainlanders his age smoking and drinking tea. When he was in college, he studied drama and he once thought he could become a broadcaster. Now he spends most of the time just sitting around with his cronies, smoking and talking, while his wife, who is also a second-generation mainland refugee, cuts up pieces of beef while watching soap operas on television. When guests come, Chou walks out slowly to the front of the shop, walking like he's shrunken somehow or petrified, as if his body is a scarecrow and his legs are just moving it around, and he waits on his customers without looking them in the eye.

But there's no food more mainlander than beef noodle soup. This is not to say that local Taiwanese don't run beef noodle shops, but the shops first became known around Taipei as businesses run by old soldiers. So you could say that in a small way, Chou is carrying on some part of the culture, or at least the memory, of the first generation. It's hard to say if it is because he was talking during the time when the DPP was in power and it seemed like the mainlanders were out of power for good, but he just won't come right out and blame the native Taiwanese for his troubles. There was a lot of fighting, he says, there was a lot of blood let out on the ground, and there were stones thrown and other violence that lasted for years. But, in the end, he concludes, as if to bring the story to a happy ending, the boys all ended up friends.

> Ultimately, we did stop the fighting. It wasn't easy. A lot of the boys held grudges against each other. But we were classmates in school. We would fight on the streets in the morning, before school, then have to sit in the same classroom, then go back to fighting after school. Eventually, we stopped fighting. It was too tiring. We actually ended up friends, if you can believe it.

Chou's hair curls in slightly above his ears. He has a boyish, eager face. He looks younger as he talks about remaining good friends with the natives for about fifteen years. For a long time he believed that he could "still become good friends" with them. It was then that he finished college and gave up his dream of becoming a television announcer—he lacked connections at the TV station. He hit the road as a salesman of cheap clothing. Taiwan was still booming out products such as shirts, pants, and coats, and he peddled them around Taipei, which was still the stronghold of the Kuomintang and the mainland refugees. His spoken Chinese had the accent of a mainlander and he looked the part for a mainlander city. Then his success brought him to the attention of his superiors, who asked him to fan out and cover uncharted territory, the vast southern reaches of the island. The headquarters of the Kuomintang had always been in the north and the south was populated almost entirely by native Taiwanese. He was leaving his island again. At first, he was merely taunted, much as the children of his childhood taunted him at first.

> I'd walk into a store and start to try to talk with the owner and the people standing around the counter would say, "You don't speak Taiwanese." So I would try to speak a little. They'd say, "You don't speak good Taiwanese. If you can't speak Taiwanese, don't come around here." I'd try to reason with them. I'd say I just wanted to do business. But they'd say, "Get out of here. Don't come back again."

Later, he would try to reason it out, to tell himself he was their superior, that if he couldn't speak their dialect it was because it was crude and shallow. His level of "culture" gave him both the rights and responsibilities of a civilized person. This seemed to fit with his more practical approach that, as a salesman, he must do whatever he could to win over his clients.

> I was a salesman. As a salesman, you have to accept the reaction of your customers. Sometimes they're not interested in what you're selling. But I didn't have to take this. In Taipei, everyone spoke Mandarin. Why should it be different here in the south? It's not like I was coming to try to take over. I just wanted to do business. Why did there have to be such a big difference between the north and the south? I was angry, sure. But I felt I had a duty to be civil. And not just because I was a salesman. We were coming from different cultures; that was all.
> I said to myself, this is just for a time. I can stand it because it's only temporary. I could endure anything if it was just temporary. But it wasn't temporary. No matter how hard I tried, they wouldn't talk to me. I tried

learning Taiwanese. But I always had an accent. It didn't work. They would only do business with a native. I hated the city of Kaohsiung, where I was based. I heard Taiwanese in the streets every day. It sounded like the people were yelling at each other.

So it seemed he just couldn't stop fighting with the natives. It was almost like he was a man doomed, cursed even by the very land that he trod on, the southern half of the island where the natives predominated. It was as if he had just finished fighting with the schoolboys, then simply waited a few decades, for him and them to grow up, then resumed the same fight with the same antagonists.

My line was underwear. There was a factory that hired me to sell it. One time, I had had enough, so I just walked into one of the larger establishments, plopped some of my stock down on the counter, unrolled a chart showing the prices and stood there, waiting for the owner to come and take a look. I knew I had better merchandise than the locals and I had changed all the prices so that they were lower than the local brand. I waited for a while then one of the local agents came over.

He said, "You know, there is a right way and a wrong way to do things here." He was speaking in Taiwanese. By this point, I could understand even if I couldn't speak it that well. He said, "By coming in here like this, without showing any consideration for us, who have been here much longer than you, you are making us lose face. Do you understand that? Can you grasp that concept?" When I didn't say anything, he grabbed my merchandise and threw it on the floor. I had had enough. I pulled back my fist and hit him right across the jaw. After that, he got up and jumped on me. We were rolling around on the floor when the owner came out and tried to pull us apart. "You come into my store," he said, "and act this way? How dare you? How dare you?"

It took a while for Chou to figure out what to do. He hired a dozen local agents to work for him. While his agents—all local Taiwanese—scoured the countryside for dealers, he stayed in his office. He finally started earning money and ended up living in the south for twenty years until Taiwan's economy ran into trouble when cheaper Chinese goods flooded the market. He and his wife loaded all their furniture into a truck and drove up to Taipei and, with the help of a friend, launched into the beef noodle shop business. The return to Taipei after twenty years was a new beginning, especially in Mucha, an area populated mostly by local Taiwanese. When there aren't many customers, it's almost like he's recreating his mainlander island again with his friends, also second-generation, sitting in front of his shop around a small plastic table smoking and drinking tea and talking loud in their mainlander Chinese.

Table 5
Population centers of mainland refugees on Taiwan (1990)[a]

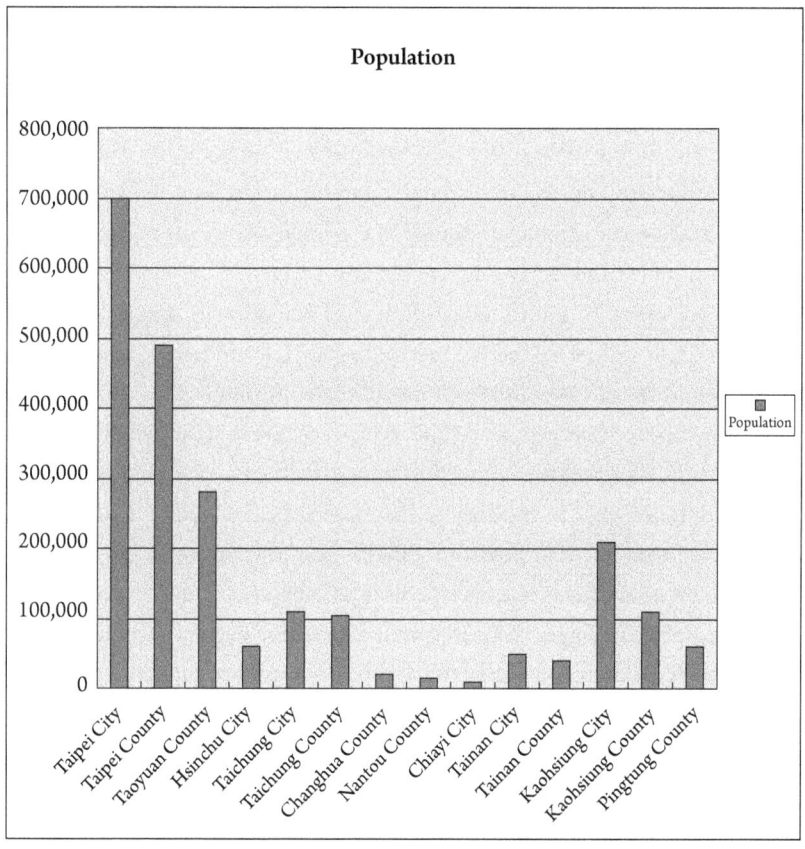

a. The concentration of mainland refugees in the northern part of the island, with the exception of the industrial center of Kaohsiung, suggests an "island." The chart is adapted from a similar one found in *Sili Donghai Dahsueh, Lishihsueyanchiusuo, shuoshilunwen, Zhanhou Taiwan "Waishengren" de suozao yu bianqian, 1945–1997* [The Vicissitudes and Contributions of Mainlanders in Postwar Taiwan, 1945–1997: Master's thesis, Tunghai University], Chai Weichen, June 1997. The graph is based on the census tolls of that year which still included place of origin.

Death outside

Sometimes it seems that the second generation is far more scared of the local Taiwanese than their parents were, maybe because some of them have parents that are local Taiwanese. But it seems to some of them that the local Taiwanese can somehow manipulate things, the environment, business deals, love affairs, in ways they cannot. It's almost as if the local Taiwanese were ghosts, or had the ability to move invisibly and quietly behind the scenes. Chou Chih-sui (who is not related to Chou, the noodle-stall owner) has always believed in a central authority. His mother, Wang Shu-chih, was just such an authority. She was the one who stood atop her housing complex and breast-fed her children during a typhoon as the water climbed up almost to her ankles. As for his father, the man was an army officer and taught Chou to put all his faith in the Kuomintang Party. As Chou got older, he joined an assortment of Kuomintang organizations for students and, in college, edited the party newspaper. Eventually, returning from Europe, where he had been studying medicine, to encounter the traumas of an earlier generation, he became one of the chief psychiatrists at the Taipei Veterans' General Hospital, an edifice with a flowering garden and cool pond, shadowed by multitudinous trees in memory of the more than one million Kuomintang soldiers who came over in defeat to Taiwan. The hospital was a gift from the late Generalissimo Chiang Kai-shek to his loyal followers. Today, it is one of the premier hospitals in Taipei and is frequented, to a large degree, by mainland settlers and their children. On a good day, Chou sees dozens of patients. They jostle outside his door, trying to defeat the phalanx of nurses. Like Chou, the noodle-shop owner, Dr Chou works and exists in his own island of time and space—the hospital. From his window, he can see the large garden, covering an entire side of the central building, with ornate, imperial-style bridges, and walkways, and a stylish array of large boulders, perhaps reminiscent of a Ming-dynasty craze for large rocks as status symbols. Trees lapse in the breeze. If Chou ever needs a reminder he is in "sacred" space, he just has to look out at the garden. It's like looking back in time, to the "old world," like being whipped back to a past he never knew, a past glorified in the structures and layout of the garden that were as real as a Disneyland castle.

As he cares for old men pushing walkers, or in wheelchairs being wheeled about by Filipina maids with pursed lips carrying their catheters, he may from time to time think of his own father, another old veteran who was killed when he stepped out of his own island of mainland space and time. Chou, at forty-three, is pudgy without being fat. His skin color is like the color of fresh cream, yet his black shiny hair and hawk nose express a personality adept at finding insights into problems that sometimes transcend the biological. In this case, the death of his father, his analysis is driven by the mysterious connections of locals, outside the mainlanders' enclosed space. He is talking about the fact that most second-generation mainlanders like him have never experienced a death in the family before. Their grandparents, for the most part, were left behind on the mainland when their parents escaped.

> I had never experienced death. I had never met my grandparents. They all died on the mainland. I suppose if I had lived through seeing a grandparent die, I would have been ready for death. I was twenty-seven when my father died. I wasn't ready. He should have died much later. But it was not just that. It was a shock for those of us in the second generation, who have never experienced the death of a family member before, to see one of our parents die. How could we know what it would be like or how we would react?
>
> My father was the first one in our family to die. I felt like I was dying. I also felt relief that I hadn't died. Then I felt guilty. Losing my father. It is something that even until now I don't understand. As I said, I had no idea what death was like, what experiencing the death of someone in your family was like.

As he speaks, Chou's voice is light, as if he is chatting with colleagues in a cafe. But as he continues, it thickens in his throat and then he begins talking faster, lighter, yet with a harder edge. His voice keeps going up and down, like a rubber band, tighter and looser. His father was killed, he says, not because he left his mainlander comfort zone, but because the Taiwanese just reached out and killed him and then fouled up the law and justice that should have served him as one of the founders of Taiwan as it is today.

> My father was hit by a truck. My mother basically stopped talking after that. But she tried to get some friends of hers to take legal action. It was impossible. There was nothing we could do because he was a local, the police were locals and the court was run by locals. When we tried to get the photos taken by the police at the scene, they somehow vanished. The police couldn't find them. They said it wasn't their policy to hold on to

them. But then when we came to court, the other side brought out a few of them as evidence.

We found out that the truck driver had family all over the area. His lawyer, who was also from the area, had been able to get the photos. It blew my mind.

As Chou sees it, the drugs that the driver was using, that had contributed to the accident, were just one more part of the society of the locals. In his way of seeing things, it's like all of Taiwanese society could be part of a plot against him and his family.

My father was killed in an area called Longtan. He was just going down the road to buy vegetables. It was the busiest time of day. There were lots of people out. But somehow the car hit him. Of all the people out on the street that day, he was the only one hit.

It was dawn. The driver was some local kid. Apparently he hadn't slept at all. Someone later told us he had been using amphetamines to stay awake. But of course, there was no evidence. We saw him weaving back and forth all over the road when he drove his truck back to the police station behind a police car. We saw that. It was in broad daylight. But what could we do? The police simply told him not to drive anymore. He was a native.

Not a lot of second-generation mainlanders are willing to accuse local Taiwanese directly. This could have something to do with an old idea that if you are to rule, you must include all ethnic groups within your Chinese empire. The idea came down from the Qing dynasty when the empire had a hold over a whole array of ethnic groups. During this time, the Qianlong emperor himself even pretended to be a part of these different groups, pretending to be a Buddhist god or a Mongol king. It was a little like an American candidate for president trying to appear Texan to Texans, or like a New Yorker to New Yorkers. But the emperor went much further: he claimed to actually become, to channel, a Buddha god king of Tibet, for example, thus giving him the right to rule over Tibet.[1] The Chinese were making claims like this almost from the beginning. When they encountered barbarians that became wrapped in the embrace of their empire, these nomads were then considered "civilized." The idea of organizing different ethnic groups under one culture was in full sway well before the Qing. But it was the Qianlong emperor that made it something absolutely essential.

Chou Hau-yi, the noodle-shop owner who used to fight with Taiwanese, doesn't want to criticize the locals outright. But, once he begins talking about the history of the island, he starts yelling. Cars and trucks rattle the glass windows of his shop. The heat and fumes come in off the street through an open door. Fumes of hatred rise from his throat. By the time he is halfway through his tirade, his face is one shade darker and he stands up, pulling his hands through his hair. The strain of his protest is similar to one his father might make. The Kuomintang saved Taiwan from economic and cultural peril, built up the island, and were now unrecognized. It is almost as if he is still fighting—only this time with no adversary.

> The Taiwanese were slaves before we came. When the Kuomintang got here, the local people had been brainwashed by the Japanese. The Japanese were here for fifty years and by the time they left, the Taiwanese had been made to believe they were slaves. Slaves to the Japanese. The Kuomintang, the mainlanders, came here and liberated them. We saved all of Taiwan. We taught the Taiwanese people that they could become Chinese again. And in that way they could escape the slavery of being second-class citizens to the Japanese.
>
> Actually, the mainlanders here in Taiwan have done a lot for the Taiwanese. Everything they have done has been for the benefit of the locals. But do they see it that way? Do the Taiwanese think they should be grateful to us? They don't. They say they have finally stood up. Yes, that's right, they've stood up. They've elected one of their own people to be president. But look at the job he's doing? Yeah, they can do anything. But for them, doing anything is just destroying the past, destroying what we've done for them.

The growing debate about the character of Taiwan before the Japanese colonized the island in 1895 is solved in an instant by Chou. He rejects the claim that hundreds, perhaps even thousands, of *xiucai*, scholars who passed the first tier of imperial examinations, lived on the island during the Qing. He rejects the idea that the island had any culture at all. He doesn't know it, but he comes closer to that view that is fashionable in Western academia: that during most of the Qing dynasty the Chinese turned the island into an agricultural colony that supplied most of the rice and sugar to the southern provinces of Fujian and Guangdong and rebelled from time to time against its masters who solved the problem by cutting off heads and butchering the rebels. What he's saying is that the place was barbaric, not some civilized outpost of learning. Chou is pulling at his hair, almost as if one of his enemies from childhood has just beaten him in a fight.

> Don't tell me about Taiwanese history. I've studied it. The Taiwanese have never been free. When in the past hundred years, or before that, has Taiwan ever been an independent country? During the Qing dynasty, the Taiwanese were basically slaves. Then the Japanese controlled the entire island. The Taiwanese have never been a free, whole people. They never realize how they've gotten to this point. We liberated them and now they have forgotten everything.

You can see he's trying to control it. But it's already too strong. It's like something inside him is broken and he's only now realizing it's broken and so it comes swarming out in anger, fury, and shame. It comes from somewhere deep inside him like a hurricane or a tornado, as black as hell. He just sort of freezes as it takes possession of him as if it is not him speaking or acting but something bigger than himself, something from the past, like a shadow that wraps itself around him. When it's all over, he tries to explain by saying that the rage comes from a place he has always kept secret—pride in his father. Now that he sees his father's generation put down and belittled, he is secretly wondering whether maybe the opposition party is right, maybe they weren't so much saviors as occupiers. He doesn't say so exactly, but you can see that there must be some other reason for him getting so mad. Or maybe it's just his father's rage and terror passed down like an old coat, or the shadow of a coat, to the son. He now takes up the 2–28 Incident, the massacre in which Kuomintang troops are accused of killing 30,000 locals in 1947. Chou is talking fast now, the words stumbling to get out. His throat is pumping to keep up, making little choking noises between breaths.

> Now people want to bring up this incident from the past. They want to link it to the Kuomintang. But does anyone actually know what happened? There are a million different explanations. Mainlanders were attacked and killed during that time. How come that never gets mentioned? People say that the Taiwanese died in great numbers. But so did the mainlanders. They never mention this. They just say now the Taiwanese have stood up. A Taiwanese can finally be president. That's all that matters to them, that he's Taiwanese. It doesn't matter if he can do a good job. No, the only thing that matters is that he's Taiwanese. Well, let them have their president for all the good it will do them.

But the one thing that bothers me the most is that they have forgotten what the mainlanders have done for them. Education, security, prosperity—all of these things were given to them for free. By forgetting this they are forgetting their roots. It is a betrayal. Not just of the mainlanders but of the Taiwanese themselves. The Taiwanese are betraying themselves.

By the end, he can hardly tell the difference between what is fact and what is imagination, if he ever could. Both point in the same direction. Taiwan would not have amounted to anything without the Kuomintang, the mainland refugees, and his father.

When your own mother is Taiwanese, there's a little bit of a problem. Who are you supposed to blame? Both of the sons of Ko Jen-tao, the police chief, call themselves "mainlanders." But their mother was a native Taiwanese. The younger one, Ko Chen-tsang, lives in a big apartment with his three children and wife, who is an aborigine. The apartment is large with several floors but it takes so long to get there from Taipei that it might as well be in a different country. During the time that the DPP was in power, Ko Chen-tsang just couldn't stop cursing the DPP president, Chen Shui-bian. "I'm going to assassinate that son of a bitch," he says. "I am Chinese." But as much as he talks about his hatred for the DPP and the local Taiwanese that constitute it, he never quite loses himself to anger. Instead, it is like a long, drawn-out pitched battle, like a dog baring its fangs and hissing for hours at its own image in a glass sliding door. You might say that he redirects his anger, since he can't allow himself to get angry at his own mother, a native Taiwanese. He lets himself get run down, physically and emotionally. He eats junk food constantly and most of his teeth fall out. It takes him years to go to see a dentist and get a set of false teeth. He wears the same clothes, the same shorts, and constant sleeveless undershirt. His plastic sandals are grimy and black around the edges. Like Chou, the noodle-shop owner, his job as a salesman, takes him deep into the southern palm plantations of the island. He does his best to sell Japanese-made foam molds for cement. He doesn't usually have much luck. Then, on the way back, it takes him about seven hours of driving up the long cement freeway which rain and sun has turned the color of lead, to reach Taipei. For most of the trip, he spends his time thinking how his life or the lives of his children might have been different—if it weren't for the DPP and their president, Chen Shui-bian.

His fury takes him beyond the confines of his own life. He gets mad, taunts a dog or curses the president or one of the other ethnic groups in Taiwan, then laughs about it with his brother. Sometimes, as he drives through Taipei, he pulls up alongside a car with a dog sticking its head out the window. Sticking his own head out the window, growling, making threatening facial gestures until the dog notices him, he can work a dog up to a frenzy in a matter of seconds. By the time the dog is crazed and yelping nonstop, Ko Chen-tsang then lets out his own bark, only one, but deep from his chest, baring his teeth even more. At first, the dog had been ready to jump at him from the other car window, barking and shredding saliva, but now, when it suddenly comes face to face with the suddenly ferocious and large red face of Ko Chen-tsang and his loud single bark, the dog falls back, whimpering into the back seat of the car.

He doesn't like the Hakka much either. The Hakka were originally a group of northern Chinese that worked their way down to the south, where the agriculture was richer. Today, they are stereotyped as hard workers, thrifty and untrustworthy. During the early years of Taiwan, when most of the first Chinese came over to the island during the Ming and Qing dynasties, they often fought with the Hakka and the aborigines. Likewise, his rage at ethnic groups on the outskirts of society is towering. All that Ko Chen-tsang knows is that they once fought against Chinese people. He might not admit, but he also sees them as outcasts, pariahs even. He tries to explain his hatred of them and talks about his childhood, when he and his brother and sisters lived with his parents in police dormitory.

> I first started hating Hakkas when I was a kid. We had this neighbor who was a Hakka and she was always coming over and complaining to my mother about everything. We called her "long-necked lizard." That was our pet name for her. We used to yell that after her when she left. When my mother heard us, she would take a bamboo switch and beat us. But I think that was just for show.

All three groups, Taiwanese, mainland refugees, and Hakkas, talk about wars and battles between Hakka pioneers and Taiwanese settlers during earlier centuries in Taiwan. But they always keep their voices lowered when they do so. After telling his childhood anecdote, Ko Chen-tsang wants to show that in reality he likes all kinds of people. "I have a friend who is Hakka," he says. But then he just can't seem to help falling back into his earlier vein. "But he has great hatred in his heart for the native Taiwanese." So the Hakka is both friend and enemy, both ally against the native Taiwanese and someone that could never be trusted, who has already betrayed the Chinese once.

For most of his life, Ko Chen-tsang has approached other ethnic groups with a mixture of fascination and rage. When he married an aboriginal woman, his parents yelled and cursed and nearly disowned him. Like many Taiwanese, they thought of aborigines as lower class, prostitutes or drunks. It was almost as if they had arranged it, on a regular schedule. He would find a way to go down to Hualien, a city on the eastern coast where the aborigines still live, and when he came back and they found out about it, they would make him kneel in front of one or the other in the living room, yelling, cursing, slowly and steadily with growing anger. "You think you've had it hard, you think you've been carrying rocks all day," his mother would yell at him, in her nightgown as he knelt before her, his head down. Ko Chen-tsang thought it was worth it, though. He had a sixteen-year-old aboriginal girlfriend with skin the color of slow mud and eyes that burned black out of two cracks. She was like a piece of volcanic lava, chipped away as it was cooling and left to harden with still some of the flame, the intensity kept inside. She was the most beautiful thing he had ever seen.

> I only had three weeks' leave. It was during my second year of military service on Kinmen. It was considered the front line so they gave us more time off. I took a boat back to Taiwan. I didn't even go to see my parents. I just went straight to Hualien to see her. If my parents had found out, they would have killed me. But I missed her so much that I couldn't stand it. And she really missed me. We were basically glued together for three weeks.

His time on Kinmen gave him the courage to face his parents. When he went to that long heap of rock, an island only several kilometers offshore from the mainland, yet still occupied by Taiwan, he was a teenager that had eaten too much fast food at night markets, bloated and soft. On Kinmen, the rice was full of weevils and there was never enough. He grew to be lean and tough. When he put on his wide and round glasses, he looked like an owl. He insists that he lived a clean, hard pure live. He says he never visited the brothel that the military kept out there, staffed with female convicts that had agreed to work off their sentences as prostitutes for the men. He was a "medic" and would go with the doctor when he did inspections. He said that even if he had wanted to go he wouldn't have because the women were all native Taiwanese. And besides, he had a picture of his girlfriend in his pocket that he looked at from time to time. Gradually, as he spent more time with her, saw her on leaves back to Taiwan, he began to see himself in a new way. He began to see himself as almost a protector of the aborigines. He started to see himself almost as an aborigine himself, an outcast from Taiwanese society who had more in common with his girlfriend's people than with the native Taiwanese or perhaps even his own.

Ko Chen-tsang just doesn't understand why his parents keep pretending. If he could, he might ask his father how the Kuomintang has survived for so long since it had been so easy for the natives to topple it. He had become disenchanted. He had always had a hard time accepting authority. He and a friend, when he was still in middle school, had once stolen a motorcycle and his father had to bail him out of jail. Now he just stopped taking authority that seriously at all. Maybe all second-generation mainlanders felt this way at the time, disappointed, discouraged, and angry that the façade of power or money their parents built up over six decades, or the elite positions they had held until recently, had suddenly seemed to have vanished. As the façade crumbled, as for instance the military fell from the grip of the mainland refugees, to be taken over by native Taiwanese, second-generation refugees like Ko Chen-tsang want to strike out at it as a falsehood. If it is no good now, he is saying, how could it have ever been good? Ko Chen-tsang fumbles his lips over his broken teeth and talks about his worst experience on Kinmen when he almost succeeded in cheating the whole military that, in a way, was cheating him out of his inherited place as one of the elite in Taiwan. When he talks about getting caught, and put in the stock house, he laughs and says it doesn't matter, he really didn't get hurt. But he can't help biting his lips and glancing around as if he is still in that stock house, or as if he is comparing it to his life in Taiwanese society now, an outcast who is being punished for only trying to help, shamed, humiliated and dishonored.

> When I was on Kinmen, I worked for this officer who was in charge of reviewing legal documents. Every time I filled out a form, I had to get a stamp from him. There were hundreds of forms we had to complete a week. So I finally went to a shop and had a copy made of his seal. Then it was easy. I just filled out the form and stamped it with my replica of his seal. I just wanted to save time, to keep up efficiency. But the officer in charge

eventually found out and said it was perjury. It became a huge deal and eventually everyone on the island found out about it.

Ko Chen-tsang laughs, raising his hand to cover his teeth. There's another side to the story. It was just another prank, the kind his father had caught him at before, when he had stolen the motorcycle and his friend's older brother and his own father were both policemen, so the matter just went away. He's proud of the days he spent in the military brig for a maneuver he would probably try again if possible. Now it almost sounds like he likes remembering his time in the brig. When he was a boy, the Kuomintang still held martial law over the island. There were similar rules telling you what you could and couldn't say, when you could sleep, and what you could do. In those days his father, a Kuomintang party member and a police officer, still possessed enough authority to order people, to punish them, to make Taiwan safe and clean. After the DPP took over, Taiwan became a different place. There were protests against the mainlanders. In school, you now had to study Taiwanese history. And his father was no longer a hero but a killer. Chiang Kai-shek believed in discipline and punishment above all else, or at least tried to make other people believe that. Ko Chen-tsang's memories are of when the Kuomintang still ruled, when Green Island was still used as a prison for political prisoners, and when his father still believed in himself. In those days, governing was somehow always connected with punishing.

> So I ended up in the stockade. They had all these rules, for example, you could keep your shoes on but you had to take off your socks. You could keep your pants on but you couldn't wear a belt. You could wear a shirt, but you couldn't button it up. The worst thing was that every day you had to stand at attention for four hours. Maybe it was three. For three or four hours, you had to stand without moving. If you couldn't do it, they wouldn't let you sleep. So you learned quickly.
>
> When you got up in the morning, you had to wash a lot of laundry. Then you could have breakfast. Then you had to do a lot of other things, like cleaning. I was in there for five days. And it was really hot. I must have lost twenty pounds. Finally, on the sixth day, the sergeant let me out but I couldn't go back to my old job. Now they only let me stand sentry duty.

As soon as he got out of detention, he took a medical leave. He told his commanding officers that his mother was sick. When he got to Taiwan, he went home to change his clothes. "What are you doing here?" his mother asked. But he didn't listen. For the first time in his life, he simply walked into his room and changed his clothes. His mother stood outside the door, yelling at him. He opened the door and pushed past her. He had a white Vespa that his brother had been riding but he still had a key and it was there, parked on the street. He rode to the train station, left the bike among a group of other motorcycles, walked inside and purchased a ticket. On the platform, he thought he saw someone who looked like his father, a short, burly police officer. But he ducked behind a post until the man passed. He got on the train and stood the whole way down the coast: he didn't have a ticket for a seat. The train swayed around the bends as it made its way, slowly, down the eastern coast. From the cliffs over which the train was traveling, the ocean spread out like a piece of blue glass that someone had left ripples in as it dried. As the train lumbered down to sea level, the swells crashed against the rocks. When he disembarked in Hualien, the sound of cicadas in the trees was like a physical presence, like a blanket draped over his head and shoulders. He moved through it as if through water. It was suffocating, cloying, and invincible. He felt invincible. He rented a motorcycle and drove up the snaking roads into Taroko Gorge, a large ravine widened and equipped with paved roads winding through tunnels that the Japanese had built during their fifty years of occupation. It was dusk and the gorge was like a tub filled with dirty, grey light. Only the tops of the long columns of rock that enclosed the gorge were touched with fingers of light. When he arrived at the apex of the gorge, a small trading outpost called Tianhsiang, he found the trinket shop where his girlfriend worked. A flood of tiny black mosquitoes rose up around him as he parked the motorcycle and extinguished the splash of light from its headlight.[2]

After they were engaged, his parents had to accept her. They outfitted one room in the family apartment to make it a suite for the couple. They put in new lights and plastered over the old cracked paint. They put up a picture of the couple that covered half the wall. They took it for granted that the girl would cook for the household. And she spent the first six months learning, from Ko Mama, how to cook in native Taiwanese style.

Then they had children. His wife bore him three daughters. "It's not that I wanted a son," he says, "it's just that I kept asking, why couldn't we have one?" Many mainland refugees of the second generation believe, as part of their cultural snobbishness, that women are treated more fairly in mainland families. Some say that women are offered more opportunities for education than in native Taiwanese families. But some things never change: a woman is still valued by her ability to bear a son. Ko Chen-tsang's subtle disgruntlement about his wife's inability to give him a son only exacerbated his anger at himself. If his wife had at one time served as a symbol of his own disenchantment and alienation, it was now his children who became his target. With eyes that reflected their aboriginal origins, that swooped up at the corners, his children, Ko Chen-tsang complained, "looked too aborigine," and that this would "hurt them in their lives." His sensitivity for outcast racial groups, given his own and his father's experience, found expression in the faces of his three daughters. His attraction to the outcast was now staring him in the face and he could not endure it.

In his apartment, in an outlying low-rent district of Taipei, there is a stillness. The eldest daughter sits on the couch, looking away. The two younger daughters are nowhere to be found. Ko Chen-tsang sits awkwardly on a chair and his hands dropped heavily on his lap. Minutes before, his wife called friends and family members from the lingerie shop she manages down the block. Her grief is plain. Ko Chen-tsang has been hitting his children again. The embarrassment all feel when the door is opened to the apartment is like a solid block of frigid air. Ko Chen-tsang pushes his head forward on his neck like a frog, as if to defy anyone to look too closely at him. The girls are not crying, although their heated cheeks suggest they have been. The entire apartment is frozen into one single moment, that moment being when his thick, callused hand smacked the faces of his children. Later, he says he only hits his youngest and eldest daughters. His middle daughter, whose obesity seems a kind of defiance, he does not strike. He does not know why.

> I am ashamed of myself almost every day. It's because of this bad habit I have. When I'm tired and come home and I'm in a bad mood, it's easy for me to lash out at my daughters. The oldest one is starting to go on dates and I don't trust her. The youngest one always talks back. If there's one thing I can't stand, it's back talk. The middle one, it's strange, I never hit her. It's strange because when I get really angry I feel like I don't have any control over myself and I lash out at my daughters. But I never hit the middle one.

His father, at least, was able to use as a reference point his family's lost fortunes and triumphs on the mainland as a guidepost to steer him in his social climb in Taiwan. But for Ko Chen-tsang, his father's efforts seemed no longer worthy. They were being eroded and undermined daily by the attacks and propaganda of the DPP, which was trying to recast history, the history of the mainland refugees, as one of violence, invasion, and destruction. Ko Chen-tsang is now merely joining in the assault on the wretched, on his father, by striking at those immediately under his care—the outcasts. Like his elder sister, who wanted to locate her identity in her Taiwanese memories, Ko Chen-tsang seems at this moment frantic, disgruntled, and like a man losing his grip on a long stairway that he has been climbing, a stairway built by his father. In his fall, he strikes out at those below him, following him.

Ko Chen-tsang talks of "lacking the ability to control himself." Control came, in childhood, from the feeling of being surrounded and penetrated by reigning customs and hope, discipline and memory. The problem for someone like Ko Chen-tsang is that the guidelines or structures that govern his life seem to have almost completely collapsed. His memories are no longer valid. There is only a wasteland where he is not sure of the value of his own life, not to mention his past. In striking out at his children, as they sit there on his white dirty couch, he is striking out at the chaos and terror of his life. Striking out, slapping, ordering are all similar actions, even if undertaken in anger. He's not quite sure if he is a man trying to teach his children through pain and anger, or if he is trying to destroy them.

His father, Ko Jen-tao, spends an increasing amount of time with the three daughters. It is as if he slides into the form of an old grandfather, with a pot belly and graying strands of hair around his face. He has purpose and stops fretting about his marriage. Ko travels from his house in northern Taipei, Neihu, the mainlander's district, the area where the buildings all rise high away from the street and night markets are absent. He travels by bus to the outlying district where open pits of construction are constant, and spends evenings cooking stewed beef for his grandchildren. His eyes that are as sad as a person's in mourning bounce happily as he watches his grandchildren play. He washes their clothes and nags them about eating enough.

Meanwhile, Ko Chen-tsang finds some freedom from his family and his self-disgust, traveling to the south of the island to sell his merchandise, mostly failing, and returning frustrated and ready to escape from his life.

A chance came when he ran into a childhood friend, a young woman surnamed Chen in a random encounter. The woman was native Taiwanese. Perhaps it was an opportunity to test the fragile union he had made with his aboriginal wife. Perhaps he felt shame for marrying an aborigine, a member of the most discriminated-against ethnic group in Taiwan, as if his marriage was one of social defeat rather than outrage. Now he recalls his wife as a sickly-looking young girl in the back of the trinket shop with graying skin, someone whose background seems to hang over her like a shadow, a slave that he would simultaneously save and identify with. In one single moment, all the romance, glamor, and passion of his love vanishes and turns to dread, changing his memories like someone in a magic show had swapped a rabbit for a dog. Perhaps now that he had a family and the experience and pride—and the power—of being a father; perhaps he no longer saw his wife as strictly an outcast—now it was his children. He had more control over them than responsibility. They were under his care and control, so they were more wretched than anyone. His despair, the despair of beating his children—beating them almost as if to prove his lack of self-worth—grew. It was at this time that he found even more despair in the arms of another woman. He describes the woman he had a romantic relationship with as "intelligent."

> I was working on construction sites at the time. I didn't talk much to anyone. Who could I talk to? Then I ran into a girl I had known in school. It was like going back into the past. We were never really friends, but I had admired her from afar. She was really pretty. But the main thing was it was like going into the past before my life had really begun. We started meeting for tea or lunch, or just talking. It was innocent. I ended up telling her everything, all my troubles. She was really comforting. She said that she had been hit as a child, that it wasn't that bad. Her mother was also Taiwanese and her father was also a mainlander. We could really relate.
> But she would never talk to me about her private life. She just wanted to listen. I started to think she was married. I thought, if she was married, she must have a really bad marriage. She always looked a little sick, too. Maybe that was why she seemed so intelligent. I always felt like I was saying the wrong thing. We started meeting more and more. We would sit for hours in coffee shops. Sometimes we held hands.
> One time, we were on a bus together, in the back, and no one else was on the bus. I put my hand up inside her blouse and she put one of her hands down my pants. I wanted to get off and go to a hotel but she wouldn't. She kept saying, just wait a little longer. Finally, I got really mad. I pushed her away. And her head hit the back of the bus. I felt really ashamed and scared. And I was still angry. I got off the bus and said to myself I would never see her again. But it was really weird, after a few days, she started to call me. She

would call me at home, late at night, and eventually my wife picked up the phone and guessed I was involved with someone else.

His wife became increasingly infuriated. Then she began to drink. Her long dark hair fell wildly over her face. Her deep eye sockets seemed to grow deeper, and her hooked nose drooped. With her vivid white skin, a sign of her Taroko tribe, and the dark circles under her eyes, she looked like she had emerged out of the grave. Eventually, she almost went there. One evening, she took a butcher's knife into the bathroom and locked herself in, planning to commit suicide. Ko Chen-tsang was out with his new girlfriend at the time. He had agreed to see her one last time. The children called their grandfather. Ko Jen-tao and his new wife, Liu Rong, rushed over and Liu Rong, the mainland wife, persuaded the wife to open the door and put down the knife.

Ko Chen-tsang had attempted to escape from the outcast position he had made for himself—to escape from the despair he knew into a despair he did not. His sister also has an escape story, which she tells after recounting a childhood idyllically set among the fern trees and palms of Bamboo Mountain. While she explains that she sought to escape from the cruelty of her mother, who threatened and abused her, she is also seeking to cast her whole life on a trajectory away from the mainlander household. To see her then, with long stringy hair, a guitar and speaking regularly in Taiwanese, one could almost imagine her a local, if not for her long nose and ivory-colored skin. She was a woman trying to escape from her mother by entering the society of her mother, enter Taiwanese society on her own, no longer the pampered daughter of a mainland police chief but an independent woman, an artist and a teacher.

At a young age, she realizes that her parents' marriage is a sham. Her father bears everything, every hint of his mother's displeasure, he swallows it down as if he were forcing himself to drink a glass of medicine.

> My father knew how to bear things. He had borne a lot. Now he had to bear my mother's temper. The Taiwanese, generally speaking, have a worse temper than the mainlanders. She was Taiwanese so it goes without saying she would have problems with anger management. My father was always reserved. He rarely yelled. But when she yelled, he just had to bear it. That was his nature. She would get all worked up about something. Or she would be yelling at one of us, and my father wouldn't say a thing. He'd just bear

with it. *He* was the real victim of their marriage. He was cursed. It was his fate to lose his home as a kid. Now it was his fate to have to endure this.

She wished she could change her entire past. Her father had no voice. Neither has she. She makes her voice even smaller, as if to hide. Her name, given her by her father, Chen-yuan, means "graceful." She has chopped it off in recent years to the simple Ko Yuan, a name that sounds artistic and free, a rebellion in a way against her roots, her legacy. She can also understand her father who if only for a single moment, a week, a month, was unable to bear his oppression and had an extramarital affair. Ko Yuan insists that the affair was the result of her father's "bearing" a bad marriage for decades. But her memory of it is also the prelude to her own act of rebellion.

> Everyone in our family is a victim or has made some kind of sacrifice. My father put up with my mother for so long, in the end he just couldn't take it anymore. At one point, when I was in my teens, my father told me that something really serious had happened between him and my mother. I immediately knew what he was talking about. I asked him how he could do this to us. He said he wasn't being unfaithful. He had gone through so much in his life that he had finally had just given up. He said it was just one time. Just one time. He said, "I have put up with so much for so long, can't you just put up with this one little thing?" When he said that, I thought to myself I must really be spoiled. I felt really ashamed of myself. That was when I started thinking about running away.

Ko Yuan must justify her need to escape. Terror. Silence. Helplessness. Her father was someone "with no voice." A mainland refugee in Taiwanese society at that time, during the most turbulent period of its democracy, he was doubly a person without a voice. After losing his position and authority, he slumped around his apartment waiting for his children to call or spending his days with his grandchildren, cooking and cleaning. How can she not be a victim, like her father, victimized by her mother and now by society? Nothing is permanent to her. Nothing is sacred. She saw her mother taking money from her father. Her own country is in upheaval. Escape is the only answer, she believes. Ko Mama, the native Taiwanese wife, is stealing from the pants of the mainland refugee in a way, a little but like the native Taiwanese, after a long climb out of repression, are finally able to start stealing from the pants of the mainland immigrants.

Whenever my mother went to visit my father at the station, in the dormitory there, she would always bring me along. It took me a while to figure out why. She'd tell me to go talk to my father while she "cleaned" his room. One time, though, I came back early because I had forgotten something and I saw my mother checking the pockets of all his clothes. She didn't see me. I saw her take out some cash from the pocket of his pants. It looked like it was a lot. Like a thick wad of bills.

After a few days, I finally had enough courage to ask her about it. She just said, "Don't ever tell your father about it, you understand." I knew in my heart of hearts that my father knew who was taking his money. But I know he just didn't have the guts to confront her about it. Why not? Because in that marriage, he was someone with no rights and no voice.

Ko Yuan also becomes a person with no voice. Her mother had asked her to keep silent about her stealing from her father. "Don't ever tell your father," she said. With no voice, she faded. She slowly disappeared.

When I was in primary school, there were many times when I tried to kill myself. I would gather up all the pills I could get my hands on at home and take them all at once. But the result was always the same. I would end up sleeping for a long time and then wake up with a hangover. My mother had no idea. She would come into my bedroom and shout at me. She'd say things like, "You just lie around all day. You know what you are—you're a pig. But at least a pig would get up to eat."

I spent a lot of time writing suicide notes. After I wrote one, I would hide it in between some newspapers in my room. One day, I came home and the newspapers were gone. I came out of my room into the living room where my mother was watching TV. She didn't even look at me. She just said, "How many suicide notes are you going to have to write before you actually do it?" She said, "You're exactly like your father. The only thing you're good at is running away from your problems."

After that, I tried to stay away from home as much as possible. I knew I was too young to run away. So after school was over, I would go to the Sun Yat-sen Memorial. It felt safe to me. I would hide behind the exhibits on the first floor or in the basement. I wouldn't leave for home until it closed for the day at seven o'clock. Then I would go home and try to sneak in without my mother hearing me.

Ko Yuan at forty-four resembles a long Chinese flute. She has a bean-pod-like body which she wraps tightly in faded jeans and a small shirt. Her long hair flies wildly in the wind as she walks. She usually wears a little grin like a child who has seen too much for her age and feels privileged above and beyond her peers by the secret. She has the high cheekbones of her mother, the long, straight nose of her father, and sleepy eyelids that seem almost mocking or disdainful. Her only apparent link now to the traditional culture that her mainland ancestors would have identified as theirs is her Chinese flute and her *Book of Changes*, which she teaches out of a studio apartment in a seaport twenty miles from Taipei. But her story of herself as a child, who later hides out in the mausoleum built for the man considered by the refugees to be their founding father, resonates with her past. Even if the mausoleum were merely the most convenient public space on her way home during that tumultuous time, her focusing on it, bringing it up out of the past, as a central reference point, suggests that it has other meanings as well. Perhaps she is thinking of the need for such sanctuaries. After the DPP took over and even after they lost power, Taiwan no longer seems safe to mainlanders. It's like the connection with the past is gone. Native Taiwanese ideologues do not recognize Sun Yat-sen as having anything to do with Taiwan.

In junior high school, she found a second life. Her friendships with teachers revived her. School became her sanctuary. But her exaggerations suggest she is still trying desperately to belong to some institution outside her familial origins. School becomes her escape. She remakes herself as the authority. As a result, she is reborn, not as a mainland refugee, but as an *enfant terrible*. She escapes her ethnicity through scholasticism. Yet, it is her belief in her heritage that helps her to thrive in school—a belief that maintains that mainland refugees are culturally superior to the natives. The teachers she remembers might readily be assumed to have a significant number of Taiwanese natives among them.

> Most of the teachers at that school were really friendly. Some of them wanted to be my personal friend. They used to praise my writing a lot. Sometimes we spent hours talking after class. I hardly got any sleep at all during those years. I felt like I had so much to do. Teachers would tell me to read certain books but I ended up introducing a lot more books to them than they had to me. They became my pupils. I felt that I had something I could share with them.
>
> They would ask me if I had read a certain book, and it would usually be something I had read a long time ago. There were a couple of teachers who had crushes on me. It was obvious. Every time I came into their classrooms,

they got really nervous. One of them was always asking me to stay after class. We would talk and she would touch my arms and my hair. It wasn't uncommon at that time for older women to have crushes on girls, especially if the girls were bright and came from a cultured background.

Home life, however, is a battle between the native Taiwanese mother and the mainland refugee father. Her mother is furious because her husband is never at home. It is his drinking, too. Ko Mama takes it out on her daughter. She throws off casual comments, cruel ones, at first. Then she adopts a new tactic, saying nothing to the daughter for days or weeks, a tactic she uses against her husband when she wants to show her anger. The daughter is caught in the middle. By showing just how terrible her family of origin is, Ko Yuan is recreating herself in the new order, a little bit like the Red Guards who denounced their parents in order to be accepted in another new order. Her Taiwanese mother is the trouble; she is the source of the problem. She just has too many memories of her mother's abuse, which are more painful given the current atmosphere instability and uncertainty.

> I could stand my mother yelling at me and calling me names. It wasn't that bad because she just didn't know that many swear words. She was from the country. She mostly called me "pig" or "slut." But when I turned eighteen, it was like a curtain dropped. She stopped saying things like that to me. She stopped talking to me altogether. She would just look up and glare when I came into a room. No matter where I went, I could feel her eyes on my back. She was crazy. I couldn't sleep. I was afraid she would come into my room in the night and kill me.
>
> My father kept nagging me to speak to my mother. I told him what was going on but he just said, speak to her, tell her I'm sorry. I don't think he realized how hard it was at home. I don't think he realized how my life had become a living hell. I was caught between my father's nagging and my mother's silence. My thoughts of killing myself came back then, almost as strong as when I was younger. Only this time I made other plans, like jumping off the roof of the apartment building.
>
> I thought about this for a while. I guess I finally figured out that I was just trying to escape my problems. But I knew that I didn't have the skills to deal with them. So I started imagining myself somewhere else, out of our house, starting a new life somewhere. I was scared, but I felt this exhilaration. I felt like, like in my imagination I was already starting to be free. In my life, in reality, I was still a prisoner. But in my mind, I felt like I was starting

to feel what it was like to be free. I think it was at that time that I felt the beginning of my true self being born.

She wanted to be free of everything. She was becoming her "true self." What was she leaving behind? Everything. Who she was in her family. She was about to flee her childhood home. Like her father, she was about to flee her home in the midst of a revolution. But unlike her father, she was fleeing not for her life, but for her identity. A new identity, starting from scratch seemed hard to aim for. But she planned carefully.

I had no idea how to get going. I started writing in my diary, trying to come up with some plans. I would write out one plan about how to get out and start a new life. Then I would write out another. It was almost like I was writing short stories. I decided I would choose one of them and then follow it. I was scared most of the time. I was scared that my mother would find my diary. I was scared I couldn't really run away or that something bad would happen if I did, something I couldn't even imagine. I always came back to the thought that it would be better just to jump off the roof. I was so frustrated because I couldn't make a decision. I think one of the problems was that my mother had always kept us isolated. My father, too. We never had any responsibilities except to do our schoolwork. We had no knowledge of how the outside world worked. Schoolwork wasn't going to get you freedom.

I also knew that once I left home there was no way of coming back. Part of me still felt like a child and I didn't want to give up my home, no matter how bad it was. What if something terrible happened? What if I got sick? I was about seventeen by then but I still looked like a kid. I felt like I was making a big mistake. I knew that the door would be locked if I tried to come back.

Another worry I had was that I wanted to make sure my mother never found out what happened to me. I wanted her to pay for what she had done. In my diary, I formulated a plan. I would find a place outside of our district or outside of the city. It had to be out of the way of any of the bus lines that ran near our house. I didn't want even the possibility of ever running into my mother if she was taking the bus. I couldn't face the possibility of that happening. I never wanted to see her again. It would be too upsetting. I wanted to move somewhere where it would be impossible to ever run into her.

I saved up money for a year. It took me that whole time to find a place. I had enough for a deposit and a few months' rent. But actually leaving was the hardest. I didn't want my mother to be suspicious. So I brought my things out slowly. I would wait until my mother was on the back porch washing clothes, then I would bring out a few clothes and books in a bag. On the next trip I would take my guitar and a bowl and some chopsticks. I just did it all bit by bit. I got out most of my stuff and most of my books. I had too many books to bring them all.

Every time I left the house, I'd say, "Mom, I'll be right back." But she wasn't speaking to me. She hadn't spoken to me for a year. I just didn't want her to suspect anything. I was afraid she might kill me or something. I thought of her cutting off chicken heads like I had seen her do in Bamboo Mountain. And, when I was going to sleep in my room, I used to imagine her coming in while I was asleep. I just didn't want her to get mad. Eventually, I moved most of my stuff to a room I had rented in Shipai, across the river.

The landlord was a bastard. It turned out I didn't have enough for the deposit. He hadn't told me it was so much. Or maybe I misunderstood. I think he changed the price. Then he told me I could stay on a spare cot in his room until a smaller room opened up. He said he wouldn't bother me and would treat me like a daughter. I got down on my knees and begged him to let me stay in the room I had already moved all my stuff into. When I started to cry, he gave in. I stayed in my new room until my money ran out. After that, I had no choice. I went to my father's station and asked him for money. He had no idea what had happened, because my mother wasn't speaking to him either, and when he came home on Sundays he would just get drunk and go to sleep. So after all that time, he had no idea I had left home.

President Chen Shui-bian and his administration said they wanted to create an island where everyone could create a new identity for him or herself. In his idealized world, a person's background wouldn't matter anymore and aborigines and mainlanders would be renamed and given smooth identities to roll right in with the rest of the Taiwanese. The approach was meant to be the opposite to the divisive politics of the Kuomintang, who forced all citizens to carry identity cards with their origins printed on the back—in effect, forcing everyone to stay "at home," with the family of one's origin. If one's father was born in Sichuan, for instance, then the child would carry the stamp of "Sichuan" as a point of origin. Under the Kuomintang, who were obsessed with mainland Chinese names, as in the city of Taipei, everyone with mainland origins had these stuck to them, like logos on the back of their shirts. The DPP, under Chen, made a big deal about trying to abolish these divisions. The island was rich and anything seemed possible—even the daughter of a mainland immigrant leaving home and entering the chaos and anonymity of Taiwanese society, adrift from her family. The local Taiwanese government renamed mainland refugees as "new immigrants." It also used the name for the batch of wives who had come over from the mainland after travel restrictions were lifted. They were also called "new immigrants." A Filipina maid who wanted to stay on and live in Taiwan was also dubbed a "new immigrant." It was an insult to the mainlanders. Should the founders of modern Taiwan, as they thought themselves, be lumped with Filipina maids? Primary school textbooks started to use the term.

Ko Yuan left home at the height of the gradual marginalization of the mainland settlers as "new refugees."[3] The new government said they could leave behind any trace of their "mainland origins." They could be considered Taiwanese, "new" Taiwanese. In her own way, that was what Ko Yuan was striving for. She talks about her escape, of taking her guitar, an instrument that seems young, hip, native, as if she is building a new childhood, a new identity for herself. Unlike the traditional Chinese opera that flooded the stages of Taiwan after the 1949 escape, the past few decades have seen the explosions of other forms of drama, more grass-roots and experimental. Along with the early rise of non-Kuomintang party activity, an underground movement of avant-garde theater, with half-nude dancers, Western instruments and scandalous themes transformed the small theaters of Taipei and the south. During these years of upheaval, these theater troupes created a culture, that the DPP claimed as its own, that was part aboriginal, part native, with chanting and drumming performances that eventually filled not only the basement clubs but the island's primary theaters. This change was part of the political revolution that swept the island. And Ko Yuan's guitar fit right in.

> Just before I left, I wrote my mother a long letter. It was seven pages long. I covered both sides of each page with writing. So actually it was fourteen pages. I told her how she had abused me, how I was disgusted with her and how I didn't want to fall into the trap of becoming like her. I said I knew that by cutting her off, I would never know if I had become like her because I wouldn't be able to compare myself with her and make sure.
>
> I had been thinking about something else for a long time, too. So I wrote that the rest of the Taiwanese were just like her, violent but in a secret way. I said that the Taiwanese had never had the chance to be violent because they were repressed. So they had become like her. Fighting in a silent, invisible way. I had thought a lot about all the history books I had read and come up

with this idea that history was basically always this kind of battle, between those who could use violence in an open way and those who had to use it in a secret way. Then I made a list of all the ways she had mistreated me. I was crying as I wrote the letter. I took my guitar with me, left the letter on the dining room table, and left.

She did not come home again for years, and only when her mother got cancer. She came home and stayed. In the final weeks, she helped her mother organize her things. Going through a drawer, she found the note she had written a years before.

The letter was still in the envelope. And the envelope was still sealed. She never even read it. I opened it and read it again. I was so sad. But I finally knew that I had been right to leave. If I hadn't left, I think I wouldn't be here now. As my mother lay dying, I thought that we had both had made a lot of mistakes. I wished I had been a better daughter.

Daniel Hu, on the other hand, another second-generation mainland refugee, spent half his adult life preparing to escape his origins—and then didn't. Tall and craggy-featured, with a face like a young Rock Hudson and skin the color of seashore sand, the thirty-seven-year-old is the eldest son of the Classics professor who escaped with his father through a refugee camp in Hong Kong and an American mother. During his childhood, he developed under the wings of his parents. His mother, a former librarian at the University of Indiana, where his father did his PhD, influenced him, he says, with her calm, steady ways. His father, on the other hand, always felt that something was lacking in his own life. Daniel always wanted to be a writer. He wanted to be a great radio playwright, like his grandfather, who led his father to safety. All these many dreams were unfulfilled. Restlessness trickled down into the veins of Daniel. While he was at Reed College, in Oregon, he ran into academic trouble. He was lazy, didn't study, and had other dreams.

I never went to a single class in college. Well, that's not true. I did go to one or two. What I really wanted was to be a writer. My writing was pretty good then. I had read a lot of novels and poetry. But I felt that my classes were harmful to me as a writer. I thought that if I read the academic writing in the textbooks it would hurt my style. I would absorb the style. And if I tried to write creatively in academic papers, the professors and TAs didn't like it.

In one class, I wrote a paper about Thucydides and religion. I used the word "skyey," which was from a poem by Shelley. But the TA crossed out

> the word. She gave me a C on the paper. After that, I just stopped going to class. I had this idea that if I could just get to New York, I could find some work there, and I could be a writer. I thought that all I had to do was get to the city. I thought that there was something about the city, that it was the center of the cultured world, so that I could write there. If I could just get there, everything would be okay. I had this idea that I would wait on tables and write.

He had never been anywhere near New York before that. But somehow he believed landing in his dream city with no more than an airy vision in his head would deliver him what he had always been looking for: if he could figure out what that was. He was like his father in one thing. Both believed that studying would not be enough—his father had told him that to major in Classics was the best preparation to pursue any career. Both father and son said that what was required in life was the necessary "preparation," which would include some sort of immersion in the past greatness of art and literature—the Classics. Both also believed that they were unfit to take up such an art because they were not able to release their emotions and vision "spontaneously."

> I knew that my grandfather had brought my father out of China. And I knew that as a result my father had never been able to achieve his dreams. I have recently been thinking that I have been trying to fulfill the dreams of my father. I want to write a novel based on his experiences escaping from China. That would be my first novel. I just haven't felt ready to start yet. I need to do some other writing to warm up. I want to be able to write from the heart. I've been able to do that a few times in a few short pieces. There's something that's been very hard for me to realize. But most of the time I think I realize it. And that is, going to New York, see, I can't even say it or even think it most of the time, is probably not going to help me write from the heart.

His father also wanted to be a writer. He wanted to know if he had what it takes. So he once asked a friend if the friend thought he could survive in Hong Kong, where he had been interned in a refugee camp, as a writer only living on one bowl of rice a day. It was like his son's asking if he could survive in New York as a writer. The friend had told him that he couldn't. So Hu had given it up.

Daniel drifted for a while, never quite completing his studies at Reed, and never quite making it to New York. His grandfather had been a leading

Kuomintang official on the mainland, then a broadcasting legend in Taiwan. His father, having given up the creation of literature, was now teaching it—Ibsen and Shakespeare to undergraduates among the palms and cockroaches of the scaly brick buildings left by the Japanese when they decamped in 1945. The family, including the white-haired American mother, lived in a flat provided by the university, across from Taiwan University. Daniel returned from the United States and hung out brooding in the tiny apartment until his uncle, engaged in a business venture in China, asked him to join. The uncle was renovating a rambling old apartment complex—into upscale short-term hotel suites for business travelers to the northeast of China. In Shenyang, the coal dust in the air filled the lungs with black phlegm, and factory waste polluted the water with heavy metals—it was the industrial capital of China—but it was an opportunity for Daniel to do something entirely different. He took it.

His uncle left him in charge of the hotel for six months while he took on other business ventures. Once in charge, Daniel tried to forget his college dreams of going to New York as an artist and tried to act like a manager, lining the staff up daily for inspection. He caught the local contractors stealing carpeting.

> I just couldn't believe it. They had no compunctions whatsoever. They were openly stealing from the company, the company that employed them. I had them line up in the lobby and I just lost it. I completely lost control. I spent a minute just looking into their faces. I remember thinking that they had never worked a single honest day in their lives. I screamed at them for fifteen minutes. I called them names. I'm ashamed of it now. I said, "You're going to have to learn right now, there's no more iron rice bowl, you're not working for the Communists anymore." By the time I was finished, I could barely breathe, I was almost choking, the air pollution was that bad.

He had found something, maybe it was the realization that he was now a man that could no longer let himself go as he had done in the past. He had returned and he had yelled at workers—perhaps even the kind who had risen up against his grandparents. He was no writer, but perhaps, in the depths of his mind, he was reasserting his rights, his prerogative on the mainland again, one that had been wiped clean away from his family—once landlords—by the communist takeover. He was almost a landlord again. He felt intense shame after losing his cool. He was no longer in control of his destiny—but he had never been to begin with, or so he felt. If he could not control himself any longer, control his tone, then perhaps he would be free in different ways. This was the first step in a subtle revolution that allowed him to eventually go back to school and finally choose something he had really wanted to study—Classics. He eventually— after gaining enough credits to graduate—went on to enroll in a PhD program in that very field. At the very least, he was able to decide that China was no place for him, that he was unwilling to explore that side of his heritage because it was too painful and dangerous: there was too much unburied grief that could leap out of him at any moment. In the meantime, perhaps because he had made a decision, because he felt some hope for his future, he found a girlfriend among the local workers, a northern Chinese girl with a snub nose who was shy and quiet, which was rare for a girl from Shenyang, where secrets are usually shouted through the street with the hoarse ring of a butcher.

The romance lasted a few weeks, then his time was up and he returned to Taiwan and is finishing a dissertation, on Aeschylus, the Greek tragedian. His career path still follows the early direction of his father. After his short romance with the mainland Chinese girl, he fell into the structured romance and love of the exiled mainland Chinese community. His parents arranged for a meeting with the daughter of another second-generation mainlander family, and the two got married quickly and had a child. He had wanted to be free for such a long time that when it finally came, in the form of his yelling at his Chinese workers, he didn't recognize it as the kind of spontaneity he and his father had wanted their whole lives. But then he felt ashamed and returned to his studies and the Classics. He had collapsed, like his people, and was now trying to rebuild himself. It was something like the old Confucian belief in the dynastic cycle, that when one era ends another one begins, the idea that all things fall and are built again. But what had he given up? Freedom of a sort? His dream of writing in New York? In his thesis, Daniel concentrates on the adjectives used by Aeschylus in such lines as:

> Low lie the shattered towers whereas they fell,
> And I—ah burning heart! —shall soon lie low as well.[4]

As he sits in his parents' apartment, writing his dissertation about such words as "shattered," Daniel wonders if such an epithet would apply more fully to his father or his grandfather. After all, his father was just a child when he was hauled out of China during war and bombing, losing everything, the privileges and opportunities of a wealthy, cultured family, only to refashion himself, as he grew up, after the fascist "lieutenant" of his imaginings, who became his role model. Or perhaps the adjective would apply more succinctly to his grandfather, the Kuomintang leader, who led his son out to safety then reestablished the family in Taiwan, braving the malaria-filled winds of early Taipei and the continuous threat of attack from China. Such a great man could surely only be "shattered" by death and an era ended. But now their whole world is collapsing, even their memories. Daniel has a deadline, too, with his dissertation. If he can complete it at the end of the month, he will enter a new job at a university here, in Taiwan, arranged for him by his father, the university don. With a wife and a new baby, he just can't let the pressure get to him. What if he lost it, like he did in China? He tries not to remember China, but he does. It is like a cage that still surrounds him. Does he ever think about his dreams of New York, of the spontaneous writer, living free, free from all the hatred and anger left over after his family lost everything in China, so extreme that it came burning out of him when he faced the Chinese who had let it happen? No, he does not. He just doesn't imagine that the one who is "shattered" is not his father or his ancestors or some character in a Greek tragedy. The one who is shattered is he himself.

And I—ah burning heart!—shall soon lie low as well.

Their parents' shame about losing the mainland and then losing their preeminence in Taiwan has rolled like a river down a slope, filling the veins of the second generation. The younger son of police chief Ko Jen-tao, who once served time in a military prison on Kinmen, is now a middle-aged father with a bank of crumbling teeth in his lower jaw. Usually unshaven in the dirty flat bought for him by his father, except when he makes unsuccessful runs as a salesman to the south of the island, Ko Chen-tsang knows that what he feels must be shame, and he just can't seem to let himself, or his family, off the hook for it. He can't help himself from hitting his youngest daughter, a ten-year-old girl who taps a balloon into the air and then dances under it. It is the same shame that causes him to have an opinion about different ethnic groups or of killing the Taiwanese president. It seems like the same shame that the noodle-shop owner, Chou, feels when he calls the Taiwanese slaves with no history they can call their own. You could call it the curse of the second generation, who have witnessed the helpless shame and fury of their parents and been helpless to save them. Ko Chen-tsang tries to get away from his shame by going back to where his life started, the gorge in eastern Taiwan where he met his wife.

One time, I walked in the door after coming home from work and I saw my daughter lying on the couch. Her hair was filthy. Her toys and pillows were everywhere. I was really tired. I got really angry. I thought to myself, she has been home all day while I have been out working. I knew that my father used to say the same thing to me, and he would talk about all he had gone through in his life. I knew this and I didn't want to be like him, but I couldn't help it.

I started telling my daughter calmly to get up and clean up the living room. She just lay there. I told her again to get up. She just ignored me and what really made me mad was that she refused to look at me. She had her back turned to me and was staring at the wall. I got so mad I walked over to her and hit her, on the side of her face. She turned around and her hair fell back and I saw that she had been listening to her headphones and hadn't heard me at all. I could see how surprised she was. She didn't even cry. She didn't say anything or make any noise but the tears started to fall down her cheeks.

I did what I normally do. I jumped in my car and just took off. I let the car go where it wanted to. I put on the radio and tried not to think about my life. This time the car took me to the new highway, the one between Taipei and Hualien, on the east coast. I just kept going. I got to Hualien about ten, then I drove up to Taroko Gorge. I couldn't see anything. The walls of the gorge are about a thousand feet high. You can't see the moon or any stars. It was completely dark. So I was driving up in the pitch dark. And then it hit me. I was going back to the place where I had met her mother.

The car stopped when I was still several miles from Tianhsiang. Tianhsiang is at the top of the gorge. It's an old aborigine settlement. I was so out of it, I had forgotten to check the gas gauge. I got out of the car and started walking. It was still warm and the air was really humid. I was in the middle of a jungle. I could hear a river down below on the rocks about a hundred feet below. There were tunnels along the road, kind of like caves, that were cut into the rock walls for cars to get through. I was coming up to one of these tunnels. Each of these tunnels was about a half mile long. I was coming up on one. I could barely see it. But there was some kind of trick of light or something. It looked like there were shards of broken glass hanging from just inside the opening of the tunnel. It looked like the entrance to the tunnel had a sheet of glass over it that had been shattered but all the shards were still hanging there.

> When I got inside the tunnel, I couldn't see anything. I thought to myself that I had come this far, I had to keep going.

When dawn came, he was still walking. He had walked all night. The way he tells it, when the dawn came he felt he had accomplished something. All night long he was nearly collapsing with fear. He says he could just barely make out the straight reflective lines down the middle of the road. He was feeling mostly with his feet by that time, it was so dark. He could feel the jungle around him. The air was wet and clammy. Spidery trees seemed to be hanging over the road, but he couldn't tell if it was just his eyes playing tricks on him. He could hear way off the sound of a river feeling its way over a bed of rocks. When a car came by, he stepped over to the side of the road and let it pass. After the sun came up, he started to believe in himself again. He had been in some dark places but had never been so scared. But he had lived through it. Then he realized that he had come back to the place where he had met his wife—the valley of shadows where her tribe of aborigines lived. This was the place his own parents had tried to stop him from going. They had tried to prevent him from marrying his wife, the aborigine. It was the place where his children's lives originated. He just turned around and walked back down the road until he reached his car.

> I let the car roll down the road until I got near to Hualien. Fortunately, there was somebody passing who gave me a ride to a gas station. What did I learn from my trip? I learned that I was cursed. It was like the glass or the light or whatever it was—I was broken, shattered. I decide to go home and apologize to my daughter. But I also realized that it wasn't entirely my fault. It was the fault of those fucking DPP. They are the ones who are destroying Taiwan.

Both of the Ko children undertook journeys, perhaps in some way reminiscent of the journey undertaken by their father when he left Nanjing at the age of ten in a naval cutter for Taiwan. The first generation had started the journey, trying to get away from their enemies, and landed in Taiwan. The second generation kept up the traveling, but in their case the journeys were shorter, repetitive and perhaps more psychological than physical. The journeys undertaken by the second generation might be seen as continuations of those undertaken by the first—the flight from danger never subsided.

Table 6
Necessary journeys

First generation	Second generation
Ko Jen-tao crossed Taiwan Strait at age 10, traveled to south of island, enrolled in naval academy, patrolled China coastal waters, toured around Taipei City as a police officer, returned home at age 55.	Daughter Ko Yuan steeled herself for years to run away from family—finally left. Son Ko Chen-tsang went to east coast to marry aboriginal bride against parents' wishes, later beat daughter and returned to east coast to expiate himself.
Hu Yao-hen traveled with mother from inner China, evading Japanese soldiers, spent time in Wuhan and Chongqing with father, taken to Hong Kong refugee camp by father, eventually came to Taiwan.	Son Daniel Hu malingered at Reed College, came back to Taiwan, worked in China for six months where he found release in excoriating workers, returned to US for PhD, then to Taiwan to write.
Lin Ching-wu traveled from his native Fujian up to the far north of China, fighting repeatedly, was wounded and then spent time in an army hospital camp near Shanghai. Still not yet recovered, he escaped to Hainan Island and eventually Taiwan where he traveled to the middle of the island and married.	Son Lin Tzu-chiang traveled in racing car around an illegal track repeatedly. During one race, a friend crashed and was killed.

Something just seems to be bothering the son of Lin Ching-wu. Maybe it's his father's optimism, his belief that if he just keeps on going, takes care of himself, that somehow he will come to a land of safety and plenty. Unlike his son, the old man rises early, eats breakfast, lunch and dinner at early hours, and keeps in shape by playing basketball with his friends. The son believes that he leads a life of sloth or indolence. Perhaps this is what makes him so angry. He keeps his own schedule, rising later, eating later, so that when he does visit his father's apartment, he never has a chance to eat or talk with his father. As a child, he never heard his father's war stories and never wondered about them until his father had them printed out and bound in a book. It's almost as if the son can't stand to see or hear his father confident in the knowledge he has lived through something that the son will never know or understand. This creates a distance between them that the son is incapable of handling, can't accept. It's almost as if his father already died in the war and he now has to listen to the gibbering ghost of him that, by virtue of his death, will never really know him or accept him. Still, the son seems happy enough to live far away in a newly-purchased apartment with his wife. His face is clad in thick deposits of flesh like he's been hit repeatedly and the skin has sealed over pockets of pus that have grown hard over the years. He doesn't smile. When he speaks, his eyes turn down as if he's looking for something in his lower eyelids. He is a large man, at least twice the size of his father, fat and muscle twisted together. He sneers at his father who still plays basketball at eighty-five. The son prides himself on the fact that he once raced cars in Taiwan, that it was illegal and that occasionally someone was killed in a crash. He triumphs, it seems, not only in defying his father and breaking the law, but in putting himself in the kind of life and death struggle that his father once faced. It is the only way to escape his father's curse, to beat it. His father lives half his life in memories, in a heroic landscape of battles and great deeds and forgotten men. Yet the son faces death in the present, here and now—by nearly killing himself at racing. And if he dies, his father won't have a descendant. Although he has stopped racing, he still talks about it as if he were still doing it, as if he was always to be found, in imagination if not in reality, behind the wheel of a car, finding the road to possible victory or defeat.

> The road is not my enemy. I have to think of it as my friend. I see it as a long runway, like for an airplane. When I begin to rev my engine, I feel free. I have a feeling of absolute freedom. Then, when the race starts, I'm only aware of the motion of my car. I don't think of anything. I don't think of my father. I don't think of my past. I don't think of the farms passing by. Sometimes I look out my side window for a second and I can see farmers working in the fields. The farmers, the locals, they don't report us. They don't care about law. Before we mainlanders came to Taiwan, there weren't any laws. Not really. When we race there aren't any laws either. It's like we're returning to the past. The police don't bother us either. They're locals, too. They let us do what we want.
>
> Sometimes we don't even race on the track. You have to know the countryside. I don't know it quite as well as some of the local guys. But I'm learning. Sometimes, we race on the freeway at about three or four in the morning. I drive a Saab. It actually belongs to my father but he doesn't use it much. Its top speed is about 130 miles an hour. But it's not the speed that really matters. It's all about taking risks. I take more risks than anyone. After

a race, someone always asks me the same question, "Are you trying to kill yourself?" Once I said to him, "I'm already dead." He said, "What do you mean?" He thought I was joking or that I meant I was going to die sooner or later on the road. But what I didn't say was that I felt I had already died, at the moment my father arrived in Taiwan, before I was even born. That was when my existence really began as a ghost.

Then a friend of mine did die. He got into a crash. It happened right in front of me. I stopped my car and got out just in time to see him fall out of his car onto the road. He died on the way to the hospital. His girlfriend was waiting for us there. I tried to help her calm down. A few weeks later, we started dating. Now she is my wife. So you could say that out of someone else's death, I found life, if you can call it that. My wife made me stop racing. That's how I put on all this weight.

These days he works as a television engineer. His mother signed him up for a course which taught him the basics. So now he has enough income to buy high-end audio equipment, which he describes as his new passion. Visiting his father's apartment, he goes up briefly to the roof to see his father then breaks off to talk to a neighbor on another rooftop. His father is painting calligraphy amid trophies from basketball games. A childhood portrait, taken with his sister, shows him at that time to be a slim and nervous child with the frown of a nascent mustache. For most of his childhood, his father was a leading military adviser to the Taiwan Normal University, which accounted for their apartment and a high standard of living. But around the time he went to college, all that ended. His father was retired, the Kuomintang lost their preeminent position, and mainlanders like his father became clowns laughed at on television rather than feared military paragons. His exit from racing took place around the same time his father and his cronies lost their political position. The son became fat, lost his wandering air, and began to frown and steel his countenance against the outside world. Perhaps the transition—from ruling party to noncombatants to outcasts—was hardest on the second generation, after all.

Social change: Taiwanese versus the rest

It was eight years only. From 2000 to 2008, when the DPP governed Taiwan from the presidential office. But a whole new range of social changes started from that time. At every level of culture, society, and education, those who claimed to represent the native Taiwanese culture, rather than the mainlander dream of reunifying China, hunted down and challenged mainland refugee culture that had shaped Taiwan for fifty years.[5] A crusade-like atmosphere rose up that infiltrated the media, teachers, and politicians, that made them toe the line, take their cues from the top, protest, and put down mainland Chinese culture.[6] Leading Taiwanese media outlets to begin to sweepingly cast mainland refugees into the same corner with the Chinese Communists and brand both of them guilty of crimes committed against Taiwanese in the distant past. According to this point of view, mainland Chinese refugees ought to have been considered as not only in the same camp, but actually brothers with the Chinese Communists. And, by the same token, both were subtly but equally guilty of any and all crimes committed against the Taiwanese people in the past. A leading website popular among supporters of the Democratic Progressive Party, entitled, *Social Force*, ran a large cartoon in a prominent position featuring a leading mainland Chinese refugee who had lived in Taiwan his whole life embracing the president of China. The slogan—"closer than brothers." Political crimes dating back half a century, including the 2–28 Incident, were tallied up against them. The message was that the mainland refugees, including those who fled to Taiwan from China directly and their children were loyal to the Chinese Communists, who wanted to take over Taiwan. The funny thing was that these aspersions were not without some truth. But the DPP supporters never caught on to the real truth. Mainland settlers, and their children, were indeed coming to appreciate the power of the Chinese Communists, but not for their ability to take over Taiwan, rather for their ability to reinvent themselves from chaos, to rise up rich and strong in the face of a hostile world.

But the DPP just didn't get that side of it. They set about attacking the mainlanders in even more scathing ways. They aired a short "documentary" among the Taiwanese elite, including local Taiwanese doctors at Taiwan's premier hospitals. The documentary pieced together film clips taken from the Kuomintang's bloody reign in Shanghai seventy years earlier, including footage of military police officers shooting political prisoners in the head. Most of the footage was spurious. A scene of Taiwanese wearing temple costumes and carrying images of a bodhisattva was purported to be a shot of locals getting ready to welcome Kuomintang soldiers as they arrived from the mainland in 1949. But the footage was too new. And no Taiwanese ever wore temple-religious regalia to meet the incoming ships of defeated soldiers in 1949.[7] Nevertheless, the makers of the documentary wove all of this together and described the bloodshed perpetrated by the Kuomintang soldiers in 1949. There were differences from past attempts to make use of the 2–28 Incident. This time the blame was cast not only upon older mainlanders, but upon their children as well. Middle-aged men like Ko Chen-tsang, who lived all their lives in Taipei and knew little more about the incident than what they learned in school, were held responsible, made scapegoats in the documentary. Taiwanese doctors, especially those working at National Taiwan University Hospital, are held in special esteem among locals since it was only the best and the brightest who could work their way through the establishment and become doctors in former years.

The society had changed faster than its politics. Just ten years ago, the media was still dominated by mainland refugees' images. One had to speak like a mainland settler in order to broadcast the news. One had to look like a northern Chinese man or woman in order to appear credible and vested with authority on television. But with the increasing dominance of the local party in politics, Taiwanese business interests began to cater more exclusively to local tastes. The models that market merchandise and news to the Taiwanese public are increasingly native Taiwanese. Broad, flat noses have replaced the peaked, ridged noses of the mainlanders. Slurred, muddy Mandarin pronunciation—the hallmark of local women on television—have replaced the crisp, ear-splitting, high-pitched twang of women with mainland pedigrees. The entire iconography of society has been turned upside down. Broad billboards hanging from the sides of movie theaters in the new eastern part of Taipei show faces that are distinctively local: the high cheekbones of the Taiwanese countryside, the wide nostrils, the distinctively softened, southern, Taiwanese look. Just a decade ago, similar billboards in the center of town, which was then the most exclusive shopping district, and closer to the Kuomintang institutions of power, showed faces that might have been seen on women in northern mainland China: thin, upturned noses, narrow cheeks and chins. For those who thought they could tell the difference, these were the faces of the mainland settlers, the faces of mostly northern or western China.

All this seemed to indicate that the dreams of the local Taiwanese were coming true. For decades, native Taiwanese politicians had been promising a sort of liberation for the Taiwanese. One major leader proclaimed that he was a Moses to the Taiwanese people. That he would lead them out of sadness and darkness. Now it seemed the promise was coming true. The background to the promise was the belief that the Taiwanese had been oppressed for centuries, first by the Dutch, then the Manchus, then the Japanese and then the mainland settlers. It was a vision of promise, of liberation, a teleology that ended with the Taiwanese creating their own promised land.[8] Some leaders of the movement, which they called "Taiwanese consciousness," believed that it was essential that Japan play a role in Taiwan's development. Overall, the theology centered on the plight of the Taiwanese and their need to gain freedom.

Mainland settlers never had that kind of teleology. The first generation did once, when they believed that Chiang Kai-shek might actually lead them to recover the mainland. After that, they had only the belief that theirs was the superior culture. The second generation, their children, didn't have anything to believe in at all. The second generation never went on the long journey out of China to shape them as wounded, retreating victims. They didn't have any justification for them to play any role whatsoever in Taiwan. Now their parents had been exposed as butchers or fools. Thus was born the tremendous shame felt by the second generation and, in some, a yearning to simply leave the island, the sight of their debacle.

There are of course exceptions.

Chou, the noodle-shop owner who fought with the Taiwanese as a child, now hopes to someday do business on the mainland. He still sits at the small table outside his shop in the heat, where his mainlander friends also sit, smoking, drinking tea and spitting. Then a downpour of rain falls swift and dense as wet laundry caught in the wind hurled from the line. A mist rises up from the street. They strike Chou, needling into his grey face and hands. "You can't make big money selling beef noodle soup," he says. "You have to go to China for that."

On the other hand, some just want to put down roots in Taiwan. Chou, the plump, boy-faced psychiatrist who lost his father to a local truck driver, built an ancestral temple near Taipei. It was his way of claiming space for himself, of putting down roots.

> After my father died, I didn't know what to do with his ashes. I couldn't decide if I should send them back to his home village in China, or find a way to keep them here. We really don't have any roots in China anymore.

> We don't even know where our ancestral tablet is. The Red Guards probably smashed it during the Cultural Revolution. But do I really think that our roots are in Taiwan? With all the recent political changes, and the division between mainlanders and locals getting worse again, I just didn't know what to do. It was my wife that persuaded me to build a new ancestral hall here. We decided that we would inter each of our family members' ashes in a box and place it there.

By this point, mainland settlers and their children are so paranoid that it's sometimes hard for them to distinguish between their own fears and reality. The fact is, the native Taiwanese government neglected to protect ancestral temples built by mainlander families for their dead. The way Chou figures it, either there was an insidious purpose behind the government's neglect of mainlander concerns, or it was simply that too many mainland families had resorted to this last-ditch effort to lay claim to a piece of land, by hastily building a small stone temple for their ancestors. Suddenly, it seemed to Chou that, no matter what the case was, mainlander families could no longer lay claim to an enduring parcel of land in Taiwan, much less in China.

Most mainlanders like to criticize the native government, but Chou does so by talking about the one thing that is the most sacred of all to mainlanders and native Taiwanese alike: burial of the dead.

> We bought a plot of land in Miaoli. We put my father's ashes and my mother's ashes there. But the government kept expanding the farmland in that area. Originally, our temples were in a large plot of open space with trees and fields. But the government bought all the land around the temple and is starting to sell it off to private developers. There is new construction going up right next to our temple. What disturbs me is that we offered to buy that land first. But the government said it wasn't for sale. They said it could only be used for farmland. But now they're building roads and shopping malls right next to our plot of land. Maybe it's an accident. But sometimes I wonder if they wouldn't have shown more respect if it were locals. Who knows? All I can say is that the old government would have had respect for the dead.

The second generation grew up squeezed into dormitories and military villages, surrounded by hostility and danger. Now their dead were facing the same fate: squeezed into mausoleums that the local government not only failed to protect but allowed developers to surround with acres of housing developments and parking lots. It's hard to know if Chou's fears are a reaction to a program by the DPP to eliminate mainlanders' burial plots or if they just come out of his own past. He isn't quite sure himself.

The grandchildren: Two sketches in memory

Mini's eyes

Mini Hu has had several operations on her eyes. She is a short, attractive mainlander of the third generation who always seems to be on the verge of hamming things up. When she comes out of a telemarketing company where she works, into the hallway, she looks like she is poised either to tell a joke or to cry, depending on what is said to her. Her mouth is large and wide and looks like it is ready to shovel out some gossip or episode from her day. But her eyes, in dollar terms, are the most valuable part of her face. So it's funny they look so delicate, like the edges of them are fringed with glass, or like someone had pinned two grasshopper wings over the place where her eyes ought to be. In a common operation among mainlanders—especially among the third generation, or the grandchildren of the first generation—her eyes have been altered several times, first under her mother's direction and second, by herself but influenced by her mother's need for her daughter to conform to the changing standards of beauty. The third generation of mainlanders is caught in a struggle between the influence of their grandparents' legacy and their parents' attempts to cope with that legacy. The third generation has one major resource that helps them figure out who they are: they are willing to listen to their grandparents' storytelling. Stories of their grandparents' flight from China, the hardships suffered during wartime and the rebuilding of Taiwan, as well as an awareness of lost honors and glories of their ancestors, fills the minds of this generation, giving them some sense of where they came from. And for those who were unable to hear their grandparents' stories, life in Taiwan is fraught with confusion and vague, heedless attempts to conform, to fit into the revolutionary program of the nativist political party, which seeks to trample on the legacy of the mainlanders.

Mini is one of those who did hear her grandparents' stories. At twenty-two, she knew, for instance, that her family came from an esteemed line of officials stretching back into the Qing dynasty. By the time of the Nanjing Republic, her grandfather was a banker, carrying on a lineage of distinguished merchants and officials. Thus the stories took on an even more thrilling sense of alarm. They fled not only for their lives, they also lost their heritage. The vagueness of some parts of the story adds a veneer of epic grandeur to her family's past, and its flight, by contrast, is seen as all the more ignominious.

> It's hard to imagine. During the time of the republican government, my grandfather was a banker. So when the government escaped from the mainland, he could get his family on a boat. But it was a really tiny boat, and it was packed with people. My grandfather was able to bring his wife and his children along. My father's older sister was only two at the time and my father was only one. When they got out of sight of land, they ran into a storm. The waves started filling up the boat, and everyone wanted to turn around and head back for shore. So the captain decided to turn back. But when they got back close to shore, they heard the sound of the Communists' gunfire. So they had to choose what to do. Other boats were turning back because of the storm. But they decided that at least they had a chance if they tried to cross the ocean. So the captain turned the boat around again. That's why I'm here.
>
> My grandfather never hurt anyone. He wasn't a landlord. He didn't exploit anyone. He was a banker. His crime was that he helped the country manage its finances. He was just a government official. He was never a landlord.
>
> I heard that our family helped manage the salt monopoly during the Qing dynasty. We sold salt for the government. That was in Zhejiang. That's where we're from. I heard we earned a lot of money and had a big family there. But by the end of the Qing dynasty, the family had separated, split up. But I heard there's still an ancestral tablet of our family somewhere on the mainland.

As Mini sees it, the contrast between the salt monopoly run by her family and the "tiny boat" in which they escaped is like the difference between what life must have been like then and what life is like now. It is a contrast between past wealth and present ruin, between past security and present danger, between life and death. But the family line stayed alive. Only its past was gone. The salt monopoly was one of the major sources of revenue for the dying dynasty, and association with it brought great prestige and importance. Her family had proof of its right to greatness—in their memories. Her grandfather came over, bringing his family, driven not only by his proven worth—as banker for the past regime—but by his memories as well, which he then passed down to his children and grandchildren. Mini, his granddaughter, about five-feet-two, with her hair bobbed, round, puffy cheeks and roving eyes, is loud and cheerful as she recounts this part of her history. She has a strong sense of her history. She knows where her family is from. She even traces it to the crucial salt monopoly during the late Qing.

Her mother didn't have the same memories, or at least they didn't mean the same thing to her. They hadn't been passed down to her by a grandfather. Instead, she had felt the full emotional force of the treachery, escape, flight, and horror experienced by her father. They were not stories to laugh at, to help her find herself. They were a whirlwind that dislocated her, filled her with terror. To her, Mini imagined, they merely meant that she had been deprived of her rightful place in a society that would never happen again. Her mother panicked. The locals, who were now ascending to power like a rising star, already made up eighty-five percent of the population. She felt like a woman crowded by enemy forces to the edge of a cliff. Her daughter needed to marry as soon as possible.

Mini never talked with her mother a great deal, and she came to understand that her mother felt a certain amount of disgust and disappointment at herself and her people, for letting the locals take over. Quickly, as soon as possible, she wanted to raise her daughter up out of the disgust and degradation her people had fallen into, like bringing up a dead cat out of a sunken field, out of the mud and into the sunlight, hoping that Mini could marry someone of her kind. It was not uncommon for women from the mainland to undergo an operation, quite simple really, that cut the eyelid then sewed it back together into a desired form. Mini had a crease in her eyelids, a sign of beauty warped, of defect and imperfection. Her mother, frantic, as if she only had so much time to sell her daughter off, as if being a mainlander was no longer a privilege but a defect, she ordered an operation to alter her daughter's eyes, at first not even sure what she wanted the outcome to be.

> My mother would stare at me and shake her head. She said that my eyes were too big. Later she said my eyes were too small. Another time she said that my eyes were crooked. My eyelids did have a fold in them and the upper part was thicker. So it looked like the upper part was a little swollen. I started to believe her. I would stand in front of a mirror and open my eyes as wide as I could and stare at myself. My mother said it always looked like

I hadn't gotten enough sleep. One time, she showed me a picture of her mother, taken in Shanghai. I didn't see any difference between her eyes and mine.

My mother arranged for a doctor in Taipei to do it. Then she changed her mind and had me come to Taichung because it was closer to home and she could take care of me after the operation. When the operation first started, it hurt so much I asked the doctor if we could stop, but my mother, who was standing by the side of the operating table, told me I had to endure it. She said we had gone through enough already and she wanted me to have a better life than she did. I couldn't really concentrate on what she said because there wasn't enough anesthetic and it really hurt. But I didn't cry. My mother did, though.

Now the memories, the stories of her grandfather, became a sort of playbook, a guide for her action. She found a way to leave her home, travel to the United States and study at the University of Washington. She still kept in touch with her mother, every day, by telephone, sometimes crying, sometimes pleading. She believed that by fleeing her home, she could achieve some kind of peace. But she had brought with her some of the frantic nature of her mother and, even though she was now on her own, in a new country, she was the one now who decided to continue altering her eyes. She believed that unless she had laser surgery to fix her vision, she would never have the slightest chance of finding her husband. Her eyes were the key. If she could fix them, get rid of her glasses and show them off, let people see what her mother had done, the single fold of smooth seamless flesh like a baby's bottom or the side of a breast, then and only then would she have a chance to get married. She felt, with a sort of mute superstition, that nothing short of altering her eyes could help her. Contacts weren't enough.

I'm fine. I knew it was risky but it was the right thing to do. I predict that I will get married within two years. I don't know why, but I have not the least doubt about that. That was why I decided to have my eyes fixed, again. Only this time it was for my vision. I started wearing glasses in primary school. Now I'm twenty-four. I think my mother had the right idea that you have to endure some things to get what you want.

My vision is perfectly clear now. The first thing I saw when I opened my eyes after the operation was light, just pure unfocused light. The doctor said the surgery was successful. Things still looked blurry. And my eyes hurt a lot. So when I got home I started to cry. I cried for four hours straight. After a while, I had to turn off all the lights. But now I can see everything clearly. I almost feel like my eyes are finally perfect. I could even say that at last I have eyes that are even better than my Shanghai grandmother's.

She takes up swimming at the university. It is not as if she has decided to isolate herself by taking up the one sport that most separates her from others not only by the fact that it is undertaken entirely alone, like jogging in a park before dawn, but by the fact that it surrounds her with a medium that can suffocate her in a matter of seconds if she is careless.

The pool is deep and cold. As she swims, tears flow out of her eyes. At first she cannot explain it. She cries as she swims the breaststroke, her only stroke. It is not the lack of sun, nor the artificial shade in the pool. She looks at the colors wheeling in the corners of her eyes as she comes up for breath. She does not think she is going blind. But she does reflect on her desire to mingle her identity with a man, with others, something which her parents makes difficult. In a way, she has to fight the struggle her parents were unable to. She has to learn to cry, she says.

> When I go swimming, I swim for at least an hour. I always swim the breaststroke. I can swim the breaststroke for a long time. Sometimes I can't even remember how long I've been swimming. I like to swim for two reasons. The first is that the water makes a special kind of sound as you swim. It's like the sound of oars in a rowboat. The second reason is because I can cry. I actually cry a lot when I swim. I guess I believe that when I cry in the water that no one can hear me or see me. I can't even hear myself. It's like it's not really happening. It's almost like I can say to myself, your eyes are wet because of the water and not because of your tears. It's like I can finally cry and it's not just me who's crying but my mother and father, too. So I like to swim.

In the suspended isolation of the frigid water of the pool, she reflects on herself. Her reflections often turn to the hardship of being a third-generation mainland immigrant. Three thousand miles from Taiwan, where her parents were raging against the heaped-up indignities faced by their group, she thinks silently and solemnly as she swims. She comes to conclusions—revelations—from hours of swimming silently in the campus pool.

> When I swim, I have time to think. And I have come up with certain conclusions.
> I feel that to be a part of the third generation is to be caught in a trap. I remember the year that Chen Shui-bian was elected, and then because of the election, ethnicity was made a huge issue.

> And I remember the people from his party, the DPP, said, "Mainland pigs go back to the mainland." They brought that slogan back from the past. I was a college student at the time. But I felt that I was also a Taiwanese. I was born in Taiwan, even if my parents were from the mainland. Maybe it was because of the election. But I've actually always felt that I'm a stranger, from someplace else. And so they attacked us.

Her mother refused to cry. Even if she had once known how, she had lost the ability somewhere in the shame and terror of her past. It was considered a weakness to show emotion, as if someone from the outside might see it and take it as a weakness to be used against you. Her parents, she said, also refused to take any action. They lived in a small dark room that was not so much pleasant but frigid with their idea of safety and survival. And to venture out of it was too dangerous to consider. Mini recalls the one time she wanted to take action, to join a protest of mainlanders against the locals' denunciations of them. Her father put a stop to it immediately.

> There was one time when a lot of mainlanders went over to the Chiang Kai-shek Memorial to have a protest. They were holding signs and sitting on the ground. And some were singing songs. I really wanted to go. But my father said, "If you go over there and take part in that farce, you'll shame your whole family. Not only that, but you'll put us in jeopardy. Don't you know that, as a mainlander, they'll be monitoring you, all the time? The media will check out your background." That was my father's shame talking. Even though I thought what they were doing was right, I wasn't allowed to get near them.

So she took refuge in expressing some of her ideas in words and posted the message in the campus chat room.

> I sat down in my room and I wanted to cry but I couldn't. So I got out a piece of paper and a pencil and wrote down everything I would have said at the rally. I wrote about my parents and my grandparents. Mostly, I just wrote about myself. I ended the article by saying, the only difference between me and other students was that I couldn't speak Taiwanese. That's all. Does that mean I can't be Taiwanese?

The article went beyond the self-pity of the second generation—the old theme that mainland immigrants are stranded, without a home, having lost their first one on the mainland, then their second one in Taiwan. Like her parents' generation, she invoked the rise of China as proof of her self-worth, as if the enemies who had once taken the land away from her ancestors' were now her only refuge. Later, however, after her first trip to Shanghai, she updated her article with a new, more realistic appraisal. She had now gone beyond the blind, romantic yearning of her parents' generation for a new model, a new way to be Chinese, a new chance to be part of a greater Chinese sphere of influence determine by economic might rather than war. But something of her grandfather's longing for a home grew until it was bigger than anything else.

> For a long time I had really, really wanted to visit China. But after I went to Shanghai, for the first time I realized that there was no way this place could be my country. There are too many differences and the differences are too great. It's not just the road signs or whatever, the differences are too great. I thought that maybe a long time ago Taiwan might have been like this, but it sure isn't like this anymore. In China, no one stands in line. So I added all this to my article.
>
> I wrote that I had realized it's not my country, in any way. If I were to go there again, I know I could never relax or fit in. I could never live on the mainland. But in Taiwan, the Taiwanese will always feel I am an outsider. So whenever people start to speak Taiwanese, that's how I feel—that I'm an outsider. I feel like I should study Taiwanese, but no matter how good I get, my accent would always be a mainlander's. There's no way in.

Her grandfather had been in perilous circumstances, an outsider. But he had prevailed, for a time at least. Mini had his stories to rely on. They were guides and they hinted at undreamed-of possibilities, of courage and bravery of the unwillingness to admit defeat. Children who have heard their grandparents' stories of hardship and ultimate survival can be more resilient than other children. During a particularly traumatic situation at high school, in which Mini was rudely deposed from a leadership position on the student council, she showed a willingness to seek help rather than fester in her rage—as members of her parents' generation might have done. Was this because she heard stories from her grandfather and had a sense of her past identity, an heir to officials in the Qing dynasty? Was it because she had more confidence, perhaps even a sense of entitlement as a result? Mini's experience of banishment and finally rehabilitation stirred up feelings related to her family's banishment from the mainland: a sense of betrayal. Perhaps this was why it triggered such a strong response in her.

I had a lot of bad luck in high school. I was head of the student council. But I ended up being attacked. It was almost like during the Cultural Revolution where students struggled against people in authority. I was in charge of putting on activities. And then all this stuff happened. And so I said to myself, if they don't want me, I'll just step down. I wasn't feeling too well at the time, anyway. They wanted to get someone else to serve in my place and I just didn't have the energy to fight it. So I gave them face. I said I was stepping down. But no one said anything.

It was during my sophomore year. We always held our meetings on the ground floor of the dormitory. One day I showed up and waited and waited and no one else showed up. I just sat there by myself for about an hour. I had been planning to talk about holding a dance.

The next day I came down and they were all sitting there. The atmosphere was really strange. I always used to say hello to them one by one so I started to do that. There were about ten of them there. But once the meeting started, they all started to criticize me at once and talk about all the things I had done wrong and say that I couldn't do anything right. They passed a motion saying they didn't want me to stay in that position anymore. They got someone else to take over my position. Wow. It was a shock.

I don't like to fight with people. I like to remain calm. So after all this happened, I just went directly to class. I remember it was geography class. I sat in the front seat all the way to the left. The teacher was a young man. My tears kept falling down my face. And I remember that the teacher came over and stood in front of me and whispered, "Do you want to go to the restroom?" But I said no, I didn't want to. I wanted to endure it.

So she kept on sitting there. But she made a decision. She decided that maybe some kind of counseling would be best for her. It was a fairly radical idea at the time. Especially for a schoolgirl. After class, she went to the principal's office and asked for help. There was the mother of one of her classmates who was working in the office as a volunteer counselor. Mini saw her for six months. She was going to a Catholic school but religion never caught on to her. But then, after the crisis, she started going to a local church. Then, when she went overseas, to the University of Washington, she started going to church again, only this time it was evangelical Christianity. She discovered a whole new type of mainlander community in Seattle. The community had accepted, and practiced, the forms and doctrines of Christianity. But they turned them into part of the dream they had lost about retaking the mainland.

The church was in Shoreline, a northern suburb of Seattle. It was fringed with dying elms, suffocating in the pollution of the major freeway that runs nearby. It was attended exclusively by mainland immigrants who had settled in Seattle after spending most of their lives in Taiwan. The church was a great barn-like structure with a high roof that could hold hundreds of congregants, the preacher speaking in Chinese, slowly, almost like a chant, almost as if he was half asleep and yawning to stay awake. The message, though, was not always about Jesus. More often than not, the preacher talked about evangelizing China. After her first service, Mini met a nineteen-year-old college student, the daughter of mainland immigrants, whose black steady eyes fastened onto her face like two beads. She told her about harrowing adventures in the interior of China, talking to converts and distributing Bibles. This was something new. It was almost as if her grandfather's dream of retaking the mainland was still alive among this mainlander Christian community with its quixotic attempts to convert a population of billions. This was something she could do. She felt something new and warm, as if she had been looking for this her whole life, as she listened to reports of these conversion attempts. The ministers seemed to have the kind of confidence she never could seem to find. She had a new vantage point from which to evaluate her homeland and the struggles raging there: Christianity. The very openness of the preachers was in stark contrast to the bitter rhetoric and invective on the nightly news in Taiwan.

> I've heard so many people preach the gospel in Taiwan. But I always found that I could never entirely agree with the minister. But when I went to Seattle, the minister responded directly to questions asked by the congregation, and I remember thinking, is this possible? The service is bilingual. Every Sunday morning, there's a time you can ask questions. I asked a *lot* of questions. There were questions I had always wanted to ask. For example: Why does someone have to be baptized? Why? Why do I have to pray? What if I forget to pray? I just asked a lot of strange questions. My questions were always about, what was the reason for doing things?
>
> His response was cool. It made me think I should get baptized. I ended up getting baptized two months later. I guess I was kind of in a hurry. I started to go in September, and after one and a half or two months, I was baptized. And I kept going.

She had found a new home in the church. In it, the dream of retaking China was still alive. She had found a temporary solution to the void faced by her people.

Aborigines

She is only thirteen, but she looks eighteen. It is the way her mouth looks. Her mouth is almost scarlet, like a splash of blood. When she was four and seven and even ten, her mouth was twisted into a smirk. Now it looks like someone has just hit her and the mouth alone betrays the bitterness and anger she feels. In fact, someone has. The mouth should have belonged to a little girl, but the knowledge it contains has already outrun the rest of her body. As she grew older, it retained the smirk even as her father began to hit her in earnest. Eventually, the hurt, the surprise moves to her eyes which are now frozen in a sort of glassy stare as if she is daring her father to hit her again. A cousin says, "Meishu better hurry up and get married, or something bad is going to happen." But the girl protects herself. She works outside home in a fast food restaurant giving her enough extra money for some independence. The oldest daughter of Ko Jen-tao's son, Ko Chen-tsang, no longer even flinches when her father slaps her.

Every Sunday she takes the train down to Hualien, the area where her mother was born, and attends classes in the aboriginal language of that region. The train passes through the jungle at the foot of green mountains that overlook the ocean. The train shuffles over its track, like an old man wheezing without stop. Strips of light come through the palmettos and the longyans and the great clumps of giant ferns bending over the tracks. When she arrives in Hualien, the home of most of the aborigines in Taiwan, she takes a taxi to her grandfather's house. The man is not really her grandfather, though. He is the stepfather of her mother, a sort of step-grandfather. She does not know that, for most of her childhood, he repeatedly abused her mother, the aborigine woman who married her father. She could not know this because her mother never told her.

As she enters the house, the grey steps leading down from the second and third floors seem to slide towards her like toilet water overflowing the rim. She greets her step-grandfather with a chipper exchange. His eyes rest on her mouth, her breasts. When she sleeps, in an upper bedroom, alone, she does not worry that he may come in the night. Her mother has not told her; her mother allows her to stay with him.

It is all for the sake of teaching Meishu about her heritage as an aborigine. Being an aborigine has become quite popular since the DPP won their first presidential election. The DPP wanted to make the aborigines into heroes, symbols of the suffering of Taiwan. During the inauguration ceremony of Chen Shui-bian, the first opposition-party president, the DPP arranged for an aboriginal pop star to sing the national anthem. It didn't matter that she was later banned from China, her and her music, almost ending her career. The DPP wanted to show that even the worst-off could rise again. The aborigines of Taiwan, who are members of the Malayo-Polynesian group of peoples, also known as the Austronesians, once were spread out into numerous tribes around the island. Then as Chinese settlers began to arrive in the fifteenth century, they were beaten back into the mountains and uninhabitable places of Taiwan. Now they are thought of by many Taiwanese as a race of prostitutes and laborers, alcoholics and gutter trash, for the most part, in some ways similar to the American Indians. But it was the Chinese who first brought them trouble. The way they live today is just the wreckage of that war. When Meishu's mother was born, the entire sea coast of Hualien was littered with tiny shacks made of spindly wood and surrounded with swarms of black mosquitoes with stingers like hypodermic needles. Driving through the region, a man would see a modern house of tile and cement suddenly spring up on the horizon, towering four stories above the surrounding countryside. This was sometimes a sign that the family had sold one of their daughters off to slavery in a brothel in Taipei or Kaohsiung run by local Chinese. With the money, they had bought the new house.[9]

Back in Taipei, Meishu wears a red T-shirt with an aboriginal painting etched in white on her chest. Her younger sister, Meilu, also wears an aboriginal motif T-shirt. Meishu's T-shirt is like her new identity, hastily slipped on. When she was growing up, she wore the usual uniform: white stockings, pleated skirt worn above the knees, and a blouse with the name of her school embroidered just above the shirt pocket. She always wore her hair in a ponytail. She was oblivious and happy. Visitors to the household would let the little girl ride on their knees, like she was riding a horse, while she pealed with laughter. She was an angel, they said. And her mother, the aboriginal girl that her father married against his parents' wishes, gave her an English name to match: Angel.

In her teens, she still wears a uniform to junior high school. But on every off-day, every moment out of school, she wears the aborigine T-shirt. "We are the proud race of true Taiwanese," the shirt says. Below the squirrelly characters, curlicued and sloping, as if a rude native hand had drawn them, is a picture of hunters and horses—as if reflecting the DPP image of old Taiwan, a place of wild horses and free lives. But the figures look like a cave painting and the short sleeves are intentionally frayed. There are tiny cuts every inch or so at the end of the sleeves—cut to make the T-shirt look as if it has been cut with jungle vines and thorns. Meishu's hair is different now. She had it cut in an aboriginal style. It is loose over her forehead, scattered and uneven like the ragged edges of her sleeves, although the style at the back is like other Taiwanese girls. Meishu's identity as one-half aborigine is also a refuge for her during these days of crisis.

> Of course, I know my grandfather was from China. But I don't know anything about his stories. I myself am an aborigine. That's what my mother is. So that's what I am. I don't think I am a mainlander. Didn't they kill a lot of people? My grandfather didn't do that. Is my father really a mainlander? I don't know. I'm an aborigine. Can't you see what it says on my T-shirt?

Her father's fingers are worn smooth from gripping the steering wheel except for the occasional callus. He loses his temper a lot these days, and when he does and she talks back to him, he slaps her. She is still too young to think: *he is a mainlander and I am an aborigine*. But she does think of violence when she thinks of mainlanders. Her grandfather, Ko Jen-tao, never told her his stories about leaving his home and coming to Taiwan, so she only learns about that part of her past through history textbooks, which were altered during the years of DPP power, to insist that mainland refugees brought only violence and corruption with them, casting the native Taiwanese and the aborigines into a holocaust of violence, forcing them to endure slavery, white terror, and imprisonment. Now that the Taiwanese are "free" from their former torturers, the new history continues, the aborigines, who were once the worst-off, are now the symbol of a new Taiwan.

One of Meishui's favorite singers is Chang Hui-mei, also known as A-mei, famous not only for her throaty love songs but also for origins as an aborigine. The DPP was fond of her, too. Wearing an aluminum-colored halter top that exposed her shoulders, with her hair piled up on top of her head, the pop star A-mei, belted out the national anthem, and across the island, people's eyes swarmed with tears. It was a historic moment, both symbolically and realistically. It was true: the aborigines, formerly considered the whores and laborers of the island, were catapulted to nation-wide attention. And the government promised to liberate them from their past.

The project succeeded to a small degree. The government renamed the boulevard abutting the presidential mansion, a brick relic of the Japanese colonial era that looks more like a school or factory, after the name of a famous aboriginal leader. A few aborigine prostitutes found work as hairdressers through a government program. Jutting, three-story houses stopped going up in Hualien. The government cracked down on trafficking of aborigine girls. And the mother of Meishu, the aborigine who Ko Chen-tsang married against his parents' wishes, changed her career. She had been working in a semi-illicit profession: behind the counter in a store that smelled of dust and perfume and sold women's lingerie. It was a little bit like the counter she had stood behind as a child selling aboriginal trinkets. The lingerie store was in a working-class district of Taipei, near the railroad tracks. She worked long hours. After the new government came to power, she gradually changed her way of living. Whether it was as a result of the general movement of society, the superficial propaganda of the DPP, or the cosmetic changes the new government had made, the theme of aborigine emancipation resounded in the media, in textbooks and in her daughter's clothing. She borrowed money from her father-in-law, the former police chief and mainland exile, Ko Jen-tao, and started her own lingerie shop in a slightly upscale suburb of Taipei. Now she works long hours still, but she is the manager.

Today the sky is cloudy, as a typhoon, entering the southern quarter of the island, has pushed a massive firmament of clouds over the top of the sky, like frosty icing on a cake. Meishu and her two sisters study in their mother's shop or run outside to play with neighbors on the sidewalk. Each of them wears an aboriginal T-shirt. They are oblivious of the aborigines' past and are completely at peace with their new identity though they are not quite sure what it is. They have grown up during the new era and, at this moment in their life, even though the Kuomintang has come back to power, fully believe the propaganda of the DPP, that the aborigines can recreate themselves. It is as if, as they scamper in and out of the sliding glass door that sighs as the air conditioner starts up each time it opens, that their past never existed. It has been replaced by ideology. The girls' new identity is as hazy as the images on their T-shirts.

After those years of change, Meishu found her identity as an aborigine a solace in the climate of anti-mainlander propaganda. Or perhaps it was just that the efforts of the DPP to wipe out the status, history and glory of the remnant of a lost civilization that had succeeded with her. She shakes her head, her floppy hair swinging playfully, her scarlet mouth pinches tight. It's just too soon to tell if she will follow in the footsteps of her father and grandfather and turn to China for a new identity. For now, she doesn't know a thing about her grandfather's side of the family. It's like it's been snapped off.

> A mainlander? I don't even really know what a mainlander is. Who cares? I know my mother is an aborigine. That's what I am. Why does it really matter?

4
Overseas Connections

Bugged: The story of Tan Zhefu

The countryside is bounded by golden fields of wheat. The grains stand stock still as if pointing at the sky, waiting for rain to come. Cicadas and grasshoppers shrill the air with their cries. The shrillness is like the sound of high-tension electric wires. For his entire adult life in the slum of tiny cement boxes where Tan Zhefu has lived with his wife and daughter, surrounded by the fields, the thrum of the insects has seemed to gain in cadence. After living there for twenty years, the ringing has transferred to the inner porches of his ears so that he can no longer distinguish the actual sound from the echo in his brain, he says.

He is the abandoned son of a mainland exile. His father, Colonel Tan Huashen, fled to Taiwan with his unit on a landing craft that gradually fell apart as they approached the island. Colonel Tan left behind him a family with two sons and a wife. For forty years, they have suffered because of his absence. And the younger Tan, now sixty-one, whose twisted nose, like a stubby tree root, resembles his father's, feels that his entire life has been cursed by what the communist regime has for fifty years called "overseas relations." In other words, because he had a relative in Taiwan—even if it was a father who abandoned him—he was beaten and humiliated during the Cultural Revolution, denied work for his whole life, and branded an outcast, unable to marry the girl of his choice. His current state of utter wretchedness, in feeling if not entirely in his material surroundings, is accompanied by the shrill throbbing of insects, as if they are the doom-chanting chorus in a Greek tragedy.

As he enters the room, a bed crouches in a corner. It is a single thin mattress atop a wooden box that is on the verge of falling apart, coated with black grease and grime. In the corner is a round table, also of wood, scattered with paper. In the center of the table floats a giant round cylinder of clear fluid with what looks like a giant mushroom floating in the middle. It is strong, blindingly-potent liquor that he bought at a roadside stand, scooping it up out of an enormous vat, now keeping it in the cylinder. The object floating in the middle is called *lingzhi*, an herb used in Chinese medicine. But it hardly seems to have any effect. Tan's eyes are bloodshot and the surface of the whites appears to be raised, as if they are coated with a thick glaze of glass. He frowns and mutters and shakes his head, mopping and mowing it back and forth.

Tan is a symbol of what happened to some families left behind when their relative—son, brother, mother, sister—retreated to Taiwan. In most cases, the consequences of having a family member in Taiwan were severe. Stunted job opportunities, perennially kept at a menial level of work, beatings, even death. Tan's father, in Taiwan, is a friend of Ko Jen-tao. Both escaped, leaving relatives behind.

Tan leans on his thick, knotted arms, burnt the color of strawberries, on the table throbbing with litter. He describes his current situation, his daily life. He has "nothing to do." Poverty is less the problem, although it is present, than what he describes as the consciousness of a failed life. As he talks, the bugs screech in the background, blanketing every word with sound. His accent is so thick, each word is cut off before it even leaves his mouth, so that his speech mimics the bugs' cries in intensity and shrillness.

> My name is Tan Zhefu. I am 61. I don't really have a job now. I just do a little bit here and there. I grow a few things. Corn and wheat. And I go out to work as a carpenter sometimes.
>
> I work outside. My second son's wife lives with us. Also, they have a small child. Because it's just the two of us, me and my wife, they can stay.
>
> I get up a little after five. As soon as I get up, we prepare food. I go to look at the crops. I pull out weeds. Water them. For two or three hours, we do this.
>
> Sometimes we go out to work. Sometimes we don't have anything to do. Each year has 365 days, but the days to work are less than 100. Because of the seasons.
>
> We eat wheat cakes. Noodles. Cut it up. Eggs. This is our breakfast. We don't have chickens. We buy them.
>
> In most cases, on the weekends, we have pickled vegetables. I drink liquor.

At noon, it's not the same thing. Sometimes, *mantou* buns, maybe dumplings, if we have enough time, we have rice.

In the afternoon, usually I don't have anything to do. If I don't go out to work as a carpenter. Like right now. Wheat sometimes needs work. The corn needs work. Then I have to work. It's seasonal work. Apart from this, I don't have anything to do and am at home.

If I'm free, I watch TV, or just talk with my wife.

In the evening, we drink first. This is liquor that you buy from the side of the road in a big tub and you fill up your bottle and bring it back. Rice liquor. It has a *lingzhi* inside. The flavor is not bad.

Every day, I drink four cups.

We go to sleep early. We don't have anything to do.

Memory, more than his current grind—which does not sound so bad, after all—is what gets him. His father was seventeen when he married a local woman from Shandong, from the countryside. Soon, however, the Kuomintang came scouring through the land, looking for men to serve in their last-ditch campaign against the Communists.[1] They laid down the law that each family must provide one son to serve in the army. Some were never heard from again, every record of their existence blotted out, lost, in the flight to Taiwan. Some like Tan Zhefu's father, made it to Taiwan, rose in the military echelon, then, cut off from their families in China, married again raising a new family. Chapter 1 follows the story of Tan's father, how he rose to colonel, married a Taiwanese aboriginal woman, then retired from the military and with his training in electronics, opened his own small shop, sired five children, who live prosperous lives—one in Japan, another a banker. But it was over forty years before the son from his *first* marriage, left behind on China, saw his father again. And during those forty years the elder Tan, the missing father, had no idea that his first son suffered not only from his absence, but also from the vengeance wrought by the Communists against anyone, any person, any family, who had the trace of a relation with someone living in Taiwan. Tan Hua-shen was persecuted because his father was in Taiwan, haled there by the Kuomintang. Both men, father and son, dreamed of the lost paradise they might have had: parallel yearnings. The father, in Taiwan, dreaming of how he and the Kuomintang might have returned *home*, retaken China, returned to the past before it was stripped away by the enemy. Tan Zhefu, the son, suffered a different, more tangible fate, dreaming of his father.

> When my father left, I was under a year old. Of course, I don't have any memories. I had a grandfather and grandmother. We had a very hard time during that period. The Kuomintang and the Communists fought for three more years. The Communists then started to track down the Kuomintang relatives.

If he had ever wondered if he had a father, lost in Taiwan, the Communists reminded him of it. He could never forget it. It was his curse. Sometimes they would come to talk with his family, to check up on them, try to reeducate them. Other times it was to humiliate them, to keep them from corrupting the rest of society that they believed they had so painstakingly and with such great sacrifice reformed, saved, liberated from the destruction and utter calamity China had suffered for centuries.[2]

> The Communists came every day. So, of course, I knew I had a father in Taiwan. The Communists. The Communists. They put a wooden placard on our home. Gave us a black sign that said we were the Kuomintang relatives, it was bad luck. It started from 1946.

This was only the beginning. The rest of his life sped up, in terms of the increasingly harsh punishments meted out to him. At the same time, his opportunities slowed down. In the middle of his narrative, he points out what his endurance, his perseverance has brought him. Denied education, employment beyond the menial tasks of farmer and part-time carpenter, he yet lived to see his grandchildren attend college. Thus, his story is also one of triumph.

> Everyone would say, all the people would say that my father was Kuomintang. When I studied, they didn't look at the scores on my tests, it was all based on your background. I always was given the lowest score.

Bitterness seeps into his account. He looks down at his hands, on the table.

> Of course, I was kept down in school. The teacher kept us down. The communist family members would be treated well. In my group, I was always treated the worst. My background was no good. I was in the group with the capitalists and landlords.
>
> Actually, we weren't called the family of Kuomintang, we were called *hei wu lei*. The five black types. Landlords, rich farmers, counter-revolutionaries. We were in this group. They lumped us all together. We were also with the "rightists," intellectuals. They were not satisfied with society.

His voice is at first dull, like metal being beaten out, forged, slowly, by hand, one blow at a time. Later, tears come to his eyes and his voice grows shriller. For now, his face is simply inquisitive, the beetroot of a nose, the swollen hands, all presenting a picture of a farmer recounting a past that seems to have no connection with the present. It is not until later that he talks about his father coming home for the first time, after forty years. Then he transforms into a mountain of sorrow and rage. Now, he is quiescent, focused.

> One class had five in this group. One class had forty students all together. Five were kept back.
> At the time, I just tried to study. I didn't know what my father was like. I just knew we were the rejects of society. I wasn't angry. I just didn't understand anything.

Then his mother remarried. For the moment, it seemed that his life might get better. And it did. His stepfather, who he hated, was a hero of the revolution, even of the famed Eighth Route Army, the name of the northern Communist military during its alliance with the Kuomintang.[3] Tan, hating his stepfather yet emboldened and perhaps with some of the prestige of his mother's new marriage surrounding him, began to shrug off some of the indignities of the past. He began to work simultaneously as a farmer and a carpenter. He got married.

> When my mother remarried, I was 29. I got married afterwards. I was living with my grandmother and grandfather. At that time, hmm, hmm, I was in a *hezuo she* [a collective]. When my mother remarried, I felt, I felt—really uncomfortable. But there was nothing I could do. My stepfather was a member of the Eighth Route Army. His position was a general.

Then the Cultural Revolution began. It was as if the cloud of his childhood had descended again. This time it was not merely discrimination. This time it was torture. He was hauled into village meetings, on account of his father, accused of being a counter-revolutionary. It was the outrage, no, not even outrage, but still shock that he would be commandeered to stand trial for a crime of association. If he had known more Chinese history, perhaps, he might have understood. That for centuries, during even the heyday of the Qing dynasty, authors, intellectuals, and statesmen were murdered, cast out of court, exiled, and punished for even the slightest of associations with tainted members of society.[4] Whether this practice was resurrected during the reign of the early Communist regime is, of course, the question of a vastly broader work. But the similarities are present. As he speaks, the same dull voice continues, the beating of metal out, word by word. Yet now his head is still and he stares straight ahead with thick bloodshot eyes that appear to have been encased in, covered over, with a film of glass. The glassy rime even appears to project beyond the case of the eyes themselves, as if outrage and shock had so projected from his brain that it formed a casing, an outer surface on its own. As if outrage itself were a physical force inhering in the eyes.

> I had never even met my father. How could I be accused of all that? Everyone accused me of things I had never even heard of. I had to stand there every day. All day. Yes, I wore a sign. Yes, I was beaten. I can't talk about it.

After that, the story is a familiar one for those of his "background." He was denied job opportunities. He was given the most menial work in the village commune. Later, he lived in a hovel that gradually caved in and he was without the means to repair it. He weathered rain filling half of his room as he cared for two babies and his meager crops. Yet, compared to others, his fate was kind. Chapter 1 chronicles the narrative of Chang Ching-tan, the shop worker who was abused by Japanese soldiers and later became a civil servant in Taiwan. His mother, he said, was forced, during the Cultural Revolution, to work with human feces, spreading them with her own hands throughout the fields of the countryside she was assigned to for the duration of the cataclysm. Others fared worse. Lin Ching-wu, the soldier who never made officer after surviving countless battles on the mainland, told of his father, who had once sailed to Southeast Asia, bringing back everything from British umbrellas to Malaysian sweets. According to the interview, Lin's father shared his wealth and largesse amply with neighbors. But during the Cultural Revolution, he was isolated in his home and "starved to death." "Not a single neighbor dared to help him."[5]

Sometimes Tan walked the road into town, the dust rising at his feet. Other members of the village would pass him. "I wished that I had a razor in my hand, each time they passed," he says. They would eye each other, the schoolmates who had passed on to paying jobs in the town, were now local officials, already corrupt, already living in houses, while he sweltered in a cement box the size of a room, living with his wife, a woman worn down by bearing children and work, with half her teeth missing and a glint of something grim and beaten in her eyes, as if the wildness, the despair had already been beaten out of them. He would pass them, the sounds of the insects shrilling in the wheat fields, the sorghum fields that he had still to harvest that he knew, even if he could do so on his own, with perhaps the help of his wife, he would still have trouble selling to the townsfolk, who shunned contact with him. Even if he could survive, there would be nothing worth surviving for because his father had deserted him and his mother had remarried one of the classes of people that had brought down upon him a curse that to this day was still not expelled.

Now Tan is on his feet, his face red and gorged with blood, yelling now in his tense, tight tones, his clipped words, his unreadable accent, his bloodshot eyes, more glassy than ever, peering down as if contemplating how much strength is in the arms of a farmer and what would happen if they were directed at those who had destroyed a life that now carries if not rage but terror for the joys already lost that could never be regained.

During his lifetime, China had gone through tremendous upheavals. The upheavals, even the curse, perhaps a superstitious historian might say, laid upon the top officials was greater than the suffering of this individual farmer. The Hundred Flowers and Anti-Rightist campaigns of 1956–58, when intellectuals who spoke out against the party, were targeted, tortured and purged en masse was the backdrop for Tan's own suffering in school.[6] As he sweltered in the tiny village school, labeled a rightist, the nation poured its own invective and shame onto the "rightists" at large. Some of the mass hysteria of those times floated down, like vapor, into the eyes and minds of the teachers in Tan's village, thus making his life worse than he could have imagined before he went to school. Then, during the Cultural Revolution, when Mao mobilized the masses, including schoolchildren and college students, to support him in a revolution against the increasingly powerful inner party leaders, the hatred inflicted upon enemies of the revolution was spat upon Tan as he stood in the circle of villagers, who spat upon him both with their mouths and through a lifetime of neglect and scorn. Finally, the economic and political changes brought about by Deng Xiaoping, himself and his family a victim of the Cultural Revolution, catapulted farmer Tan into a new phase of his existence. His father came to visit.

Like other refugees, the elder Tan brought gifts and television sets. He at first did not tell his son about the new family he had raised in Taiwan. But when he did, the farmer trembled with hatred.

> I wanted to kill him. Can you say that about your own father? I wanted to kill his family. Where had he been my whole life? Yes, I had suffered because of him. That's right. He brought these gifts. What were they to me?

His father helped him—with money—repair his crumbling cement house. He built another one so that the younger Tan's daughter, recently married, could have her own space. Today, the two cement blocks stand catty-corner to each other. A chicken runs outside. Garbage litters the grass. The fields throb on the perimeter. Outside the shacks, the family members wait. His father visited twice. Then the two families separated and they remain so.

> Yes, I do look just like him. That's what people say. When he came to the airport. We went to meet him. I recognized him right off. No, I don't think we are alike. We talk on the phone sometimes.

In Tan's assessment, his life has been a waste. If his life is measured by his economic prosperity, one might point to his increased quarters, or to the television set that sits perched in his room. He and his wife always have enough to eat. In the same way, no matter how skewed between city and countryside, China's development, over the past half-century seems somehow justified, to journalists and historians alike, by the very speed of the economic growth, much of which was started by investment from Taiwan.[7] But the farmer does not see it that way.

> If I can speak truly, my life has been a waste. A waste![8] You say, forty years wasted! I never had a chance. Never. And now look at me. I'm nothing. I could have been something better. I have spent my life paying for my father's running away. Okay, he didn't run away. He had to go. He had to. The Communists were too strong. But what was I supposed to do? We couldn't be together, that's right.

As he stops speaking, the high-pitched throbbing of the insects returns, as if they have reached in with all their myriad feelers and now touch his nervous systems. Tan has tears in his eyes and his body is shaking. His wife and the rest of the party come back in.

The factory worker

Ko Jen-tao sailed across the Taiwan Strait in 1949, leaving behind his mother and seven siblings. One of them, an older brother, Ko I-jen, spent the next forty years searching for a sense of wholeness. As the eldest in the family, it hit him the hardest when the family collapsed after his father's death. As the eldest male in the family, he assumed the role of the father, sacrificing his education so that his younger brother, Ko Jen-tao, who later became a police chief in Taiwan, could attend a naval academy in Shanghai. The trauma of the role foisted upon him comes through as he describes how his younger brother was beaten to death, shortly after Ko Jen-tao left for Taiwan. As he describes the circumstances, he also seems to be subtly showing resentment for the flight of his younger brother to relative safety. Having spent most of his adult life working in a factory, attending political meetings, and being punished for having a relative in Taiwan, he is cagey enough not to let on that he envied his brother or resented him his life in Taiwan. But the fact that he emphasizes, at the end of the passage, that his brother had no knowledge of the death of a brother suggests that Ko Jen-tao was somehow shirking his duty to the family.

> It was my youngest brother, just before liberation, that was beaten to death. He was working as an apprentice in a noodle shop. He was working in a relative's shop. I can't remember what relative it was. As an apprentice, he once went to gamble with the son of the owner. He came back quite late. His life as an apprentice was rough. He worked until late and sometimes the boss's son would come back and call him to come down and open the door.
>
> There was this one night when he had to come down from the upper storey. He had to come down to open the door and of course he was unhappy. He said, "You've been out gambling and come home so late and now I have to get up to let you in." The boss' son took a stick and hit him on the top of the head. Actually, they were relatives. But later my mother took legal action. They paid 400 renminbi.
>
> My second youngest brother didn't know. Later, he came from Taiwan to the mainland and then he knew. He learned then that our youngest brother was dead. Then he knew. He was really heartbroken.

Ko I-jen is talking about the benefits that economic liberalization has brought him. After the mainland's economic changes under Deng, the economy began to heat up like an oven and eventually roar like a fire.[9] The eldest Ko was able to buy his own apartment.[10] But at the time of the beating, the society was still pre-liberation capitalist. Ko, in despairing over his brother's death, perhaps blamed the system—in which a young man could be made so vulnerable. He is ambivalent about the changes the new economy has brought for; in some way, it resembles the old. The factory where he worked for forty years after his brother left has left him a crippled man. His neck is twisted to the left, his face shriveled as if it has been held to a flame and like wax had melted at the neck. His heavy grey hair is the only sign of vigor. And yet he just isn't sure about some things. The factory, an aeronautical factory, was his home. And he must be speaking to some extent directly and sincerely, since when he entered the factory in 1951, he had just lost half his family to war and its precursors. His father, one brother who fled to Taiwan, and another brother who was killed by the cruelty of the old society. He must have, through his forty years, been longing for a sense of wholeness, safety even, that to some extent, at least, the factory work gave him. It supplied him with a wife—he met her there—with every part of his life, his apartment, his monthly food budget. Perhaps it was a substitute for the Taiwan that his brother had escaped to or, perhaps, after forty years of living under the communist regime and in a factory where labor was strictly controlled through political manipulation, he is still in the habit of speaking well of his former employer. As he speaks, fatigue of forty years' manual labor hovers over his every movement and every word. It is as if the machines he served for decades have exacted their revenge. Even his smile is lopsided. Physically, then, even his body cries out for a return to wholeness, one which is always elusive.

> Nanjing was liberated in 1949. After the liberation, I didn't go to school. I didn't graduate from primary school. Our family was so poor that I had to go to a capitalist's store as an apprentice. What did I study? I studied how to make noodles. To make noodles. I was that kind of apprentice. Being an apprentice was really tough, you had to get up at three in the morning—all the way until 1951, when I was freed from my apprenticeship.
>
> At that time, in Nanjing a factory was hiring workers. I had some of my relatives make the necessary introductions and in November I went to work in the factory. The factory was originally a national defense factory. It was aeronautical. It was an aeronautical factory. I went to that factory.
>
> I grew up in that factory. When I started working in the factory, I was still young, I was only seventeen, or even sixteen. I felt that now I was truly liberated. Our lives were not bad before liberation until our father died in 1945. Then things got quite tough. It was not until after liberation in 1949, when I went to the factory, that my life started to turn around. That was a real turning point. I had a guaranteed job for life. It was a national factory. The factory officials cared about us. It was quite like being in a big family.[11]

> The leadership caring for me and guiding me bit by bit from apprentice to worker and then from worker to cadre, all the way to retirement, was part of this feeling, this experience. I was in the factory from the year 1951 to the year 1994. Then I retired. I was working in the factory that whole time. So now you can say I am a grandfather of every piece of machinery in the factory. I grew up in that factory.

A clue to the ambivalence he feels towards the factory is revealed in a slip of the tongue. He refers to his starting a "factory," rather than a family. He has already confused the two.

> In 1958 I got married and started a factory. My wife was also a worker in the factory. We were in the same work unit. And that's the way we met.

His dissatisfaction, even torment and torture, from working in the factory also comes through loud and clear. He describes how hard and patiently he toiled over the course of a decade, only to be denied promotion because of his "overseas connection," meaning his brother, the police chief Ko Jen-tao. Other family members were affected as well. Referring to his nephew's attempts to join the army, the only trusted way to rise out of poverty, his bitterness seeps through his account.

> During the Cultural Revolution, if a family member was in Taiwan, during the '60s and '70s, at that time, it was big trouble. I'll tell you, my older sister, her son wanted to go in the army, and they wouldn't let him in.
>
> Because my work unit was a government factory, they would pay more attention to you because your brother was in Taiwan. The pressure was greater than in other places. In most cases, the workers around me, they didn't know my brother was in Taiwan, but the leaders knew. There was some pressure put on me. Take when I tried to join the party. I started working in the factory in 1951, but I wasn't allowed to join the party until 1960. That was because my brother was in Taiwan.
>
> They really focused on your work. If you did a good job, they would keep you on. But if your work was not truly outstanding, and you had a relative in Taiwan, they would make a connection between the two and you would be in trouble.

But that was not all. Still another brother was sent to the countryside. The seeming injustice of it was that, normally, poor workers such as the Kos who remained on the mainland might not be sent to the countryside. Their father had been wealthy, but he was a doctor and not a Kuomintang soldier or official, as in the case of Tan Hua-shen, the farmer. But, because of their "overseas connection," one was singled out and sent to exile in the hinterland to live among the nightsoil-drenched fields of inner China.

> In some work units, if you had overseas relations, they would send you down to the countryside. To work in the fields.[12] It depended on what work unit it was. For example, my other brother, he was considered suspicious. He was sent down to the countryside. His whole family was sent down to the countryside. Originally he was in an agricultural company. It was called Agricultural Products Company. His wife was in Weisheng Xuexiao [sanitary school]. The two of them were sent to the countryside because my second brother was in Taiwan. Just like that, sent to the countryside.

Ko I-jen resembles his brother. His voice has a similar cadence as if their voices were fixed during childhood. They use the same words and have the same accent. Instead of saying *hei* for "black," they both say *heh*. They both greet a visitor with the same show of enthusiasm, the same anxious entreaties to eat, the same form of subtle manipulations over the dinner table: "What? You haven't eaten anything. I've been watching. You haven't eaten anything." And then of course the visitor is obliged to eat more although his stomach is bursting and his face sweating with the spicy food. Yes, Ko I-jen is not only like his brother, he is aware that he is like his brother. He says that his mother favored Ko Jen-tao and grieved so hard when he went to Taiwan that she cried without stop for a year. It was hard for him when he realized, suddenly, that the factory he was in was producing weapons, particularly airplanes, to strike against Taiwan. His hand may have been touching the very steel that would plummet down thousands of feet to land on the head of his brother, who he knew was in Taiwan's navy. He was preparing, in this sense, to kill his younger brother. His brother was alive, he guessed. But perhaps he would soon lose his life in the ongoing skirmishes between the Communists and the Kuomintang. Ko I-jen might be the instrument of his brother's death. There was no way to warn his brother. They couldn't reach him to tell him of all the airplanes the factory was spewing out. They couldn't tell him to watch the skies.

> In 1949 or 1950, we knew he was alive. But when he went to Taiwan he couldn't get in touch with us. There was no way to get in touch with us. One letter did get through, at the very beginning. But we didn't know how to get in touch with him. He said he was in the navy on a boat and that there was

no way to get in touch with him. After that, we didn't hear anything from him for fifty years. After that one single letter, we heard nothing, we knew nothing for fifty years. *But we knew he was in the navy, that he had graduated from naval school, and we also knew that there was serious fighting between Taiwan and mainland China. We knew in the factory, the airplanes we made were going to be sent against Taiwan, probably against their navy. I thought of that every day I went to work. We all wondered if he was still alive or not.*[13]

He begins to talk about his childhood memories of Japanese bombing, as if to call attention to the danger of airplanes and air raids to human life, to his brother. Since he is several years older than Ko Jen-tao, who only remembers walking out of his home in Wuhan to see his school demolished by Japanese bombs, Ko I-jen's memories of the War of Resistance against Japan are much more vivid. He talks about them, after expressing his worry about his brother being killed by airplanes. Ko I-jen, on some level, is talking about one thing: the dangers of bombing. It's as if his memories of Japanese bombing help him to realize just what kind of danger his brother was in. Only this time it wasn't about Japanese bombs, but communist bombs, bombs that he had helped to drop. The memory is six decades old, but it squirmed into his consciousness as he began talking about the danger of the bombing his brother faced at the time. But the major difference is that he was with his brother in Chongqing, when the Japanese bombed it. When he was producing airplanes in Nanjing, after his brother had gone to Taiwan, he was alone.

When the Japanese bombed Chongqing, my clearest memory is of the air raid sirens.[14] As soon as they let off the air-raid sirens, you would know the Japanese planes were coming. You'd run into the air-raid shelters.

Life was pretty miserable. The Japanese would come and bomb the whole area where we lived. They would burn it up completely. That was really scary. The air-raid siren sounded like, woooOOOOoooo, woooOOOOoooo. Most of the time, though, after they set off the air-raid siren, it wasn't long, maybe three or four minutes, before the airplanes came.

Chongqing had more air-raid shelters than other cities. Chongqing had a lot of air-raid shelters. The big air-raid shelters were mostly safe. The small ones were no good.

I remember, we were hiding in an air-raid shelter, the alarm was just over, and we had just come out. Only a few seconds later, the air-raid siren went off again, and so we jumped into the air-raid shelter again. The life we led then was really one of constant fear.

It is hard to imagine a life of fear in Ko I-jen's present surroundings, although constant toil seems to have left him shriveled and stooped. Soon after he joined the factory, he was allotted a small apartment where he lives today. The apartment is utter dilapidation, with pipes running along the ceilings, clotting the air space. The floors are frayed concrete. Each room's door is slightly unhinged. The kitchen is a cement hole. And the living room is cluttered with boxes and old chairs. Yet the apartment has a comfortable, lived-in feeling. One feels that generations have been raised and raised again in the confines of the very small living room and the two bedrooms, the bathroom and the kitchen. There is something comforting about the way of life it represents among the economic reforms coursing through China today. In airports and on street corners young people talk about the cruelty of present-day life in China. Some have easy jobs while others worry aloud about being laid off and sent into the vast pool of hundreds of millions of poor farmers and workers who are unemployed as factories and industries are transferred to semi-private ownership, or simply become obsolete.[15] Yet in the circle of the factory—the apartment block where Ko I-jen lives with his family—which is only a stone's throw from the factory itself, a semi-feudal system still prevails. The children continue on in the line of work of their father. Ko I-jen's daughter now works in the factory. He expects his grandchildren to work there, too.[16] The factory is not at risk of closing down, because it is still a national defense factory. Now that he is retired, he draws a small pension and, with his wife's pension from the same factory, it is enough to get by and even to save from. Now he occupies a variety of roles related to the factory. He is still involved in the community of dormitories—apartment blocks—that cling to the outer edges of the factory complex. He makes his nightly rounds. He still seems part of the old communist China, before reforms spread first anxiety and later wealth across half the nation.

> It was after 1994, after I retired. I became a member of the community organization and did a lot of small jobs for the community. I worked on behalf of the people. Most of them were in the factory. I helped take care of our community. Safety, hygiene, I did it all in order to serve the people who live here. One reason was because at the time I retired I was vice chairman of the factory union. The vice chairman of the factory union! The factory union was founded for the sake of the people.

When his brother returned to Nanjing in 1988,[17] after restrictions had been lifted on travel across the Taiwan Strait, Ko I-jen's resentment came to the surface. His brother was bringing back money and gifts, almost as if to show he had succeeded whereas those left behind had starved and failed. "He saw us as backward," said Ko I-jen. Even the language of his younger brother was laced with classical allusions, proverbs and cant he had picked up in Taiwan where education is still tied closely to traditional texts.[18] It was as if he had come back bigger, bigger than anyone had ever imagined to the grey streets and stunted trees, the factories and the swarms of people in his home city. It was understandable that his brother would feel resentment.

> When he talked, he used different words than us. My brother told us that we were living in terrible poverty because everything was so difficult to buy. I had to admit that was true. But I don't think I had ever been ashamed of it until then. He said there was a huge difference between his life in Taiwan and ours in the mainland. I couldn't deny that. No, we didn't think he was looking down on us. It was just that he felt *sorry* for us ... he had *sympathy*.
> When he first came to our home, he saw that we had quite a small television. It was a twelve-inch black-and-white TV. He immediately ordered a new television for us—from Hong Kong. We had never even seen that kind of television before. We hadn't been using our original television that much anyway. Then he saw that we didn't have a VCD player. Eh, so he immediately went and bought some from Hong Kong. He gave one to my eldest brother and one to my younger brother and one to my younger sister. He gave one to everyone.
> We knew that we were poor. Compared to his lifestyle in Taiwan, our kind of lifestyle must have seemed primitive. We knew that. There was a big gap. But my younger brother made it seem like we had nothing. He looked up at the ceiling, all the pipes, and he asked, "What is it like to live in this kind of wretchedness?"
> But at least this place, at least I bought it after the economic reforms. I bought it. We used to live in public housing—that was even worse.

The small dormitory-apartment where the family hunched over a tiny, wooden table, stained with decades of use, was his now. He had saved enough money over the years to buy it—a possibility that the economic reforms had made possible.[19] Deng Xiaoping had not only encouraged people to find extra work, to make more money, the reforms he led also encouraged people to buy their own homes—indeed, had made widespread private ownership of homes possible. So as Ko I-jen sat in his living room, around the tiny wooden table, he was proud. He began to narrow down the differences between him and his brother, as if to make up for the lost forty years. Of course, some of this was due to economic propaganda launched by China Central Television that touted the progress of such cities such as Shanghai and Beijing. The airwaves, at the time, were flooded, for instance, with commercials about the upcoming Olympic Games in the capital, showing sleek city scenes and impeccably-dressed spectators. But Ko I-jen wanted to go deeper. How did his brother see them? At first, he was blind to any change, according to his younger brother living in Nanjing.

> Our economic reforms are changing peoples' mindsets. My brother's viewpoint about politics and ours are starting to have a lot of things in common. They were quite different in the past. But during his first visit, he hadn't quite understood what kind of changes we'd been through, so his overall feeling was that our lives hadn't changed at all. The mainland was poorer than Taiwan. That was all he saw. And he said that Nanjing hadn't really changed at all in all this time. He said that in forty years it hadn't changed. The streets were filthy. Chaotic. He went on and on about this. The buses were crowded. The traffic was terrible.
>
> But actually, things have changed a lot in these last few years. The economic reforms have really made quite a difference. It's true that until recently, the buses were no good. And there were a lot of beggars on the street.

When Ko Jen-tao visited, Nanjing was a city torn in half by the reforms. The old spindly trees of twenty years still crouched and leaned on the sidewalks. Stray dogs still chased pedestrians. Beggars lay face down on sidewalks. But at the same time, construction noise tore at one's ears. The hammering, drilling, and pounding exploded like the sound of a train passing. Tall hotels jutted into the air like signposts advertising the power of the city. People walked fast on the streets. The crowds of people pushing to get on busses were gone. Ko I-jen had lived through all the changes and didn't want to argue with his brother.

> We admitted that what he was saying was true. We admitted there were still a lot of problems. We admitted that life was still hard. Things hadn't really changed that much. We admitted it. I said that the main problem was the population. The population on the mainland was just too big.

Resentment mingled with regard. On one hand, Ko I-jen also seemed to blame his brother for disregarding his filial obligations to his mother by absconding to Taiwan.

> My brother's biggest problem was that he felt guilty that he hadn't been able to look after his mother for forty years. He wasn't able to be a loyal son. So he took his guilt out on us. He wanted to make us feel bad [his wife interjects: "he looked down on us"].

Ko Jen-tao came back to Nanjing as if he were bringing life to the dead. He showered imported hand lotion, gold and cash onto his relatives. While the two brothers had been talking about the family, the forty years had melted away. But as Ko I-jen remembered the gifts, the proof of the life his brother had led, Ko he began to grow jealous, bitter.

> We talked about Taiwan. We talked about our family. Our children. We talked mostly about things like this. Afterwards, he gave us money. He gave his mother money, he also gave us some money. He gave us some golden bracelets. He gave money to his younger sister, he gave us rings. He said people here are poor, they don't have things like rings. He gave and he gave and he gave. So I should be thankful. My brother had a good heart.
>
> When his wife got seriously ill, I told him I would send him some herbal medicine. I had heard that there was a special treatment for cancer in Zhengzhou. So I took a train to Zhengzhou. I bought the medicine. I bought it and I mailed it to him. Brothers are always brothers. They never lose their love for each other. I made a lot of trips to Zhengzhou.

Deep down, Ko I-jen felt sad, as if he had lost the most important things a man can have: time and hope. He had lost the forty years he might have spent with his brother. He had also lost something bigger, decades of wasted political campaigns that left the people poor and afraid. Now the two losses seemed to grow bigger as they mingled together. Ten years later, when his brother visits again, Nanjing will be richer, richer almost than Taiwan after a growth rate of ten percent a year. But even then, it will seem to his brother that he was simply born at the wrong time. His grandson will be a stock broker or a banker, he may imagine. But for the moment, he remains in his tiny apartment, which he at least owns now, eating the same kind of rice, the same kind of food, he has eaten for forty years. The mattresses on the beds are as soft and limp as old sweaters. The family sleeps split up between two of them and have to get out of bed carefully so they don't hit their heads on pipes hanging from the ceiling. You can almost tell what Ko I-jen is thinking, that he might have had a different life if he had been able to go to Taiwan with his brother.

> If he had stayed in mainland China, his life would have been pretty much the same as mine. He might have still been involved in photography. Before he left, he was an apprentice in a photography studio. He had to work with harsh chemicals. If he had done well, maybe he would have become the boss or a cadre. His life would be similar to ours.

Ko I-jen keeps whispering the same thing over and over. "Forty years, forty years." He's like a man waking up out of a dream, with a strange, tired expression on his face, as if he still can't make up his mind if the dream were real or not. He is wearing a blue factory worker's coat and dark pants that look like they have been worn every day for years. His brother, when he first arrived, was wearing a leather coat, the kind Ko I-jen might have seen on television in foreign movies, and an expensive wrist watch. His face was full and thick, bronze-colored and well-fed. When his brother left, China was in chaos. It had just gone through a long period of invasion, division and war. After forty years, it is growing rich and stable again although problems still remain. Some of its economic growth depends on an army of hundreds of million migrant workers, unemployed or partially employed that gather routinely in the big cities on the coast or work in factories at low wages or become prostitutes or beggars. In central China, farmers and coal miners riot over corruption and dangerous working conditions.[20] Forty years passed like a hurricane, uprooting some things, moving other things around, realigning people's relationships with each other, bringing Taiwan closer to the mainland. His brother's return from Taiwan was not just a single moment of pain and pleasure for a family; it was also part of a general rearrangement of wealth and communication between China and Taiwan. Ten years later, as the forty years stretch into fifty and then sixty and China's economy continues to grow, some cities in China will come to make Taipei look like a poor distant relative wearing old, frayed clothing standing next to a man in a custom-made silk suit driving a Bentley or a Rolls Royce. But that was still twenty years in the future, like another dream that both men had just put their toes into, just testing the temperature of the water, without even thinking of taking a plunge.

The first time he came back, I knew his voice immediately. He was already in Guangzhou. He had gone from Taiwan to Hong Kong and then taken the train to Guangzhou. As soon as he got to Guangzhou, he could call us. When I picked up the phone and heard his voice, I knew it was my brother. I was so excited I was laughing and crying at the same time.

I couldn't stop laughing and crying and I didn't know which one was the real emotion—sadness or pure happiness. It had been forty years. Forty fucking years! I hadn't heard his voice in that long. Forty years! Now, suddenly, I was listening to his voice. It actually didn't sound that much different, just deeper, maybe a little sadder. It was like those forty years no longer existed. He asked me if I was alright. And I still couldn't stop laughing and crying at the same time.

He took a flight to Nanjing. Our whole family went to the airport. Only our mother stayed behind. She was too old. Or maybe it was that she was afraid. Maybe she was afraid that he wouldn't know her anymore. My sister, my eldest brother went. We got to the airport really early. His plane was scheduled to get in at five o'clock in the evening. We got there at noon. When he walked out of the exit, I recognized him immediately. I knew him immediately! He was wearing a black leather coat and pulling a piece of luggage, but I knew him. I knew him!

Forty years. What do you say about something like that? It was gone, passed. And now he was here. I looked around for his wife, but she hadn't come with him.

It hit me again. It was forty years. Gone by. Wasted. He was still standing on the other side of customs, but we all rushed over, yelling his name, but they didn't let us go in. After he finally came out, we all hugged him. We hugged him all at the same time. We were all crying. We cried and it was both happy and so sad. We cried because it had been forty years. And now, at last, we were together again.

After we went back home, I had a better chance to look at him. He looked good. He was healthy and in good shape. He was even a little bit fat.

Ko I-jen remembered that his brother liked to eat braised beef as a kid. He had his wife cook some. The family bought dozens of different kinds of meat and spread them out over the table. When his brother left, to go back to Taiwan, he filled a duffel bag with roast duck, dried beef and other food he imagined he might not be able to get in Taiwan. His imaginings of what life must be like in Taiwan were probably not that far off from what other Chinese in the cities thought and believed. It was almost like Taiwan itself became a beacon, a marker of what China could develop into. The two men were brothers but they lived different lives, lives that were not coming together. They ate together, exchanged gifts and would continue to think of each other in new ways when they separated.

> We were always close as kids. We were just immature. Sometimes we'd fight or get into arguments. I would want something and maybe my brother wouldn't want to give it to me. It was normal. But my brother was always fair, he never did anything mean.
>
> He went through a lot of hard times when he was a kid. It was hard to get a job and he ended up working in a photo studio. It was really hard on his hands because the papers had to be kept in freezing water. He was constantly exposed to harsh chemicals. But he never told our mother. He was afraid it would make her worry too much. He went through that for us. So when he went to Taiwan, I used to believe that it was so he could escape from his work in the photo studio. I thought he was trying to escape from a really tough life.

It was hard for Ko I-jen to let go of his brother, even after they came together. In a way, they couldn't really come together until their lives had started to come closer, until the places that they lived, the food that they ate and the apartments they lived in had started to resemble each other. That took another twenty years and even then personal healing seemed almost to lag behind economic healing as Taiwan and China evened out in wealth. One thing helped, early on, that was when Ko Jen-tao brought his Taiwanese wife along with him to Nanjing. She had grown up poor and Ko I-jen felt she wouldn't judge them the way his brother might have. But when she died and his brother married a second time, this time to a woman from Qingdao, a northern Chinese city that had experienced great economic growth, Ko I-jen wasn't so happy. He felt she looked down on them, was judging them, even more than his brother had.

> The next time he came he brought his first wife with him. We liked her. We felt like she didn't look down on us. She brought us a lot of stuff but she didn't make us feel small. She was very good to our mother. She said that we had to struggle for everything but now in Taiwan you can get anything. She said when she was growing up in Taiwan, things were hard, too. We could communicate with her.
>
> She was right. Fuel, rice, oil and salt are all hard to get. She said she would bring all of it on her next trip. She had been poor as a child, so she understood. She was very filial to our mother. Overall, we had a good

impression of her. So when she got sick, we were really worried. We tried to find doctors. We heard that she had worked in a television factory, so she also went through a lot of stress and difficulty.

Now as for this wife, we just don't really know her, she's only come to visit a couple of times. At least she's come to visit.

Liu Rong: Stranger in a strange land

Liu Rong has a wide, round face, with round, wide eyes, as if her face and her eyes are both frozen in astonishment at the turn her life has taken. She had an uncle who went to Taiwan and it changed her life in two ways: she was sent to the countryside during the Cultural Revolution at the very end of the movement, believing she should not have been. Second, she married a man from Taiwan, diving into the marriage without looking. She is fifty-one years old, tall, attractive, a native of Qingdao in China. When she speaks, she has a way of lisping and hanging on words in mid-syllable so that she sounds as if her tongue catches at the roof of her mouth as if she is in the middle of a long, slow kiss. When she is displeased by something, her lips are tight. As a result of her marriage to the man in Taiwan—her uncle introduced her—she stays in Taiwan for months at a time, working feverishly as a nurse's aide in a hospital. As she describes her childhood, the past takes on a baffled, helpless quality. When she was small, as if in anticipation of her unjust sojourn in the countryside and then purgatory-like life in Taiwan, away from family and friends, she says she was mute, unable to speak. She was already, even at age four, a stranger in a strange land: a child without the ability to touch anyone verbally, a theme that would dominate the rest of her life.

> I never spoke when I was a child. I only listened. That was actually convenient for my parents. So my father could take me everywhere he went. In those days, my father was a cadre. Wherever he went, meetings, anywhere, he took me with him. I learned a lot. I watched and I listened to a lot. I never talked.

She grew up in a family of seven siblings. She learned sewing from her grandmother and then, during the Cultural Revolution, her older sisters became Red Guards. She stayed at home and performed in the courtyard of her parents' dormitory nightly. Eventually, she was sucked into the violence. But she attests her purity—she was so pretty and she danced and performed so well, she must have felt that her innocence saved her from any real complicity.

> When I was little, I was really pretty. White skin, cheeks like two apples, bright red. During the Cultural Revolution, every living area had a propaganda team. I played a big role in our propaganda team. I would get my father and mother and grandmother to come and sit in the courtyard and be my audience. Then I would sing songs for them and dance for them. And they would always give me a round of applause. I just sang any song.
>
> For example, Xinjiang Ge [she starts singing], or there was one about a butterfly. It didn't have anything to do with politics. I sang for them every song I knew. I just sang anything I knew. I was only in the first grade. First or second grade.
>
> During the Cultural Revolution, every courtyard put on its own performances. We had no idea what was really going on outside. We didn't have any television. We were just kids putting on our own shows.
>
> My parents, on the other hand, were affected a little bit by the Cultural Revolution. My father was the chairman of a union so he eventually was a target. When the Cultural Revolution started, my father quickly came running home. He kept asking, did we have any of the "four olds"? We've got to destroy them.[21] My grandmother had been a landlord. She was the daughter of a big landlord family. Anything we had that was worth anything belonged to my grandmother. She burned in all up.
>
> I remember one thing. My father had a ring. There was a photograph of my father on the ring. My parents even destroyed that. They were so careful that we didn't have a single one of the "four evils"—I mean the "four olds"—left. Basically, they just destroyed our family's antiques and our family's paintings. Whatever. They destroyed everything from the past or that was part of Western culture. It was really a shame.
>
> When the Cultural Revolution was over, I was in my sophomore year of high school. I felt that my studies had been disrupted. And they had been chaotic, so I had to review everything all over again. Yes, I grew up in the Cultural Revolution. When it started, we were in school studying and at first we studied the normal subjects. At first, things were strict. We weren't allowed to have any romances.

Then, suddenly, she was thrust out of her innocence.

> I remember one time when I was in primary school. My sisters were Red Guards. I heard there was a student who was going to arrest a teacher. My sister took me along.

> We kept going and going and I asked my sister, "Why are we going to get that teacher?" My sister said, "Keep your mouth shut. He must be arrested. He is an intellectual. He must be punished for his mistakes."
>
> I didn't understand what she was talking about. I just kept going along with them. They just kept walking, and as they were walking, they used chalk to write on the walls that they were going to arrest that teacher. I couldn't go along with them. I was too afraid. Later, I asked if the teacher had been arrested.
>
> My sister said, "Yes."
>
> And do you want to know what happened in the end? He was beaten up and died. I felt really bad. I thought, how can they kill a teacher? I thought I should have done something to stop it. I had let him die.
>
> "Oh, he made mistakes, it was right that he was beaten to death."
>
> Those Red Guards seemed like they were really pure. But they didn't know themselves what mistakes that teacher had made. They were just following along because he had been accused. I felt really, really bad. A good teacher was beaten to death. And I had let it happen.
>
> I was seven years younger than my sister. I was pretty young. When schools opened again, my sister didn't do very well. Now she works in a restaurant. She makes noodles in the back.

Even at that young age, the events of the time were moving so fast she could only stand back and watch, or so she says. Her sister, on the other hand, was responsible not only for killing someone but for making Liu Rong lose her innocence, grow up too soon. Yet she paid for it, by ending up living a life of labor. But the worst was yet to come for the family. Her uncle had fled to Taiwan years earlier, around 1949, when the Kuomintang retreated there. During the latter days of the Cultural Revolution, Liu Rong and her sisters were sent to the countryside at a time when most college students were returning. Although her father was a cadre in an agriculture cooperative, his high rank failed to prevent her from being sent into exile. It was on account of her "overseas connection." The authorities had finally found out about it.

> I always knew I had a relative in Taiwan. When the Cultural Revolution started, I immediately thought of my uncle in Taiwan. My father came back and asked my mother, "Should we include this? Should we include this?" My father's work unit wanted to check up on each family's history. My father was really afraid. Actually, it didn't matter if my father included it in his report or not. But my father was afraid and left it out. So when they

did their own background check, our whole family lost our jobs. Everybody lost their jobs including my sisters and older brothers.[22]

They all had to go to the countryside to work with the peasants. My sister went to Qinghai. My brothers were sent somewhere else. I had to go to the countryside, too. All seven of us siblings had to go to the countryside.

By the time we were sent to the countryside, those who were supposed to go down to the countryside had already all been sent. And a lot had returned and could work.

I wasn't afraid because I knew I had an uncle in Taiwan. Even though it was because of him we had gotten into trouble, I hoped that someday he would come and save us. But my father, of course, had never been able to reach his brother. He was afraid his brother had died. My father's work unit told him to make a confession. Actually, my father didn't have anything to confess.

I was sent to the countryside for two years. I went with my father's unit. They sent the family units to a village. The village was not too far from Qingdao. We were just like farmers, we had our own plot of land, we grew crops. Part of the time, we worked in a factory, doing the same work as the workers. It was hard work. We had to carry things by pole. We had to go down to the river to get water and carry it back. We had to carry water into the fields, or carry fertilizer. That was really hard work. We had to carry the fertilizer up the side of a mountain and then dump it into troughs. This was traditionally men's work. Women were doing it, too.

We lived in a big house. The students who had been sent out to the countryside slept in the courtyard. One side of the house was for men, the other side was for women. We lived in that house for two years.

Then we came back.

Liu Rong's life seems to fall into different stages, each one connected but transparently different. When she returned home, she worked in a sewing factory, using the skills her grandmother had taught her. Then she had an accident.

When I came back from the countryside, I found a job right away. I started working in a factory that made sports clothes. Sports jackets and things like that. My job was to sew together fabric. It was really hard work. I worked the night shift. I was living in my father's old house. Normally, I'm not the kind of person who can stay up late. It's hard for me to sleep when it's light out. So when I would come to work, I would always feel exhausted.

I remember one time. I was working the night shift. I got off at six in the morning. Qingdao is in the northeast, and it still wasn't light then. I came down the mountain and when I came down I fainted. I don't know if it was fainting or slipping, but I fell down. I blacked out.

And the next thing I remember was pushing my bicycle through the doors of a hospital. There were a lot of patients waiting to see the doctor. I looked at the clock. I had lost my consciousness for four hours. I couldn't remember anything else. I didn't know what my name was. I didn't know where my family lived. After four hours of sitting in the hospital, I remembered where I lived. My father came and brought me home. After that, I never worked the night shift again.

I was living with my family again.

Her story sounds dreamlike, almost as if she were absent from the events, as if the events were happening to someone else. Her whole life has been like a dream, a childhood when she sang and danced for her parents every night while students butchered each other in the streets. Her uncle was sent to the countryside for having a relative in Taiwan. Her fall from her bicycle is almost the only time in her life she realizes how cut off she really is from her family and herself. She has been a sleepwalker through her life. Then she falls off her bike and wakes up, gets some sense of her absence.

She then went into business for herself, which is now allowed by government reforms. She sold clothing in a market in Qingdao. Her family introduced her to a man, they married, and he began to abuse her, verbally and physically, sleeping with other women. She contracted a disease, was treated and cured. Yet in many ways, she seems to identify with her ex-husband. They both have bicycle accidents. They both go through stages where they can hardly speak a word.

> My former husband used to drink a lot. Sometimes he would get drunk and crash on his bicycle. He would crash and afterwards his whole face would be covered with blood. When I saw it, I just felt irritated. And when he drank, the smell of his breath was grotesque. Even our son couldn't sleep when he was nearby. It was like living with a rope around my neck while trying to raise a child. After a while, I just couldn't stand the smell of that liquor anymore. Our sex life went down the drain also. I just lay there.
>
> He was really a grouch. It was because he was just really stupid. He couldn't even express himself properly. He would say one word and that was it. I really was pretty. Even though I had a child, I still put my hair up on my head. I wore my hair up really high. But I never thought of trying to get another man. What I wanted was to make money.

My family was really poor. I just thought if I could earn some money, maybe learn some skill or something, I could help out my family. My husband had affairs and he was cheap and petty. Before we got divorced, he would come down to where I worked and ask for money. I would give it to him. During the first year of opening my own business, I gave him a washing machine and a television set. I bought them all for him.

The next year we got divorced. After I got divorced, I took my son and went to live with my father. But after I got divorced, this is really interesting, I also used my connections, and my former husband used his connections, to try to win custody of our son. My connection was the school principal. His was a department head. We used our connections because we both wanted my son. In the end, my son was given to me.

Her son came to live with her. But, about that time, relations were reestablished, unofficially, between Taiwan and China; travel was possible.[23] Her lost uncle began writing letters. In one letter back to him, her father asked him to find a husband for her. The uncle, who was a policeman, thought of Ko Jen-tao, his colleague, a police chief, who had recently lost his wife to cancer.[24]

It was lucky for me that by that time we had been able to contact my uncle in Taiwan. He introduced me to Mr Ko. I was so relieved I could leave this place of suffering I was in. My uncle had come back from Taiwan for the first time. He was very warm. He was very interested in me.

He said, "What is the secret of your business success?" I said, "Sincerity. You have to have the right attitude towards your customers. And your product has to be good. If you have a new customer, you have to really take the time to introduce him to your product."

And he said, "Oh? Not bad, not bad, not bad."

He felt that I had a good sense of responsibility. So he promised to introduce me to someone in Taiwan.

Even though she had never met him, she immediately felt her uncle was different than the way he must have been in his youth on the mainland. She already had an image in her mind of what Taiwan was like: sophisticated, rich, and culturally advanced. Later, however, she says she changed her mind. This was after she had lived in Taiwan for a while, with her new husband, Ko Jen-tao.

My uncle had been changed by Taiwan. It wasn't just the way he talked or acted. It was almost like he was higher quality than all of us. I admired him a lot. If I look at him now, however, I don't see any difference. But at the time, we were backward compared to him and he was more foreign. You could see it in his clothing, in his way of speaking, and in the way he held himself. It was all more advanced than any of us.

By that time, he was just a relative. Nobody cared whether he was Kuomintang. Then she met Ko Jen-tao. Smiling, happy, jocund, he came to Qingdao to meet her. He stayed in an expensive hotel with a swimming pool and attendants in the lobby. He lavished gifts and cash on her and her family. Since he had only seen her photos before, it was a shock when he met her: she was more beautiful than he imagined. In the photos, she appears hoydenish and jolly, leaping onto a bed in a dress, laughing, her bare dimpled thighs showing, like curdled cream. Her hair is short and wavy. Her face is round. The contrast with the women he met in Qingdao, whose hair was long, cheeks were white with makeup, and who seemed as slender as a wand, made him gasp. She, on the other hand, was disillusioned. She turned pragmatic, but not overly so.

> When I first met Mr Ko—in other words, my future husband—everyone thought he had a very warm laugh. For me, however, I just wondered how old he was. When I was running my own business, I didn't really have much interaction with people who were old. It wasn't hard for me to find a match. It was just that getting married to someone twenty-two years older seemed a little strange. I would have to change my thinking. I thought that at first we could just talk and chat and I could see if I felt any disgust. I didn't. That was a good sign.
>
> After he decided he liked me, he started to throw around a lot of money. He promised me immediately he would buy me a house. I remember thinking at the time, "it takes a small fortune to buy a house." If I worked for ten years, or even twenty years, I probably couldn't afford one. I was also getting a little tired of running my own business. I needed rest. And that was how I started thinking about it from an economical point of view. He was a pretty good guy, after all. I just felt that there was a big difference between our ages.
>
> So that's how I made the decision.

He bought her a villa on the coast of Qingdao. In the mornings, the fog comes in off the water and coats the fake brown wood, carved into European patterns, with beads of moisture. A fountain shoots out drizzly strings of water in the midst of a garden cut in rough imitation of a French garden. The house, they decided immediately, should be rented out to a Japanese businessman, partly to pay for the expenses of her son from the earlier marriage. They returned to Taiwan, where she immediately began working to save money to send her son overseas, to New Zealand or someplace where he could escape the drudgery of life in China. Ko Jen-tao is inconsolable. His wife, on whom he has lavished millions of New Taiwan dollars,[25] is now absent from his home eighteen hours a day. When she is at home, she is too tired for sex. He stops running, complains about bone spurs, grows fat. He begins to complain, a constant whining growl that persists every time she is at home. What makes the situation intolerable, however, is the hate that Ko's children from his previous marriage bear towards her. Some of their hatred is kindled by general stereotypes held in Taiwan against mainland Chinese. Liu Rong also feels that the children are afraid she will rob their father—and them—of his savings, houses and possessions. The situation becomes intolerable.

> When I first went to Taiwan, I wanted to commit suicide every day. My husband was very kind to me. So I didn't want to do anything to make him angry. But his sons kept trying to pick a fight with me. If my husband was home, they wouldn't dare to do anything. But the minute he left to go somewhere, they attacked me.
>
> They would say something like, "How can you let our father do any cleaning? That's your job. Don't you know how old he is?"
>
> I wouldn't say anything.
>
> But after they kept talking that way, I finally talked back. I said, "I haven't forced your father to do anything. I do as much as I can around here. Your father just wants to help me a little. Besides, that's his business. I didn't ask him to do anything."
>
> They said, "It doesn't matter. You have to do what we tell you to do."
>
> This was just the beginning.
>
> One day, their father went to Kaohsiung.[26] The two sons actually took the day off. They came home together. The entire family was living together at the time. I could tell they wanted to have a fight. And I was spending half my time looking after their children, too, while they were at work.
>
> The two sons came in and said, "We want to talk about money." They accused me of marrying their father for his money. They said everyone who comes from the mainland just wanted money.
>
> They were yelling at me. I was really afraid they would hurt me. I thought they might try to kill me. Their father wasn't at home and no one would know what had happened. I just kept backing away until I got to the

window. I said, "If you do anything, I will scream as loud as I can and the neighbors will hear."

They left and went back to work. I have a loud voice, and if I had screamed, the neighbors would have heard it.

Later that night, they came back. I had been thinking of how much time I had spent babysitting their children. While they had been attacking me, one of their children was sleeping in the other room. I wasn't scared anymore. I was furious. I made sure when they came back, I was holding the kid. "Wait," I said, "I'll have dinner ready in a minute."

They came into the kitchen. I turned off the stove and turned around. I was holding the child in one arm. In the other, I was holding a butcher's knife. When their father came home that night, I didn't say anything. I was too upset to talk. I had written down what had happened. I wrote, "Your two sons attacked me. They threatened to kill me. They said I was just after your money." I was too upset to talk about it.

As soon as he stepped in the door, he saw that I was crying. He read my note. When his sons got home, he yelled at them and threatened them. One of his sons called me. He said, "Auntie, auntie, please come out. You be our witness, we didn't do anything to you."

I said, "So you were putting on a play? The two of you were here threatening me. Now that your father comes home you're changing the story. I'm not going to take it."

I said, "You wanted to kill me."

As soon as he saw his father was on my side, he got angry and ran out and smashed a window with his hand.[27] It was the window in the bathroom. Then he ran out of the apartment and down the stairs and out.

How her fortune had changed! She thought she was moving to a new life on the other side of the Taiwan Strait. She felt affection, even love, for Ko Jen-tao. But she didn't know what it would be like to marry a man twenty-two years older. But what did it matter? She cared for him and it would secure a future for her son and herself. Ko's temper was good, he was placid, soothing, like butter. But now this. She was at a loss for what to do. Then she hit on the idea. "You can hear the neighbors talking and smell their cooking smoke. It's impossible to live here," she said one day. "We must move." Ko listened to her, and then came the great change in the family's finances since his first wife died. As chronicled in Chapter 2, Ko divvied up his resources. Each child was given the down payment for a flat. It seemed, to the children, as if this was all her doing, that she had tricked him, changed him so that he had no desire to want to solve the situation together, as a family, just a dry, loveless sense of responsibility or, worse, just a selfish desire for her body. She and he moved to a spacious flat on the outskirts of Taipei near a hill and a lake and a military academy that was empty for most of the day so that the apartment enjoyed a pillow of quiet coming from the jungle on the hill and around the lake.

At first it was idyllic. They took long walks together in the hills. They cooked and ate. Then the issue of her son began to crop up again. Ko refused to support him. On a visit to Qingdao, he caught the son cheating, or preparing to cheat, on an exam. "I will not support a cheater," he said. "I, who never had the chance to go to school, to college, should support a cheater, a liar!"

Then the fights began. First it was over sex, as she worked out of the home constantly. Then, on trips to Qingdao, which they took in the height of summer to escape the melting oven of Taipei, it was over other, often petty things.

> We have been married over ten years. Maybe it's my age. I'm almost fifty. I may have a bad temper sometimes or flare up. I feel that when two people fight, it's not that big a deal. I don't know. When the two people were married in the past, the two sets of children can influence their relationship a lot.
>
> If one of you says something that's insensitive, and you feel hurt, you should let it go.
>
> But at this age, you can't let it go. And your partner won't either. I can't stand it either when he loses his temper. It's usually about something very small. I think he's been spoiled. Compared to me. I can't stand it.

On one occasion he was going to buy beef for a stew. According to Liu Rong, the argument lasted over a day. Ko simply disappeared. This was in Qingdao, in late July. She came home and he was gone. And Liu Rong said to herself, "Something very serious has happened." It was about the beef.

> I said to him, "Don't buy too much, you're the only one who is going to eat it." He said, "How much?"
> I said, "Three *jin*."
> "That's not enough!"
> I said, "You're the only one who's going to eat it."
> "How about your son?"
> "My son isn't going to be back for a long time. He doesn't want to eat dinner here, anyway. He likes to eat at his grandparents.'"

He got angry. Just because I said that one little thing, he has to try to hurt me.

"I'm leaving. This isn't my home."

I said, "Then where are you going?"

I was speaking calmly. I was watching TV. But he was furious. It was because I just mentioned my son. I said my son wouldn't eat his beef.

The problem was that my husband used to cook for my son and wash his clothes. But when the two of us fought, he would throw it at me. He would say, "I wash your son's clothes, I cook for him."

So I finally said, "Then don't wash my son's clothes anymore, and don't cook for him. I'm tired of listening to this."

So when he brought up the issue of where my son was going to have his dinner, I just couldn't go through it all again. I said, "My son is not coming here for dinner. He's going to his grandparents.'"

He would bring it up over and over and over. "I washed your son's clothes. I cooked for your son."

But I will not put up with his hounding. I've been listening to it for ten years.

Her complaints become more general, and move backward in time, almost as if she wished she could retrace her steps to arrive at the moment before she met him.

We have a terrible sex life. When his skin touches me, I want to shrink away. It actually hurts, for his skin to touch my skin. I tried putting powder and oil on my face and body. But it doesn't make a difference. He has been trying Viagra. He's seventy-two. It's not going to last that much longer.

I realized I didn't love him anymore. I realized this after we had been married for four years. The marriage wasn't fun anymore. It had destroyed me. I was broken and hollow. I couldn't stop crying. He called his son's wife[28] and she came over and tried to get me to tell her what had happened. I just kept crying.

It was like I was sick. I couldn't stop crying. I tried to stop. I drank a lot of water. I never asked for a perfect life. Women need support, we don't have any interaction. We just say, hey, come eat with me, come help me wash clothes, come wash the floor. Once in a while, we go out. We meet his friends. That is when we are at our best. We go to see movies. Maybe it's just that his age has made him unable to be open. Maybe if he were younger, it would be different.

Liu Rong, on her good days, knows what Ko has gone through. But she often forgets that his childhood was filled with war and loss of a father and family and home. While he eats he says nothing but gulps the food as quickly as he can, stuffing rice and candied fish into his mouth with his chopsticks. So rapid is his eating, as if the Japanese bombs were still raining around him, as if his father were still dying, as if he were still a young man on a ship off of Taiwan, that it looks as if he will never get enough to fill himself up completely, to blot out the memories. This is what Liu Rong must now be sensing. Adding to her grief is the fact that her mother is dying of colon cancer. In the hospital in Qingdao, a place where the floors are coated with dust and grime, there is not even a bed for the old woman. Finally, a doctor makes space for her in an office shared by several doctors. As Liu Rong enters the room, the doctors are sprawled out over the desks, heads on their arms, their greasy hair shining under the fluorescent lights like oil. The mother is a sack of old clothing and dull metal-coated teeth.

Her father, who is also there, describes his own life as influenced by "overseas relations." It was his brother who fled to Taiwan, meaning that he, who remained, could never rise above his job as machinist in a metal factory. Several times, he was promoted, he said, only to be shot down on account of his relation in Taiwan. The mere mention of "overseas relations" makes the scraggly old man stammer and gape, momentarily ceasing his pacing by his wife's flecked-white-paint bedstead.

"There was a ceiling I could never penetrate," he said.

Missing

Her cutesy voice changes into one of fatigue—a middle-aged woman with wrinkly eyes and a head like a lump of clay, brings with her a middle school girl with zits on her face who is shy and says little. Her relatives, brothers and sisters, are laid off, she explains.

> They are all, let's say, underemployed. They are Mongol. They are all still in Inner Mongolia.

But this woman, named Lu Xiuqi, in her mid-fifties, is the provider for the family. And she doesn't know when she will be laid off. Even as the economy changes and creates jobs in the new sectors, the old, government-run industries no longer offer permanent employment, generally speaking. Lu Xiuqi is a heroine to her family. Her story about herself is heroic.

I came to Beijing in 1973. I had been admitted to the postal university. It was like climbing a mountain. I felt I had been climbing all the way from our village in Inner Mongolia. Suddenly, I was at the top. I studied electronics and mobile phones there. That was cutting-edge research. When I was growing up, most people in Inner Mongolia had never even heard of these things. After I graduated, I worked in the same area. I was in the University of Research Electronics. I worked on technical applications. I researched strategy for communications. I was the only one from Inner Mongolia there. I was basically working on the next wave of mobile phones. I had helped make it possible for someone to call from Beijing to my home town.

A novelist might say that communication is the theme of her life. Her uncle has been missing for sixty years, missing even from before she was born—and she has tried every single thing she can think of to communicate with him: shamanic rituals, letters, the Red Cross, the Bureau of National Security, and now a foreign researcher. She is in a small hotel room in Beijing. Outside the air is palpably grey. Coal smoke smothers the sky. Grey light filters in the window. She is with her niece, a girl of thirteen.

I have a husband and a child. We were college classmates. He wasn't prejudiced because I was Mongol. He's a Han. He does the same thing I do. We both work on telecommunications. But we don't work in the same place.

We have a son. He's in his thirties. He also works in telecommunications. He also went to the postal college. He's married. He doesn't have children. He's been married for three years. His wife was also his classmate. We are all that way.

Soon her voice changes. It is no longer the tired old postal worker, but a cutesy almost simpering voice, as if all the fifty-odd years of her life were nothing and she were suddenly a teenager intoxicated with her own wishes. Her uncle was taken by the Kuomintang sixty years ago as the war was dying, as the Communists were scouring the country clean of their enemies. So now, she hopes, he made it safely, somehow, to Taiwan. She has faith he made it there before the Kuomintang armies on the mainland were destroyed. Or perhaps it was her grandfather who had the faith. After all, it was his son who was lost.

So when we were little, we knew there was a Taiwan and that our uncle was in Taiwan. My grandfather was the one who talked about this, because after my uncle disappeared, my grandfather really missed him.

As a Mongol, she along with her family, had apparently adopted a practice common in her homeland: shamanism. The shaman told them that the uncle was still alive. This was about twenty years after he went missing.[29]

> And we went everywhere to ask about him. Finally, it was proven true. Do you know what "proven true" means? "Proven true" means that the person who would tell you, a shaman, whether a relative was living or not, also said that he was still living but that he couldn't come back. He said that he had gone in a southeasterly direction.
>
> The army unit he was in had headed in a southeast direction, so everyone knew that they were heading for Taiwan. So when we were little, we knew that our uncle was probably in Taiwan.

She never met her uncle. She was born after he was taken. But she entertains an image of him based on how her father looks; he must have looked the same—handsome. He has already begun to assume the larger-than-life proportions that he assumes for her later in her life. She knows she can probably never see him, but if she can somehow get some knowledge of where he is or what happened to him, she might be able to put to rest that image she has created of him, something fantastic and terrible and tragic, like a ghost seen here and everywhere.

> My father had two brothers. The uncle I'm talking about was the youngest. He was four years younger than my father. My father used to say that his younger brother was tall and strong. And that he was very handsome. He said he was so handsome that he would go into town and everyone couldn't stop looking at him. Children, men, women.
>
> My father was also very handsome. They said my uncle looked like him a lot. But my father said my uncle was by far the best-looking. They said he was as beautiful as a woman. More beautiful.
>
> So people said that my uncle was very good-looking. Very handsome. He also knew how to work hard. He was working on our farmlands before he was captured. In those days, we had a lot of land.

For her entire life her family has remained clenched like a fist around the memory of her uncle. If she ever wants to escape from the fist, the curse, she needs to pry open the fingers and see what she is dealing with, what kind of man he is and what her relation with him might have been. Because he went missing before she was born, he never had the chance to know her, to love her. She never had the chance to prove to him that she was worthy of being loved.

> I wasn't even born yet. I never even knew him. I feel like I knew him. I feel like I loved him. But he was gone before I was born.
> He was caught in 1947. He was caught at our home. The Kuomintang army came into our house to take soldiers. I don't think they came with guns. Maybe they had some guns. If the men had worked together, maybe they could have fought them off. There was this officer, called a, some kind of officer, and that officer was in charge of capturing soldiers, and then he caught, he caught . . .

Actually, it is a love affair with more than her uncle. If he hadn't gone—instead of her father—she would not exist. Because her uncle made the greatest sacrifice—his life—he allowed his elder brother to stay and build a family of his own. This is what troubles the middle-aged woman's mind, perhaps the most, the sacrifice, the self-sacrifice of a young, good-looking man, a man as beautiful as a woman, who then vanished off the face of the earth for her entire lifespan.

> Actually, I heard that at first they got my father, but my uncle, he wanted to go in place of him, so the two of them, neither wanted to let the other go. They argued about it. Then they fought each other. And my uncle was bigger, he won. Finally, he said, "I'm going, I'm going, you're staying." So in the end, he went. They took him. You had to have one person go from each family.
> My uncle thought it was no big deal. He thought that it wasn't right to let his older brother be taken. Actually, my uncle was the one with a family at that time. He had just gotten engaged. My father, his older brother at that time didn't have any family. But in the end, it was my uncle who went.

Her uncle lost everything, even his fiancée and the chance to start a family. He gave up his happiness and his life not just for his brother, but so that his brother could have his own family.

> His fiancée gave up waiting for him to come back. He had been gone for so many years without coming back, so she got married to someone else. It wasn't that my uncle didn't like that girl, it wasn't for that reason that he went with the Kuomintang. There had to be one man from each family. It was called, "When there are two nails, you grab one." If your family has two sons, you have to give up one.
> They both knew how dangerous it was to be taken to fight. They both wanted to go in the other's place. But my uncle was stronger. And he was the younger brother.

The family was changed by it. The father prayed to the sun, in the direction where he thought his son was fighting. He knelt, he bowed, he touched his forehead to the ground. Partially, it was out of guilt, because the father was the one first wanted by the Kuomintang troop leader. This was the way—corvee—that the army supplied men to serve their dying cause. But the father "ran away." So they took one of the sons. And the father spent his whole life living with the guilt and passed it down to his son, who then passed it down to his daughter, who was here in a hotel room pleading with a foreigner to find the missing man, her uncle.

> My father also wanted to go in his place. He said, "I'll go, I'll go, I'll go." And my uncle said, "I'll go, I'll go." So they took one of them away; they grabbed my uncle and took him away. It was just that everyone was yelling, "I'll go, I'll go, and you stay." The soldiers didn't want to waste any time. They just grabbed my uncle.
>
> Of course, their father was heartbroken. He felt that way for his whole life. Ever since then, his father—my grandfather—couldn't stop thinking about him. Actually, to tell the truth, the soldiers originally wanted to take my grandfather. But he ran off. The soldiers tracked him down and brought him back. My uncle was there. And that's when he and my father started fighting, about who would go in their father's place. They were good sons. My grandfather really missed my uncle after he was gone. He would often get down on his knees and kowtow to the sun. Or he would light incense, burn incense, to ask for protection for his son. He was asking, praying for someone to protect his son.
>
> He would only kowtow to the sun when the weather was good. When it wasn't too hot and he could see the sun, he would face the southeast, the direction he thought his son must have been taken, and then he would get down in the sand and kowtow. I also remember him burning incense when I was little. He would let me burn it too.

In Inner Mongolia, an old baldheaded man with desert all around him, prayed in the direction of the sun which he believed was the direction of Taiwan, for the gods to protect his son. Then he taught his granddaughter to do the same, praying in the direction of Taiwan, where they believed their lost relative had perhaps ended up, praying, kowtowing, as the incense smoke smothered them.

As time progressed, and it became apparent that no amount of wishing would bring her uncle back, Lu gradually began to cast around for other methods of trying to locate him.

The way we thought about it at the time was that we didn't know when Taiwan would be liberated. What we meant by liberated was that it would become part of our country again. We just had no idea when this would happen. If it were liberated, then he could come back. Or we could get in touch with him. There was no communication at that time between Taiwan and China.

We felt that he was alive because we went to see that shaman. The shaman said he was still alive.

In 1978, I wrote a letter to the Red Cross. My father was looking for his younger brother. We looked for him at the Beijing Public Security Bureau and they didn't have any record of him. Then I thought, why don't we just write a letter? A lot of people were starting to come back from Taiwan. But he hadn't come back. So we wrote a letter to the Red Cross. I wrote it. This letter here. I sent it off. I never received a response. I still have a draft. Here it is.

Dear Red Cross of Taiwan,

I have great hopes in writing to you. I would like to ask you to help me find my uncle who has been lost for forty years. Ever since last year in November, Taiwan compatriots could return to the mainland to visit relatives. Not a day goes by that my father and aunt don't wish that their brother could come home and the whole family can be reunited. This is what we have been praying for forty years.

We've been hoping against all odds but up until now there still hasn't been any news. My father has actually gotten an illness because he missed his younger brother every day for so many years. He has never recovered. I pray that after forty years my father and aunt can see their younger brother again. We would like to know if there is any way you can help us find him and give him this letter and ask him to write us. Please understand what we have been going through for so long. We know you probably have many cases to deal with, but please help us, please help us check on him. The loss of my uncle has also caused my mother grief for her whole life since she is the one who must look after my father. Below is my address.

Perhaps, in part, she was hoping for some form of assistance, or reparation, from the Kuomintang government, for the illnesses and loss suffered by her family. But how do you ask for compensation for a war, when the war itself seems to have never quite petered out?

> My grandfather and father were able to get the names of the Kuomintang officers who took my uncle. When they were taking him away, they also got the number of the unit and troop he would be in. They thought that would help them later, to find him.

Lu included all this information in her letter to the Red Cross. The organization had contacts around the globe. They could bridge the hostile space between China and Taiwan. They would check to see if her uncle was alive in Taiwan—or somehow perhaps find out if he had died on the way there.

> No one answered. A lot of people were coming back from Taiwan at this time. It was mostly old soldiers, a lot of them returned to the mainland. But we hadn't gotten any news about our uncle. That was when I wrote my letter. When he was taken, he was about twenty. He should still have remembered his family. I kept asking myself why he didn't come back with the rest.[30]

But his living niece, Lu, does not want to face the possibility that her uncle is in fact dead. She needs to believe in a man alive out there, waiting to return, perhaps unable to get in touch with his family. Her guilt, or her anger over her father's illness, lives on. She tries every means possible to reason her way out of the obvious—that he was killed in battle.

Even if he had a new family over there, he would have come back.

> He loved his family. He sacrificed himself for them. Maybe he was angry about it. As I said, a lot of old soldiers are coming back to find their families. There are also those who don't come back. Everyone knew that he probably wouldn't make it back.
>
> On the other hand, if he had gotten some high position in Taiwan, he would never abandon his family here. The concept of family is still very strong for the Chinese. It is very deep.
>
> Taiwan and China have tensions; that is true, but he would still remember his family ...

She shrugs off the possibility that the Cultural Revolution might have scared him off. Although they had "overseas connections," they were not targeted, perhaps because they were an ethnic minority.

> At the time, he might have been persecuted if he had come back. But eventually our country allowed them to come back. During the Cultural

Revolution no one bothered us about him. We didn't have any problems on his account. It didn't matter that the government knew. There were too many cases like that. It didn't matter. The government also felt we were in a terrible situation—for your family member to be missing all those years. The government didn't do anything.

Because of her "overseas connection," even if it is an imagined one, she has always paid close attention to Taiwan. Now, as news from the island streams over to the mainland, and is edited to suggest that Taiwan is a place of chaos—a traditional view held by the Qing court, with some truth—she buys into it wholeheartedly. She grows anxious and she talks about her despair as if it were the uncle himself, how after her grandfather had given up on shamanism, she took matters into her own hands and made a pilgrimage of sorts knowing the while that it would fail but also knowing that she would never forgive herself if she failed to undertake it. Several years ago, she traveled to the coast of Fujian Province, just across the strait from Taiwan and its accessory island, Kinmen. She climbed a tower, and in her madness and despair, shouted out his name. The wind blew in stiffly off the ocean. On a clear day, the wind comes in from the sea and pushes away all the air pollution and people standing on the coast can look out across the strait and see Kinmen, the island, knowing that it's not Taiwan but that it is connected to it politically. During the continued fighting in the 1950s, the Communists and Kuomintang took turns shelling each other for months. As a result, every tree on the island of Kinmen was denuded. The place, where Lu was now peering at (not even the real Taiwan itself), was simply a hulking rock crouching in the sea, windswept, rain-battered. She couldn't see a single thing on the island, not the barbed-wire slung along the beaches nor the stone houses built by the survivors out of the only material left on the island after the shelling. She shouted her uncle's name in the wind, hoping somehow it would reach Taiwan, or at least the Kuomintang still stationed on Kinmen. Somehow, as she yelled, looking down at the final river before the ocean, she knew that word would get through. Then she recalled that the river was the site of one of the bloodiest battles in the entire war. The remaining Kuomintang soldiers, trying to reach the coast and the safety of boats to take them to Kinmen or even closer islands were slaughtered en masse by communist airplanes, machine guns, and artillery. It had turned the river blood-red, she had learned. She wondered if her uncle's bones were buried there, under the water. She suddenly felt like part of her had died there, too. She had never felt so far from her birthplace, the barren, sand-swept capital of Inner Mongolia.

> We are really anxious to see my uncle. He's been gone for sixty years. So now he is about eighty. I feel that he's been gone so many years; maybe he has forgotten us a little. But I've been gone from our home for thirty years but I still have deep feelings for home.
> I saw on TV that there was some kind of political struggle going on in Taiwan, about a new government. It seems a little barbaric to me. I feel it's a little barbaric. We could never have seen stuff like that on TV before. It was all propaganda.

Beyond Kinmen, beyond the river was Taiwan. Even on a good day, it cannot be seen. The horizon is a single line of black-blue. A ship rounds into shape, pulling off the curve of the earth and heads towards China. She had wanted to "see" what it was like.

> I have no idea what Taiwan is like. So one year I went to Fujian, and I climbed up a tower, because they say from there you can see Taiwan. When I got to the top, I saw the Ma River was really wide, and I heard some people saying that when the Kuomintang went to Taiwan, they crossed that river and a lot of people died in the crossing. So when I was up on this tower, it finally came home to me that he probably died crossing this river.

Now what she wants is recognition for her uncle. More than that, she cannot stomach the idea of a man disappearing entirely—without a trace—almost as if he had never lived. She is touching on a notion of the importance of history that is transcendent, almost as if she is suggesting that people do not exist unless they are known in a community.

> It's not that we want any money he might have. The reason why we keep searching is that ever since he left we can't get out of the habit of hoping he would come back. After all these years, it's become a habit. It's a feeling of helplessness. So we have to keep trying to do something about it. For example, if he were in our own territory, or in Xinjiang, and we knew that he was alive, we would go there. But being in Taiwan, we can't go there, right?
> I wouldn't be mad. Why would I be mad, if he were still alive? Because he's been in Taiwan for so long and he hasn't gotten in touch with us? It would definitely be because he had his own problems to deal with.

Conclusion: The Other Shore

It started, as much as anything can be said to start, during the high point of the last dynasty. It involved officials, officials who became technicians instead of scholars. Until the Manchus took over China in 1644, Chinese officials had mostly spent their time writing poetry and other efflorescences of a culture steeped not only in its own tradition but in the stewing, masticating and swallowing of that tradition over thousands of years. Under the Manchus, a hardy, clever and ruthless people, Chinese officials became something new: they became experts at statecraft. That meant they had to manage markets, control river flooding and, most of all, prevent famine. Famine was probably the biggest killer, the biggest cause of rupture with the past in all history. It was under the Qianlong emperor that the officials took these techniques to new heights. They erected granaries around the empire to feed the hungry in times of famine, to succor the farmers when prices were too high and to retain stability in a wildly unpredictable terrain of droughts, pestilence and an overabundance of human population.

The plan backfired. Not only because the officials could not see beyond their shortsightedness. Not only because they could not see that if you feed a hungry population, that population soon doubles and then even if you have planned ahead, as these officials did, you soon do not have enough to feed anyone. Not only were they unable to see that the very success of their policies must irreparably undo the very successes they had been striving to achieve. But that it would jeopardize their own lives and the lives of their families as it was they who had brought the dynasty to ruin in the very act that, under different conditions, say, under conditions of only partial success, would have saved it.

When the population of China exploded at the end of the Qing dynasty, resources became so scarce that desperate, hungry, and bedeviled people sought their way out of the impoverished land by any means possible. They went to Southeast Asia to work in guano factories and pits. They foraged for sand banks along rivers fronting the ocean, places where seed might take hold, where they might find food for their families. Some of them went as far as Hawaii and eventually San Francisco. Some went to Taiwan. The great and last Chinese diaspora had begun, set off not only by the utter defeat of the policies that had been implemented to prevent it, but also by the final attainment of Chinese empire-building, the greatest area ever achieved, the greatest number of people fed, the most complicated institutions of government. As R. Kent Guy puts it, the Qing dynasty was too successful.[1]

So it fell, in 1911. But the reckless, frightened flight out of the land that had begun a century earlier continued. There were more horrors to flee now, besides just the worst of them all, the granddaddy of horrors, famine. Now there were foreign invaders, new droughts, and pestilence. There were warlords, opium, and the Japanese invasion. The flight continued. Eventually, those two parties which, because of the nature of their founding, continually bickered for the right to save China, began to fight among themselves. Only when the civil war ended in 1949, and China was overrun again with a single entity, did it look as if the flight was over.

It was not. At each stage of the exodus, the Chinese migrants had sought to invent themselves, then reinvent themselves. As their old institutions crumbled—which, according to their way of viewing history, was expected to happen every several hundred years—they had been forced to align themselves with the new dynasty, a somewhat mild form of shifting allegiances if not identity. But when the dynastic system itself crumbled, both students and their teachers tried to invent for themselves a new image and a new identity. Thus, when the two political parties promised to carry on the new identity, many of those same students and teachers were filled with a kind of hope. It was as if the very dreams of hope and enfranchisement that had brought down established governments before had now brought down five thousand years of Chinese history and were now going to fire a new kind of politics. Thus, the Kuomintang set out to lead the country out of its stale, backward past, a past so corrupt that it nearly ended the Chinese race. When the Kuomintang failed, the Communists, claiming an equal right to carry on this new dream and new identity, promised to further the aspirations and stunted hopes of all the Chinese. A Lincoln writing in the first part of the twentieth century might even go so far as to say that the combatants were fighting not so much over land, which is what they thought, but over the very claim that they represented the new destiny of the Chinese people.

So destiny—which in imperial times was simply called by another name—by right of force and victory, came to rest in the hands of the Communists under Mao Zedong. The losers, the final refugees in the long, terrified flight out of China, settled in Taiwan, bereft of home, of land, and of destiny. They no longer had a role to play in the history of the Chinese race. And without that role, they quite rightly came to believe that they would suffer not only dissolution but actual death, not only at the hands of their enemies across the strait but at the very people who they had displaced in Taiwan.

Thus began the long process of escape. Escape not so much from the past or even from a specific place or land. But rather escape from flight. Escape from the soundless, mindless flight from terror, from the loss of order and meaning and confidence. They simply stopped. Nor was this stopping something new. It was Confucian; it was tradition. "Stop and then you will be settled. When you are settled, you can be still. When you can be still, you can be safe. When you are safe, you can ponder. When you can ponder, you can gain advantage." Thus, the beginning of the Great Learning, one of the central, core texts, memorized for a millennium.

Taiwan was a stopping place. Not so much physically, although that was the case, but also a stopping place for "pondering," for reflecting, and for rebuilding. Many of the attempts failed. The map of China affixed onto Taipei failed to convince the mainlanders that they would ever retake China. Hatred and fear of the locals only forced them to question the democratic developments on the island. Each attempt was followed by another attempt, as if they were reliving in their hearts and minds the many phases they had passed through, sometimes as children, to escape from China, from their homes. These phases now defined them, as they imagined and re-imagined their identities. They traversed the long, personal histories of escape and reinvention just as they had trekked out of China.

And they were helped. They were helped by the economic rise of China. Their former enemies now became their guides. A mythic China, a China devoid of the differences between Communists and Nationalists, was rising. Their reunifications with relatives, their failed business ventures, and their exposure to the horrors encountered by their relatives during the Cultural Revolution did little to shake this new dream, this new way of imagining themselves. China was strong. China was rising again. The circle was closing, soon to be complete. They would get back what they had lost, if not in material things, if not in land or even in the prospect of any increase in wealth or prosperity, but in the conception they formed of themselves. They were now Chinese again, allied against anyone through the overwhelming belief that their race was rising again. They became part of destiny again, if not its masters, caught up in the tide of a new destiny, a destiny distinctly Chinese. They had come from there, the land, the old land to which they still laid claim in their blood. They did not ever expect to recover it but it marked them, freed them from their current petty and trivial lives. The land itself was now rising up, and it would pull them back if not in person, then in effigy. They had reinvented themselves as Chinese.

Notes

Introduction

1. William Kirby, *Germany and Republican China* (Stanford: Stanford University Press, 1984), pp. 169–70, 176–83, 264–5, 308.
2. Lai Tse-han, Ramon H. Myers, and Wei Wou, *A Tragic Beginning: The Taiwan Uprising of February 28, 1947* (Stanford: Stanford University Press, 1991).
3. Ya Hsien, "Salt," translated by the author (Hongfan: Taipei, 1981).
4. The group of Chinese who retreated from China to Taiwan around 1949 are referred to as both "mainland immigrants," "mainland refugees," "mainland settlers," and "mainlanders." In other places, books and magazines, they are referred to as *neidiren* (people from the hinterland) or *waishengren* (people from other provinces).
5. http://www.thelastndr.org/home-the-last-generation-of-ndr.html#eversion. Used with permission of the author.
6. Kent Guy, *The Emperor's Four Treasuries: Scholars and the State in the Late Ch'ien-lung Era* (Cambridge: Harvard University Press, 1987).
7. The following sketch is based on the oral history of Ko Jen-tao and my personal observations. I lived as an exchange student in his house from 1987 to 1988 and have remained almost as close as another, albeit foreign, son to him ever since then. This sketch is meant to "set the stage" for the following history by showing the state of one mainland refugee after a life of exile and toil in Taiwan for over fifty years.

Chapter 1

1. Steven J. Hood, "Political Change in Taiwan: The Rise of Kuomintang Factions," *Asian Survey*, Vol. 36, No. 5 (May, 1996): 468–82.
2. A documentary, *Japanese Devils*, features interviews with retired, aged Japanese soldiers who recounted the atrocities they committed while Imperial soldiers invading China in the late 1930s.

3. From the French accouchement, "to give birth." Thus meaning, "to give birth to again" or "to be given birth to again."
4. Lai Tse-han et al., *A Tragic Beginning*, p. 45.
5. R. Kent Guy, *Qing Governors* (Seattle: University of Washington Press, 2010).
6. Taipei municipal historians have erected marble stellae around the city offering accounts of the city's history that differ with Western scholarship. One such, in the suburb of Mucha, describes the area as having been named for houses built out of wood to fend off the rampant numbers of wild horses in the area during the Ming dynasty.
7. John Shepherd, *Statecraft and Political Economy on the Taiwan Frontier, 1600–1800* (Stanford: Stanford University Press, 1993).
8. Wu Hung, *Monumentality in Early Chinese Art and Architecture* (Stanford: Stanford University Press, 1995). Using Wu Hung's conception of the religious role of architecture, Taipei can be seen as more than a monument, but as rather something with a more spiritual purpose, almost as something living.
9. Documents taken from archives of Taiwan Provincial Government, which stores archival material from earlier periods of Taipei Municipal Government and Interior Ministry. These are copies of telegrams received between August 30 and December 18, 1946. *Taiwan Sheng Hsingcheng Changguan Kungshu Kungpao*, nos. 668–84. Available in *Taiwan Sheng Chengfu Kungpao Wangchi Luchahsun Hsitung*.
10. *Chungyang Ripao*, January 25 and February 27, 1947, microfilm, Taiwan National Chengchi University Shetsisuo.
11. Lothar Ledderose, *Ten-thousand Things: Module and Mass Production in Chinese Art* (Princeton, NJ: Princeton University Press, 2000).
12. Taking possession of a new territory often involves naming rituals. When the Spanish "took possession" of the New World, they read Latin texts to the trees. Yet the fact these rituals referred back to a distant power often suggested that they would have trouble fully transforming the new territory. See Patricia Seed, "Taking Possession and Reading Texts: Establishing the Authority of Overseas Empires," *The William and Mary Quarterly*, 3rd Ser., Vol. 49, No. 2 (Apr. 1992), pp. 183–209.
13. The "New Thought" is covered extensively in Jonathan Spence, *The Gate of Heavenly Peace: The Chinese and Their Revolution, 1895–1980* (New York: Penguin, 1982).
14. The reference to the leather cape comes from Lin Ching-wu (see Chapter 1). The transfer of the imperial collection of art works from Beijing to Taiwan is recorded in the 50th Anniversary of the PRC special edition of *Newsweek*, in an article I wrote entitled, "Stolen Treasures."
15. Julia Ching, *To Acquire Wisdom: The Way of Wang Yang-ming* (New York: Columbia University Press, 1976).

Chapter 2

1. Timothy Brook, *The Confusions of Pleasure* (Berkeley: University of California Press, 1998).
2. In 1978, the US broke off diplomatic relations with Taiwan, and it was kicked out of the United Nations as representing "China." The government in Taiwan still continued to debate the claim up until the early 1990s.
3. *The Chinese Pen*, Summer, 2006, pp. 40–63.
4. Lai Tse-han et al., *A Tragic Beginning*, Chapter 2.
5. You Chien-ming, "Dang Waishengjen Yudao Taiwan Nuhsing: Chanhou Taiwan Paokanchung te Nuhsing Lunshu (1945–1949)" [When mainlanders encountered Taiwanese women: Explorations into women in post-war Taiwan], *Chungyang Yenchiuyuen Chintaishih Yenchiusuo Chikan*, No. 17 [Academia Sinica Modern History Research Journal, No. 17].

Chapter 3

1. Pamela Kyle Crossley, *A Translucent Mirror: History and Identity in Qing Imperial Ideology* (Berkeley: University of California Press, 1999), part 3.
2. I am deeply familiar with the details of this trip because I was present for most of it.
3. About the same time, the government began to destroy one of the major "islands" of mainland refugee life and identity: the military villages in which many grew up. The decision involved demolishing the old communities and erecting, in their place, apartment buildings that would fit in with the characterless façade of the rest of the island, where identical concrete stacks of apartment blocks fill every city street.
4. Last lines of the play, *Agamemnon*, translated by E. D. A. Morshead, as part of the M.I.T. online classics, http://classics.mit.edu/Aeschylus/agamemnon.html. The lines are spoken by Cassandra, who has the ability to foresee the future.
5. Some mainland refugees believed that these social changes made it easier for Taiwanese to propagate violence against mainland refugees. For instance, they expressed fear over the shooting assassination of a mainland-refugee politician on May 23, 2007, Taipei County Councilor Wu Shan-jiu. Second-generation mainland refugees said he was shot because he was exposing the corruption of local Taiwanese.
6. In May, the central government voted to change the name of the Chiang Kai-shek Memorial Hall to "National Taiwan Democracy Memorial Hall." While such a change, from the perspective of Taiwanese leaders who wanted to "retake" their history was of course justified, the action prompted a military-style confrontation between agents of the central government and the city government, which was still held by the Kuomintang.
7. A leading Taiwanese activist, Peng Ming-min's descriptions suggest that the Taiwanese who came out to meet the ships arriving from China were dressed in

in Japanese-style clothing. See Peng Ming-min, *A Taste of Freedom: Memoirs of a Formosan Independence Leader* (Upland, CA: Taiwan Pub. Co., 2005).

8. Most coverage of Taiwan by Westerners follows this theme. For example, Jonathan Manthorpe, *Forbidden Nation: A History of Taiwan* (New York: Palgrave Macmillan, 2009). Taiwan is called "A Leaf of the Waves."

9. This is a situation that I wrote about as both a newspaper and magazine reporter.

Chapter 4

1. Recruits were sometimes tied together by the necks with rope to prevent them from running off. They also were sometimes stripped of clothes at night also to keep them from absconding. See Lloyd E. Eastman et al., *The Nationalist Era in China, 1927–1949* (New York: Cambridge, 1991), p. 140.

2. The Chinese Communists proclaimed, after Liberation in 1949, that they had eradicated all forms of "traditional exploitation" in society. See William Hinton, *Fanshen: A Documentary of Revolution in a Chinese Village* (New York: Vintage, 1966), p. 9.

3. In rural China, the Eighth Route Army gained almost mythic proportions in people's memories as purveyors of everything desirable. Hinton, p. 168.

4. Kent Guy, "Fang Pao and the *Ch'in-ting Ssu-shu-wen*," in *Education and Society in Late Imperial China, 1600–1900*, edited by Benjamin A. Elman and Alexander Woodside (Taipei: SCM Publishing, 1994), p. 154.

5. See the account of Lin Ching-wu from Fujian in Chapter 1.

6. Liang Heng, *Son of the Revolution* (New York: Random House, 1983), p. 8.

7. After the Tiananmen massacre, Taiwanese investors were among the first to rush back in to China to invest. Up until 2007, Taiwanese have invested at least $57.5 billion in China, according to Taiwan's Government Information Office. See: http://www.gio.gov.tw/ct.asp?xItem=34875&ctNode=2462&mp=807. Unofficial investment is much higher.

8. Even the generation younger than Tan's felt "fooled and cheated" by the incessant political campaigns orchestrated by Mao over decades. See Jonathan Spence, *The Gate of Heavenly Peace*, p. 359. The feeling of wasted decades was also felt at the highest political levels. Mao's doctor seemed to sum up the feelings of an entire generation of top elites when he wrote of "how good and talented people living under his [Mao's] regime were forced to violate their consciences and sacrifice their ideals to survive." See Li Zhisui, *The Private Life of Chairman Mao* (New York: Random House, 1994), p. 638.

9. Personal income per capita (in renminbi) rose from 400 yuan in 1982 to 2,400 yuan in 1993, for city dwellers. In the country, the growth was less stupendous. Rural per capita income over the same period rose from about 300 yuan to about 900 yuan. See Cheng Li, *Rediscovering China: Dynamics and Dilemmas of Reform* (Lanham:

Rowman and Littlefield, 1997), p. 118. Since 1993, China's economy has continued to grow at around ten percent a year.

10. Despite the rise of material affluence, the government still imposed strict regulations on families, such as the "one-child policy." See Deborah Davis and Stevan Harrel, (eds.), *Chinese Families in the Post-Mao Era* (Berkeley: University of California Press, 1993), pp. 75–76.

11. The workplace, in the Chinese Communist system, was usually coterminous with the party branch, giving the party secretary wide powers encompassing all aspects of life. For Ko I-jen, the factory encompassed all aspects of his life. He worked there, his housing was assigned from there, he was introduced to his wife there. See Deborah Davis-Friedmann, *Long Lives: Chinese Elderly and the Communist Revolution* (Harvard: Cambridge, 1983), pp. 22–23.

12. The movement to send people who had "problems" down to the countryside started during the Anti-Rightist campaign with intellectuals who had criticized the party. It continued through the Cultural Revolution when "educated youth," usually children of intellectuals, were sent to the countryside to "learn from the peasants."

13. My emphasis.

14. Between 1939 and 1941, the Japanese bombed Chongqing (Chungking) 286 times in an attempt to break Chinese morale. The Nationalists had moved its headquarters there in 1937–38. See Eastman et al., *The Nationalist Era in China*, pp. 122, 135.

15. In cities such as Shanghai, the floating population, even as far back as the late 1980s, made up over one-quarter of the population. As of 2003, there were a total of 140 million people in the floating population, mostly rural migrant laborers without residency rights in cities. Many went to Guangzhou, the center of the "world's factory." See Kam Wing Chan, "Internal Migration and Rural Migrant Labor: Trends, Geography, and Policies," in *The Labor of Reform in China*, edited by Mary Gallagher, Ching Kwan Lee, and Albert Park (New York: Routledge, forthcoming), pp. 8, 26.

16. Ko insisted that his grandchildren will work in the factory. His insistence may belie a certain level of anxiety. Migrant workers from the countryside are now granted a form of household registration in some cities, allowing them to take up factory jobs at rates lower than skilled urban workers. See Xiaobo Lu and Elizabeth J. Perry, *Danwei*, pp. 296–7.

17. This was one year after I made the visit. By that time, Ko Jen-tao had retired from the police force and so was allowed by Taiwanese authorities to visit the mainland.

18. Until recent DPP reforms to Taiwan's educational system, more time was spent on classical Chinese texts than on any other subject in Grades 1 through 12. See Douglas C. Smith, *The Confucian Continuum: Educational Modernization in Taiwan* (New York: Praeger, 1991), p. 117.

19. Privatization in the housing system has given people the chances to own homes. The rate of homeownership in cities has changed drastically, from twenty percent

in the 1980s to seventy-two percent in 2000. See Youqin Huang, "The Road to Homeownership: A Longitudinal Analysis of Tenure Transition in Urban China (1949–93)," *International Journal of Urban and Regional Research*, 28, no. 4 (2004): 774–95.

20. Riots have become common in the countryside for a variety of reasons, including the closing of factories, but also on account of such factors as corrupt officials selling off farmers' land.

21. On August 18, 1966, Mao called on over a million young people assembled in Tiananmen Square to "smash up the four olds," meaning "old ideas, old culture, old customs and old habits." Groups of Red Guards, mostly teenagers, raided people's homes all over the country and smashed anything remotely connected with traditional culture. Nevertheless, there were some efforts to defend old temples and other artifacts, oftentimes attributed to the intervention of Zhou Enlai. See "To Protect and Preserve: Resisting the Destroy the Four Olds Campaign, 1966–1967," in *The Chinese Cultural Revolution as History*, edited by Joseph W. Esherick et al. (Stanford: Stanford University Press, 2006), pp. 64–93.

22. Initially, the program of sending urban youths to the countryside was a way of stemming urban unemployment, disposing of middle-school graduates with no future educational prospects, and an attempt to enhance rural development. Between 1956 and 1966, 1.2 million urban youths settled in the countryside. But after the onset of the Cultural Revolution, the program expanded greatly and at least 12 million were sent between 1968 and 1975. See Thomas P. Bernstein, *Up to the Mountains and Down to the Villages: The Transfer of Youth from Urban to Rural China* (New Haven: Yale University Press, 1977).

23. Taiwan lifted its ban on travel to mainland China in 1987. In 1988, roughly 440,000 Taiwanese visited China. By 2005, the number had increased to 4.1 million. Source: Taiwan's Government Information Office yearbook, which can be accessed at: http://www.gio.gov.tw/taiwan-website/5-gp/yearbook/.

24. According to Liu Rong's narrative, she and Ko Jen-tao only began communicating after the death of his first wife. The children suspect it was earlier, before the wife died.

25. Or, tens of thousands of US dollars.

26. A major city near the southern end of Taiwan, roughly a six-hour car ride or one-hour plane trip from Taipei.

27. This was Ko Chen-tsang, the younger of the twins, who beat his daughters. See Chapter 3.

28. The wife is the aborigine woman that Ko Chen-tsang married. Perhaps because of her marginal background, Liu Rong felt closer to her than to other members of the family.

29. For a discussion of shamanism in Inner Mongolia, see David Sneath, *Changing Inner Mongolia: Pastoral Mongolian Society and the Chinese State* (New York: Oxford, 2000), pp. 234–44.
30. She asked me to try to find him. I contacted a number of government agencies in Taiwan and did my own research. This is what I found. Her uncle was never registered with the Tuifuhui (Ministry of Retired People), which means he probably did not make it to Taiwan alive. The archivist at the Ministry of National Defense, Mr Kuo Kuan-ling, provided a few details about her uncle's unit. The commander of his unit was named Lu Yinglue. On New Year's Eve of 1948, the unit was assigned to protect the Beiping-Hankou railroad. After being defeated by the Communists, Lu (the commander) committed suicide. Almost the entire unit had been destroyed. Some had surrendered to the Communists, who promised the Nationalist soldiers that they could keep their same rank. In February, the remaining men were ordered to the area between Beiping (as it was called at the time—Beijing) and Tianjin. This area was held by the 101st Division, whose commander was named Ru Zuoyi. He was killed in battle and the remaining soldiers died or surrendered.

Conclusion

1. R. Kent Guy, *Qing Governors and Their Provinces: The Evolution of Territorial Administration in China, 1644–1796* (Seattle: University of Washington Press, 2010).

Index

aborigines, 34, 35, 134, 135, 136, 148, 156, 173, 174, 174, 176
Aeschylus, 120, 153, 225

Bamboo Mountain, 77, 78, 109, 121, 122, 142, 148
Beijing, 110, 115, 117, 194, 211, 215, 224, 229
Bergman, Ingrid, 60
Bo Yang, 3, 94
Book of Changes, 120, 121, 145

calligraphy, 79, 93, 94, 95, 159
Chang Ching-tan, 9, 18, 33, 54, 96, 98, 117, 184
Chang Hui-mei (A-Mei), 175
Chen Lu-an, 6
Chen Shui-bian, 6, 18, 133, 148, 168, 174
Cheng Ch'eng-Kung, 62
Chiang Kai-shek, 2, 3, 5, 13, 25, 33, 34, 45, 48, 58, 65, 79, 92, 93, 94, 95, 106, 128, 137, 162, 225
Chiang Kai-shek International Airport, 92
China Airlines, 83, 84, 85
China Central Television, 194
Chinese civil war, 16
Chinese Communist Party, 2
Chinese Communists, 21, 23, 72, 160, 226

Chongqing (Chungking), 28, 39, 157, 191, 227
Chou Chih-sui, 5, 120, 128
Chou Hau-yi, 120, 122, 131
Christianity, 171, 172
Chuang Yen, 45
Confucius, 6
Cultural Revolution, 64, 68, 96, 97, 98, 103, 104, 163, 171, 179, 183, 184, 185, 189, 199, 200, 201, 216, 221, 227, 228

Democratic Progressive Party, 2, 16, 21, 49, 70, 122, 160
Dutch, 162
dynastic cycle, 153

Fujian, 9, 15, 18, 25, 33, 34, 54, 91, 92, 98, 117, 131, 157, 217, 218, 226
Fuzhou, 20, 54

Great Learning, 221
Green Island, 3, 94, 137
Guangdong, 34, 41, 116, 131
Guangxi, 39
Guangzhou, 102, 197, 227
Guy, R. Kent, 220, 223, 224, 226, 229

Hakka, 134, 135
Hong Kong, 29, 40, 41, 42, 46, 48, 96, 97, 98, 101, 102, 104, 105, 150, 151, 157, 193, 197
Hu, Daniel, 120, 150, 157
Hu, Jason, 6
Hu, Mini, 164
Hu Yao-hen, 9, 37, 45, 53, 98, 117, 120, 157
Hualien, 63, 135, 138, 155, 156, 173, 174, 176

Inner Mongolia, 210, 211, 214, 218, 229

Japan, 2, 12, 15, 16, 17, 18, 19, 20, 21, 28, 30, 33, 34, 35, 37, 38, 41, 44, 45, 46, 47, 54, 64, 65, 66, 77, 78, 87, 93, 95, 102, 106, 112, 113, 118, 122, 131, 132, 133, 138, 152, 157, 162, 176, 181, 184, 191, 205, 210, 220, 223, 226, 227

Keelung, 32, 59, 60
Kinmen (Quemoy), 57, 59, 72, 73, 74, 135, 136, 154, 217, 218
Ko Chen-tsang, 120, 133, 134, 135, 136, 137, 139, 140, 142, 154, 157, 173, 176, 228
Ko I-jen, 186, 187, 190, 191, 192, 193, 194, 195, 196, 197, 198, 227
Ko Jen-tao, 8, 9, 15, 16, 17, 21, 22, 53, 57, 68, 76, 78, 90, 98, 101, 107, 114, 116, 120, 121, 133, 140, 142, 154, 173, 175, 176, 180, 186, 187, 189, 190, 191, 194, 195, 198, 204, 205, 206, 207, 223, 227
Ko Meishu, 173, 174, 175, 176
Ko Yuan, 120, 143, 146, 149, 157
Ku Chi, 9, 17, 21, 30, 31, 87, 90, 93, 98, 115, 118

Kuomintang, 2, 3, 4, 6, 7, 8, 12, 15, 18, 21, 22, 24, 25, 26, 27, 28, 33, 35, 36, 37, 42, 43, 44, 45, 49, 53, 58, 59, 61, 65, 70, 71, 72, 73, 76, 83, 85, 86, 87, 89, 90, 92, 93, 94, 97, 99, 103, 105, 106, 110, 114, 120, 122, 125, 128, 131, 132, 133, 136, 137, 148, 149, 152, 154, 159, 160, 161, 176, 181, 182, 183, 186, 190, 201, 205, 211, 213, 214, 215, 216, 217, 218, 220, 223, 225

Lin Ching-wu, 9, 15, 24, 26, 90, 97, 98, 117, 120, 157, 184, 224, 226
Lin Ju-lin, 120
Liu Rong, 10, 11, 12, 81, 110, 111, 112, 113, 115, 142, 199, 201, 202, 206, 208, 209, 210, 228
Lu Xiuqi, 210

Ma Ying-jeou, 27, 116
Manchus, 162, 219
Mandate of Heaven, 45
Mao Zedong, 2, 221
martial law, 20, 23, 106, 137
Matsu, 57
A Midwife's Tale: The Life of Martha Ballard, Based on Her Diary, 1785–1812, 9
Ming dynasty, 7, 45, 62, 128, 224
Mongol, 130, 210, 211, 212
Mucha, 62, 126, 224

Nanjing, 9, 26, 36, 53, 57, 68, 70, 71, 78, 82, 85, 98, 101, 102, 110, 111, 115, 116, 118, 121, 156, 165, 188, 191, 193, 194, 195, 197, 198
Nationalist Party (*see* Kuomintang)
(National) Chengchi University, 43
Nei Di Ren, 5, 6

Neihu, 61, 120, 140
new immigrants, 149
new refugees, 149
New Zealand, 10, 12, 112, 114, 206

overseas relations (*haiwai guanxi*), 179, 190, 210

Peking University, 37, 39, 85, 116, 117
Peng Ming-min, 225, 226
Philippines, 57

Qianlong emperor, 130, 219
Qingdao, 10, 12, 29, 109, 110, 111, 112, 113, 114, 116, 198, 199, 202, 203, 205, 208, 210
Qing dynasty, 7, 50, 61, 62, 117, 130, 131, 132, 165, 170, 183, 219, 220
Quemoy (*see* Kinmen)

Red Cross of Taiwan, 215
Red Dragon, 81
Reed College, 150, 157
Republic of China, 93, 105, 114

Seattle, 171, 172, 224, 229
shamanism, 212, 217, 229
Shanghai, 9, 12, 17, 28, 30, 31, 32, 33, 35, 45, 48, 71, 79, 83, 88, 89, 93, 96, 98, 115, 116, 118, 157, 160, 167, 168, 170, 187, 194, 227
Shen Hsueh-yung, 9, 62, 68, 78, 117
Shenyang, 152, 153
Shoreline, 172
Sun Yat-sen, 11, 145
Sun Yat-sen Memorial, 109, 144

Taipei Veterans' General Hospital, 120, 128
Tan Zhefu, 179, 180, 181

Taoyuan Airport, 92
Taylor, Elizabeth, 60
Taipei, 2, 5, 6, 13, 27, 28, 33, 35, 36, 37, 42, 43, 45, 49, 53, 58, 60, 65, 67, 73, 82, 86, 90, 92, 99, 106, 11, 112, 119, 120, 121, 122, 124, 125, 126, 127, 128, 133, 134, 139, 140, 145, 148, 149, 154, 155, 157, 161, 162, 167, 174, 176, 196, 208, 221, 223, 224, 225, 226, 228
Taiping Rebellion, 37
Taiwan
  elections, 4, 27, 119
Taiwanese
  consciousness, 162
  dialect, 5, 83, 125, 126, 142, 169, 170
  discrimination against mainlanders, 17, 22, 28, 29, 41, 75, 77, 83, 87, 89, 123, 225
Taiwan Strait, 4, 16, 24, 36, 44, 45, 57, 119, 157, 186, 193, 207
(National) Taiwan University, 77, 152, 161
Tan Hua-shen, 9, 21, 22, 24, 29, 181, 190
Tiananmen Massacre, 226
Tianhsiang, 138, 155
2–28 Incident, 2, 132, 160, 161
2–28 Massacre (*see* 2–28 Incident)

Ugly Chinaman, The 3
United Daily News, 74, 86
United Nations, 65, 225
United States, 44, 104, 152, 167
University of Indiana, 150
University of Washington, 167, 171, 224, 229

Wang Shu-chih, 3, 9, 46, 102, 118, 120, 128
War of Resistance, 16, 30, 191

Weiwei Furen, 9, 68, 98, 104, 118
White Terror, 3, 5, 45, 79, 175
Wuhan, 38, 39, 40, 41, 157, 191

Xinjiang, 200, 218
xiucai, 37

Ya Hsien, 3, 223
Yangtze River, 45
Yellow Crane Tower, 40
Yin Tsai-chun (*see* Weiwei Furen)

Zhejiang, 165

www.ingramcontent.com/pod-product-compliance
Ingram Content Group UK Ltd.
Pitfield, Milton Keynes, MK11 3LW, UK
UKHW041914140426
5217IPUK00011B/144/J